Capitalizing on Nature

The basic unit of r
which we can thin
because this capita
dant, and always ;
Capitalizing on Na
ital can help us to
overuse of so mucl
ecosystem as natura
including landscapє
ence and collapse, ѕ
The book conclude
to be overcome in
scarcity and how v
conservation.

EDWARD B. BARI
the Department of
has over twenty-fivє
economist, working
opment issues. He
icy, including *Natu*
A Global Green N
Economies Have L
(2011), all publishec

SOAS, University of London

18 0757654 8

Capitalizing on Nature

Ecosystems as Natural Assets

EDWARD B. BARBIER

CAMBRIDGE
UNIVERSITY PRESS

CAMBRIDGE UNIVERSITY PRESS
Cambridge, New York, Melbourne, Madrid, Cape Town,
Singapore, São Paulo, Delhi, Tokyo, Mexico City

Cambridge University Press
The Edinburgh Building, Cambridge CB2 8RU, UK

Published in the United States of America by Cambridge University Press, New York

www.cambridge.org
Information on this title: www.cambridge.org/9780521189279

First published 2011

Printed in the United Kingdom at the University Press, Cambridge

A catalog record for this publication is available from the British Library

Library of Congress Cataloging in Publication data
Barbier, Edward, 1957–
    Capitalizing on nature : ecosystems as natural assets / Edward B. Barbier.
        p. cm.
    Includes bibliographical references and index.
    ISBN 978-1-107-00727-7 – ISBN 978-0-521-18927-9 (pbk.)
    1. Ecosystem management. 2. Environmental economics. I. Title.
    QH75.B268 2011
    333.95–dc23
    2011019267

ISBN 978-1-107-00727-7 Hardback
ISBN 978-0-521-18927-9 Paperback

This book is dedicated to Lara, Becky, James, and Charlotte. Future generations are, after all, what it is all about.

To waste, to destroy our natural resources, to skin and exhaust the land instead of using it so as to increase its usefulness, will result in undermining in the days of our children the very prosperity which we ought by right to hand down to them amplified and developed.

Theodore Roosevelt, seventh annual message, December 3, 1907

We could have saved the Earth but we were too damned cheap.

Kurt Vonnegut, Jr.

Contents

List of figures   *page* viii

List of tables   x

List of boxes   xi

Acknowledgments   xii

   Introduction   1

1 Ecological scarcity as an economic problem   6

2 Ecosystem services and ecological landscapes   26

3 The basic natural asset model   85

4 Spatial variation in ecosystems   129

5 The open economy   152

6 Ecological collapse   199

7 The way ahead   232

8 Policies in the Age of Ecological Scarcity   269

Index   311

Figures

1.1 The ecological scarcity tradeoff   *page 7*
1.2 Long-run global land use change, 1700–1990   14
1.3 Global agricultural and forest land use change, 1961–2005   16
1.4 Human-induced threats to coastal and marine ecosystems   21
2.1 Key interrelated steps in valuing ecosystem goods and
    services   34
2.2 Ecological landscape conversion to development   44
2.3 Irreversible ecological landscape conversion to development   46
2.4 Economic valuation of ecosystem goods and services   49
3.1 Optimal landscape conversion in the basic model   93
3.2 Landscape conversion when ecosystem services are ignored   93
3.3 The ecological transition and optimal landscape restoration   97
3.4 Land use change and the forest transition curve   98
3.5 Changing land use values and the forest transition   101
3.6 Number of coastal natural disaster events per year in
    Thailand, 1975–2004   115
3.7 Mangrove area (km²) in Thailand, 1961–2004   115
4.1 Nonlinear wave attenuation across a mangrove landscape   134
4.2 Nonlinear habitat function across a mangrove landscape   135
4.3 Mangrove land use with spatially uniform ecosystem values   136
4.4 Mangrove land use with spatially variable storm protection
    values   137
4.5 Optimal conversion of a coastal landscape with spatially
    variable benefits   139
4.6 Simulation of the spatial model   142
5.1 The rural poor and population on fragile lands in
    developing economies   157
5.2 Fragile land population and GDP per capita in developing
    economies   159
5.3 Resource dependency in exports, 1960–2006   161
5.4 Optimal landscape conversion in the open economy model   170

5.5 The effects of a change in the terms of trade   172
5.6 The effects of a rise in international payments for ecosystem
      services   174
5.7 The provision of global ecosystem services   186
6.1 Optimal landscape conversion over time with a risk of
      ecological collapse   207
6.2 Optimal coastal landscape allocation with risk of collapse 210
6.3 Simulation of the spatial model with a risk of ecological
      collapse   212
6.4 Optimal landscape conversion over time with ecosystem
      resilience   222
7.1 The capital approach to sustainable development   236
7.2 Biodiversity, productivity, and stability in ecological
      communities   258
8.1 Reversing the vicious cycle of "unsustainable"
      development   273
8.2 The transaction costs of environmental policy change   276

Tables

1.1 Magnitudes of global environmental change, 1890s
 to 1990s   *page* 12
1.2 Trends in global forest area (10^6 km^2), 1990–2005   15
1.3 Trends in cultivated land to 2050 in developing regions   17
1.4 Water withdrawal by volume and by share of total
 renewable supplies   18
1.5 Developing countries and regions with relatively scarce
 water supplies   19
2.1 Examples of wetland ecosystem services and valuation
 studies   36
2.2 Ecosystems classified in terms of source and level of
 energy flow   39
2.3 Various nonmarket valuation methods applied to ecosystem
 services   51
2.4 Losses in floodplain benefits versus gains in irrigated
 production, net present value   59
2.5 Comparison of land use values per ha, Thailand,
 1996–2004   64
2.6 Tradeoffs in landscape use scenarios, Willamette Basin,
 Oregon, 1990–2050   69
2.7 Forest ecosystem service values, Great Britain   71
5.1 Distribution of world's population and rural poor on
 fragile land   156
5.2 Low- and middle-income economies and patterns of
 resource use   165
6.1 Major ecosystem state shifts and their causes   215
8.1 Global status of key ecosystem goods and services   271
8.2 Financing mechanisms for funding global ecosystem
 conservation   279

Boxes

2.1 Ecosystem functions and services   *page* 29
2.2 Valuing water supply to New York City by the Catskills
    watershed   56
5.1 Resource dependency, fragile land populations, and rural
    poverty   163
6.1 Diversity and adaptability of ecosystems   216
6.2 The value of ecosystem resilience in the Goulburn–Broken
    Catchment of Southeast Australia   223
6.3 Land clearing and ecological disturbance in tropical forest
    ecosystems   225
7.1 Sustainable development as systems Venn diagram   234
7.2 How does economic development affect mangrove loss?   251
7.3 Estimating a supply curve for ecosystem services   253
7.4 Ecological resilience in coastal and marine ecosystems   256
8.1 Replanting mangroves in Thailand: the institutional and
    policy challenge   298

Acknowledgments

This book would probably not have happened without the prompting of Richard Carson. In June 2008, Rich approached me with the idea of writing a short monograph on the economics of ecosystems for the journal that he co-edits with Kip Viscusi, *Foundations and Trends in Microeconomics*. As Rich explained to me, many contributors to the journal expand their short monographs into book-length manuscripts. The publisher of the journal, Now Publishers, actually encourages this practice.

I am therefore grateful to Rich Carson and Kip Viscusi for suggesting that I publish the original article in their journal, and ultimately expand it into a book.[1] I also appreciate the support of Zac Rolnick of Now Publishers, who facilitated my seeking book publication of an expanded article.

I would like to thank Chris Harrison of Cambridge University Press for enthusiastically backing this project from the outset and commissioning this book.

Amy Ando, Jeff Englin, and Marty Smith assisted with extensive and useful comments on the original book proposal. Amy Ando, Rich Carson, Dave Finnoff, Duncan Knowler, Charles Perrings, Jason Shogren, John Tschirhart, and Amos Zemel provided helpful comments and suggestions on my *Foundations and Trends in Microeconomics* article. The transformation of the article to book also benefited from comments received in reaction to my keynote address at the 11th Annual BioEcon Conference, "Economic Instruments to Enhance the Conservation and Sustainable Use of Biodiversity," Venice, Italy, September 21–22, 2009.

---

[1] The original article on which this book is based is Barbier, E.B. 2008. "Ecosystems as Natural Assets." *Foundations and Trends in Microeconomics* 4(8):611–681.

While writing this book, I also produced two related journal articles, for *Annual Reviews of Resource Economics* and *Ecological Monographs*. I am grateful to Amy Ando, Ian Bateman, Dave Finnoff, Rick Freeman, Nick Hanley, Kathy Segerson, and John Tschirhart for helpful comments on my *Annual Reviews* article, which also proved extremely useful to me in writing this book. In addition, I am indebted to my co-authors, Sally Hacker, Chris Kennedy, Evamaria Koch, Brian Silliman, and Andrew Stier, for the article in *Ecological Monographs*, as well as the editor Aaron Ellison, for advice, assistance, and suggestions.

Special thanks go to Joanne Burgess, who read over early drafts of the manuscript and provided detailed comments, suggestions, and edits. Her careful attention to the first chapter of this book was especially valuable. I am also indebted to Margie Reis for helping with the preparation of the manuscript for publication.

rising carbon dependency of the world economy. Contemporary unease over natural resource scarcity, energy insecurity, global warming and other environmental consequences is to be expected, given the rapid rate of environmental change caused by the global economy and human populations over the twentieth century … At the beginning of the twenty-first century, therefore, we are more accustomed to viewing "the exceeding bounty of nature" to be running out, rather than providing unlimited supplies for "our genius for enterprise." Rather than enjoying a new "Golden Age" of Resource-Based Development, we seem to be entering a different era, the "Age of Ecological Scarcity."[3]

Fortunately, over the past several decades, a number of important developments have occurred that provide some grounds for optimism.

Increasingly, economists, ecologists, and other environmental scientists are realizing that progress in analyzing and mitigating problems of ecological scarcity requires interdisciplinary collaboration.[4] Although calls for such collaboration have been routine for some time, an important catalyst was the Millennium Ecosystem Assessment (MEA), which made two important contributions.[5] First, it confirmed what has been suspected for some time: global ecological scarcity is a serious problem. Approximately fifteen out of twenty-four major global ecosystem services have been degraded or used unsustainably, including freshwater, capture fisheries, air and water purification, and the regulation of regional and local climate, natural hazards, and pests. Second, the MEA offered a succinct definition of *ecosystem services* as "the benefits people obtain from ecosystems." Such a definition has facilitated inter-disciplinary collaboration, because it means that environmental researchers now have shared goals in exploring how the structure and functions of an ecosystem provide various goods and services to humans and in determining the value of these ecosystem benefits.

---

[3] Barbier (2011), p. 3.
[4] Throughout this book, I use the term "environmental scientist" very broadly, to include not only natural scientists who study various biophysical aspects of the natural environment (e.g., geographers, geomorphologists, hydrologists, soil scientists, etc.) but scholars from history and social science who also study human interactions with the environment (e.g., anthropologists, environmental historians, political scientists, sociologists, etc.).
[5] MEA (2005).

The MEA has been part of a long line of international studies calling attention to the international plight of the global environment and, in particular, how environmental considerations are intricately linked with sustainable economic development. The notion of sustainability received a major boost as a policy objective in the 1980s, thanks to the consensus reached by the World Commission on Environment and Development (WCED).[6] The WCED (1987) defined sustainable development as "development that meets the needs of the present without compromising the ability of future generations to meet their own needs." Sustainability gained further prominence at the 1992 Earth Summit in Rio and the 2002 follow-up in Johannesburg, and the concept has served ever since as a guiding principle for international cooperation on development. Most recently, The Economics of Ecosystems and Biodiversity (TEEB) study is an international effort of collaborative research that draws attention to the global economic benefits of biodiversity and ecosystem conservation to foster policy debate on the practical actions moving forward.[7]

The linking of sustainability and environmental concerns has also helped boost the concept of ecosystems and the environment as *natural capital*. Nature has provided ecosystems and their benefits to us for free. On the other hand, perhaps because this capital has been provided freely to us, we humans have tended to view it as limitless, abundant, and thus perhaps always available for our use, exploitation, and conversion. As this book aims to show, the concept of an ecosystem as natural capital can help us analyze the economic behavior that has led to the development, as opposed to conservation, of so much ecological wealth. If we can understand this behavior better, then perhaps we can also find ways to manage and enhance what is left of our natural endowment.

This concept of ecosystems as a form of wealth is the key theme developed throughout this book. That is, if ecological scarcity is an economic problem, and if ecosystems can be viewed as *natural assets* that produce a flow of beneficial goods and services over time, then the standard approach in economics of modeling natural resources as a special form of capital can be extended to ecosystems. Much of this book involves developing such models as an illustration of this analytical approach to treating ecosystems as natural assets.

[6] WCED (1987).   [7] TEEB (2010).

However, this book is much more than about developing conceptual models. It is also about moving interdisciplinary research collaboration forward. From my early career as a Ph.D. student, one of my principal interests in economics has been how the economic analysis of natural resource and environmental problems can benefit from the concepts and lessons learned from other disciplines, in particular ecology. I have been fortunate over my career to have benefited from collaboration with numerous ecologists and other environmental scientists. In writing this book, I am trying to appeal to this broader scientific community just as much as to my fellow economists. Again, this reflects my belief that progress in combating ecological scarcity will require interdisciplinary collaboration, which will only come about if environmental researchers from different disciplines are willing to learn from each other.

Finally, this book is ultimately about improving environmental policy. The role of policy in controlling excessive environmental degradation requires implementation of effective and appropriate information, incentives, institutions, investments, and infrastructure – the five *i*'s as I call them. The last two chapters of the book try to chart both the way ahead for future ecological and economic research to guide better environmental policy and to outline the key policy challenges that the world faces if it wishes to overcome ecological scarcity. I think, in some ways, these are the most important chapters of the book. If our ecological and economic research does not lead to policy change, then the problems of ecological scarcity, energy insecurity, global warming, and other environmental consequences of unsustainable economic development will truly usher in an Age of Ecological Scarcity.

References

Barbier, E.B. 1989. *Economics, Natural Resource Scarcity and Development: Conventional and Alternative Views.* Earthscan Publications, London.

2011. *Scarcity and Frontiers: How Economies Have Developed Through Natural Resource Exploitation.* Cambridge University Press.

Millennium Ecosystem Assessment (MEA). 2005. *Ecosystems and Human Well-being: Current State and Trends.* Island Press, Washington, DC.

The Economics of Ecosystems and Biodiversity (TEEB). 2010. *The Economics of Ecosystems and Biodiversity: Mainstreaming the Economics of Nature: A Synthesis of the Conclusions and Recommendations of TEEB.* TEEB, Bonn, Germany.

World Commission on Environment and Development. 1987. *Our Common Future.* Oxford University Press, New York.

1 | Ecological scarcity as an economic problem

> The fundamental scarcity problem ... is that as the environment is increasingly being exploited for one set of uses (e.g., to provide sources of raw material and energy, and to assimilate additional waste), the quality of the environment may deteriorate. The consequence is an increasing *relative scarcity* of essential natural services and ecological functions ... In other words, if "the environment is regarded as a scarce resource," then the "deterioration of the environment is also an economic problem."
>
> (Barbier 1989, pp. 96–97)

Introduction

One of the most critical problems facing humankind today is the rapid disappearance and degradation of many ecosystems worldwide. The key question is: How can we humans allow the continued overuse and destruction of nature, which is so essential to life and valuable? A pertinent reply is:

We are using natural capital because it is valuable; the reason we are losing natural capital is it is free.

Such a reply conveys an important economic view of the global problem of environmental loss: the basic unit of nature – the ecosystem – is a special form of wealth, which we can think of as a stock of *natural capital*. Humans depend on and use this natural capital for a whole range of important benefits, including life support. Hence, our ecological wealth is extremely valuable. But unlike skills, education, machines, tools, and other types of human and human-made capital, we do not have to manufacture and accumulate our endowment of natural assets. Nature has provided ecosystems and their benefits to us for free. However, perhaps because this capital has been provided freely to us, we humans have tended to view it as limitless, abundant,

6

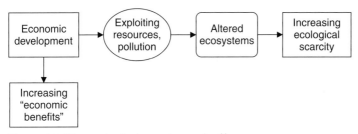

Figure 1.1 The ecological scarcity tradeoff

and always available for our use, exploitation, and conversion. The concept of an ecosystem as natural capital can help us analyze the economic behavior that has led to the overuse of so much ecological wealth. If we can understand this behavior better, then perhaps we can also find ways to manage and enhance what is left of our natural endowment.

The purpose of this chapter is to provide the rationale for the treatment of ecosystems as natural assets. The starting point for this approach, as the above quote suggests, is the growing concern over the economic problem of ecological scarcity. For our purposes, *ecological scarcity* can be defined as the loss of the myriad contributions that ecosystems make to human well-being – or *ecosystem services* for short – as these natural systems are exploited for human use and economic activity.

Ecological scarcity arises through a fundamental tradeoff in our use of the natural environment. This tradeoff can be depicted in a simple diagram (see Figure 1.1). Economic development cannot proceed without exploiting natural resources for raw material and energy inputs or using the environment to assimilate pollution and other waste by-products. On the positive side, economic development also leads to the increased production and consumption of human-made goods and services. As these goods and services contribute to overall human welfare, they can be considered the "economic benefits" of development. However, the exploitation and use of the natural environment by humans for raw materials, energy, and waste assimilation also leads to the alteration of *ecosystems*, which are the interacting systems of biota with their physical environment that are found throughout nature. The disruption and destruction of ecosystems affect, in turn, their various contributions to human welfare, such as the use of aesthetic landscapes for recreation, the maintenance of beneficial species, the control of erosion, protection against floods or storms, and so forth. The loss of these "ecological benefits," or ecosystem services, as the consequence of economic development is what constitutes increasing ecological scarcity.

Once we begin to see ecological scarcity as an economic problem, it is not difficult to view ecosystems as natural assets. Because ecosystems generate services that contribute to human welfare, they can be considered a form of wealth. The tradeoff of increased economic benefits versus increased ecological scarcity is therefore really about a tradeoff between different assets. On the one hand, we are creating economic wealth; on the other, we are sacrificing our available "ecological wealth" to do so.

The recent literature on ecological services also implies that ecosystems are assets that produce a flow of beneficial goods and services over time.[1] For example, as Daily *et al.* (2000, p. 395) state, "the world's ecosystems are capital assets. If properly managed, they yield a flow of vital services, including the production of goods (such as seafood and timber), life support processes (such as pollination and water purification), and life-fulfilling conditions (such as beauty and serenity)." Ecosystems should therefore be treated as an important asset in an economy, and in principle, ecosystem services should be valued in a similar manner as any form of wealth. That is, regardless of whether or not there exists a market for the goods and services produced by ecosystems, their social value must equal the discounted net present value (NPV) of these flows.

This concept of ecosystems as a form of wealth is the key theme developed throughout this book. That is, if ecological scarcity is an economic problem, and if ecosystems can be viewed as *natural assets* that produce a flow of beneficial goods and services over time, then the standard approach in economics of modeling natural resources as a special form of capital can be extended to ecosystems. For example, an important contribution of natural resource economics has been to treat the natural environment as a form of capital asset (e.g., see Clark 1976; Freeman *et al.* 1973; Dasgupta and Heal 1979; Herfindahl and

---

[1] See, for example, Barbier (2007, in press); Daily (1997); Daily *et al.* (2000); EPA (2009); MEA (2005); NRC (2005); Pagiola *et al.* (2004); Polasky and Segerson (2009); TEEB (2009); WRI (2001).

Kneese 1974). Initially, this approach focused only on certain valuable renewable and natural resource stocks found in the environment, such as mineral ores, energy reserves, fisheries and forests, as stores of wealth. But even in the early development of natural resource economics, there was growing recognition that the capital approach to the natural environment should be extended to natural areas and ecosystems (e.g., see Freeman *et al.* 1973; Howe 1979; Krutilla 1967; Krutilla and Fisher 1975).

For instance, in the early 1970s, Freeman *et al.* (1973, p. 20) proposed that the environment should be considered a "capital good" for the diverse "services" that it generates:

[We] view the environment as an asset or a kind of nonreproducible capital good that produces a stream of various services for man. Services are tangible (such as flows of water or minerals), or functional (such as the removal, dispersion, storage, and degradation of wastes or residuals), or intangible (such as a scenic view).

However, it is only in recent years, with rising concern over the problem of ecological scarcity – the continuing disappearance and degradation of many of the world's ecosystems and the subsequent loss in the many benefits they provide – that this natural capital concept has gained more widespread acceptance. As summarized by Barbier and Heal (2006, p. 1):

A new paradigm is emerging in environmental economics. It views the natural environment as a form of capital asset, natural capital ... Natural capital consists not only of specific natural resources, from energy and minerals to fish and trees, but also of interacting ecosystems. Ecosystems comprise the abiotic (nonliving) environment and the biotic (living) groupings of plant and animal species called communities. As with all forms of capital, when these two components of ecosystems interact, they provide a flow of services. Examples of such ecosystem services include water supply and its regulation, climate maintenance, nutrient cycling, and enhanced biological productivity.

The main aim of this book is to demonstrate how the concept of an ecosystem as a capital asset – natural capital – can inform a wide range of conservation and development decisions. Such an approach not only builds on the notion of ecosystems as critical assets for sustaining economic activity and human welfare but also facilitates analyzing the fundamental ecological scarcity tradeoff depicted in Figure 1.1. Although one of the objectives of the book is to develop and extend an economic model of ecosystems as a natural asset, much of the book is written in a nontechnical style that should broaden its appeal. The book also includes extensive discussion of real-world examples, scientific developments, and policy applications.

In developing and extending its basic natural asset model, the book explores research on ecosystems and their services from economics, ecology, and environmental science. Thus, an additional aim of the book is to discuss the major developments in the ecological and economic analysis of ecosystem services and to identify the areas for further interdisciplinary research collaboration. The topics covered in this book will also interest academic researchers and students from the different disciplinary backgrounds concerned with environmental management, and not just economists.

To summarize, the main purpose of this book is to show how the standard approach in economics of modeling natural resources as a special form of capital can be extended to ecosystems, and why such an approach should be of interest not just to economists but also ecologists, other environmental scientists, and general readers interested in the latest developments in the economics of ecosystems and their services. After all, progress in understanding how ecosystems contribute to human welfare – and what is being lost through increasing ecological scarcity – will require much more interdisciplinary research involving economists, ecologists, and environmental scientists. Such research is also essential to ecosystem conservation and development decisions, which will continue to be a major policy focus for the foreseeable future.

These aims of the book are developed over the subsequent chapters in the following way.

Chapter 2 examines the "capital" approach to ecosystems and ecological services in more detail. It discusses the economic implications of ecosystem services, reviews examples of valuing these services, and looks at how the concept of an ecological landscape can be employed to define ecosystems as natural assets. This background is essential for demonstrating how the standard approach in economics of modeling natural resources as a special form of capital can be extended to ecosystems. As shown in Chapter 3, the starting point for a basic natural asset model is the assumption that any ecological landscape that is conserved must compete with the other assets in the portfolio of wealth owners in the economy. The model shows the importance of valuing ecosystem services to determine the optimal allocation of landscape among competing uses. It includes the possibility of an ecological transition, when it becomes technologically feasible to restore developed land as ecological landscape. The basic model is then extended to allow for the value of an ecosystem service and the costs of maintaining this service to vary with the spatial distance across the ecological landscape (Chapter 4); for the implications when the economy is opened to trade and payment for ecosystem services (Chapter 5); and, finally, for examining the effects of the risk of ecological collapse (Chapter 6).

In addition to developing and extending the basic natural asset model, Chapters 3 through 6 also include many examples and discussion of its application to specific ecosystems and landscapes, such as estuarine and coastal ecosystems, forests, watersheds, and marine systems. Chapter 7 discusses further advances in research, especially collaborative research by economists, ecologists, and other environmental scientists, which will be required to develop and apply further the type of policy-relevant analysis advocated in this book. Chapter 8 concludes the book by focusing on the major policy challenges that need to be overcome in order to avert the worsening global ecological scarcity problem.

The global problem of ecological scarcity

As suggested by Figure 1.1, the main rationale for treating ecosystems as natural assets is the growing problem of ecological scarcity. There is now substantial evidence indicating that this scarcity problem is accelerating on a global scale, and is manifesting itself in the loss of many ecosystem services.

Contemporary unease about the extent and scale of this process is understandable, given the rapid rate of environmental change caused by the global economy and human population over the twentieth century (Table 1.1). The long-term trends of this change depicted in Table 1.1 also reveal the fundamental ecological scarcity tradeoff. On the positive side, and reflecting increased economic benefits, the world

Table 1.1 *Magnitudes of global environmental change, 1890s to 1990s*

Indicator	Coefficient of increase, 1890s to 1990s
Drivers	
Human population	4
Urban proportion of human population	3
Total urban population	14
World economy	14
Industrial output	40
Energy use	13–14
Coal production	7
Freshwater use	9
Irrigated area	5
Cropland area	2
Pasture area	1.8
Pig population	9
Goat population	5
Cattle population	4
Marine fish catch	35
Impacts	
Forest area	0.8 (20% decrease)
Bird and mammal species	0.99 (1% decrease)
Fin whale population	0.03 (97% decrease)
Air pollution	2–10
Carbon dioxide (CO_2) emissions	17
Sulfur dioxide (SO_2) emissions	13
Lead emissions	8

Source: Adapted from McNeill (2000, pp. 360–361) and McNeill (2005, Tables 1 and 2).

economy, industrial output, cropland area, energy use, water use, urban areas, marine fish catch, livestock populations, and human populations have expanded significantly. But these trends are also important drivers of major environmental impacts, such as decreasing forest area, declining wild species, and increasing pollution. As we continue to encroach on and pollute fixed natural environments and habitats, the result is continuing decline in the remaining ecosystems and their services.

Over the past fifty years, ecosystems have been modified more rapidly and extensively than in any comparable period in human history, largely to meet rapidly growing demands for food, fresh water, timber, fiber, and fuel. The result has been a substantial and largely irreversible loss in biological diversity, ecosystems, and ecological services that they provide. Approximately fifteen out of twenty-four major global ecosystem services have been degraded or used unsustainably, including freshwater, capture fisheries, air and water purification, and the regulation of regional and local climate, natural hazards, and pests (MEA 2005). Over the next fifty years, the rate of biodiversity loss is also expected to accelerate, leading to the extinction of at least 500 of the 1,192 currently threatened bird species and 565 of the 1,137 mammal species (Dirzo and Raven 2003).

Global land use change has been a major cause of the alteration and loss of terrestrial ecosystems. As indicated in Figure 1.2, for the past three hundred years, global forest and woodland area has declined by about 10 million sq. km as cropland area has expanded dramatically. Since 1950, the pace of global land conversion has shown little sign of abating. However, underlying these global trends are significant differences in land use changes in developed and developing countries.

During the late nineteenth and early twentieth century in developed countries, cropland area slowed its growth, and eventually stabilized and then declined slightly by the late twentieth century. Throughout the twentieth century, abandoned cropland increased and then rose quickly in the last decades. As a result, the decline of forest and woodland has halted in developed countries in aggregate and, since 1990, total forest area has increased (see Table 1.2). Not only has primary forest area recovered but the growth in plantations has also been strong.

But on the whole, the long-run land use change for tropical developing countries is continuing and there is a rapid decline in forest area (see Figure 1.2 and Table 1.2). In the late twentieth century, cropland area in the tropics was still expanding, and consequently, forest area declining. Over the past fifty years, the contrast between changing agricultural versus forest land use in developing as opposed to developed economies could not be more dramatic (see Figure 1.3). In the major developing regions of Africa, Asia, and Latin America, the demand for new land required for future crop production growth shows little sign of abating in the near future (see Table 1.3). Almost one-fifth of

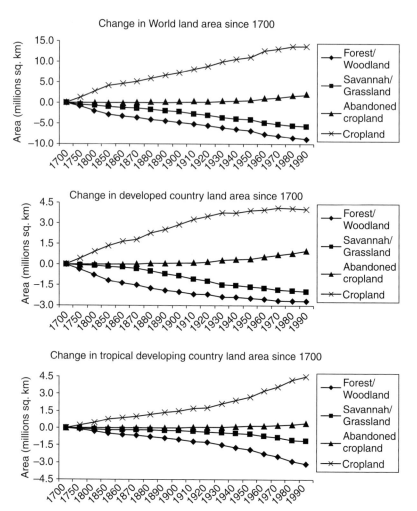

Figure 1.2 Long-run global land use change, 1700–1990
Notes: Developed countries include Europe plus Australia, Canada, Japan, New Zealand, and the United States. Tropical developing countries comprise the entire regions of tropical South America, Mexico and Central America, tropical Africa, South Asia, and Southeast Asia.
Source: Ramankutty and Foley (1999, Tables 3.a and 3.b).

Table 1.2 *Trends in global forest area (10⁶ km²), 1990–2005*

Region	Total forest				
				Percentage change	
	1990	*2000*	*2005*	*1990–2000*	*2000–2005*
World	40.77	39.89	39.52	–2.17%	–3.07%
Temperate developed	17.99	18.08	18.11	0.53%	0.71%
Tropical developing	18.55	17.49	16.95	–5.70%	–8.60%
Region	Primary forest				
				Percentage change	
	1990	*2000*	*2005*	*1990–2000*	*2000–2005*
World	14.03	13.73	13.38	–2.10%	–4.65%
Temperate developed	5.30	5.47	5.43	3.24%	2.55%
Tropical developing	8.29	7.84	7.52	–5.41%	–9.19%
Region	Plantation				
				Percentage change	
	1990	*2000*	*2005*	*1990–2000*	*2000–2005*
World	1.03	1.27	1.40	23.68%	36.18%
Temperate developed	0.45	0.56	0.59	24.32%	29.15%
Tropical developing	0.24	0.28	0.30	17.71%	27.37%

Notes: Developed countries include Europe plus Australia, Canada, Japan, New Zealand, and the United States. Tropical developing countries comprise the entire regions of tropical South America, Mexico, the Caribbean and Central America, tropical Africa, developing Oceania, South Asia, and Southeast Asia.

Source: FAO (2006).

Table 1.4 *Water withdrawal by volume and by share of total
renewable supplies*

Region/country	Total water withdrawal (km³)			Total withdrawal as a percentage of renewable water supply (%)		
	1995	2010	2025	1995	2010	2025
Asia	2,165	2,414	2,649	17	19	20
Latin America	298	354	410	2	2	3
Sub-Saharan Africa	128	166	214	2	3	4
West Asia/North Africa	236	266	297	69	81	90
Developing countries	2,762	3,134	3,507	8	9	10
Developed countries	1,144	1,223	1,265	9	9	10
World	**3,906**	**4,356**	**4,772**	**8**	**9**	**10**

Source: Barbier (2005, Table 1.5); adapted from Rosegrant *et al.* (2002, Table 4.1).

of extreme water scarcity. Other countries facing worsening water
stress and scarcity include Pakistan, the Philippines, South Korea,
and Mexico.

Coastal and marine ecosystems are also some of the most heavily used and threatened natural systems globally. They can start up
to 100 kilometers (km) inland, extend to the continental shelf, and
include ocean systems with waters up to 50 meters (m) in depth (MEA
2003). The distinct ecosystems found in these environments include
estuarine and coastal wetlands, such as marshes and mangroves,
sand beaches and dunes, seagrass beds, coral reefs, and coastal and
open-water marine ecosystems. However, coastal human population
densities are nearly three times that of inland areas, and they are
increasing exponentially (UNEP 2006). The resulting deterioration in
coastal systems due to human activities is intense and increasing, such
that 50% of salt marshes, 35% of mangroves, 30% of coral reefs,
and 29% of seagrasses are either lost or degraded worldwide (FAO
2007; MEA 2005; Orth *et al.* 2006; UNEP 2006; Valiela *et al.* 2001;
Waycott *et al.* 2009). Overfishing has also been a persistent and growing problem in all marine environments (Beddington *et al.* 2007; FAO

Table 1.5 *Developing countries and regions with relatively scarce water supplies*

Region/country	Total water withdrawal (km³)			Total withdrawal as a percentage of renewable water supply (%)		
	1995	2010	2025	1995	2010	2025
Huaihe	77.9	93.7	108.3	83	100	115
Haihe	59.2	62.1	62.9	140	147	149
Huanghe	64.0	71.1	79.5	89	99	111
Changjian	212.6	238.5	259.1	23	26	29
Songliao	51.5	59.2	67.6	26	30	34
Inland	89.5	98.9	111.2	299	330	371
Southwest	8.3	9.7	12.3	1	1	2
ZhuJiang	77.1	84.9	96.9	19	21	24
Southeast	38.8	41.4	47.7	27	29	33
China total	678.8	4,356	845.5	26	29	33
Sahyadri Ghats	14.9	18.7	20.8	14	17	19
Eastern Ghats	10.5	13.7	11.6	67	87	74
Cauvery	11.8	12.8	13.1	82	89	91
Godavari	30.2	33.3	38.8	27	30	35
Krishna	46.2	51.4	57.5	51	57	63
Indian-Coastal-Drain	34.8	46.9	43.6	108	145	135
Chotanagpur	7.2	10.9	14.3	17	26	34
Brahmari	25.5	27.2	31.0	24	22	26
Luni River Basin	41.9	43.1	50.8	148	140	166
Mahi–Tapti–Narmada	31.4	34.3	36.3	36	39	42
Brahmaputra	5.5	7.2	9.2	1	1	1
Indus	159.1	178.7	198.6	72	81	90
Ganges	255.3	271.9	289.3	50	54	57
India total	674.4	750.0	814.8	30	33	35
Pakistan	267.3	291.2	309.3	90	98	105
Philippines	47.0	58.2	70.0	24	29	35
South Korea	25.8	34.9	35.9	56	75	78
Mexico	78.6	86.2	94.2	24	26	29
Egypt	54.3	60.4	65.6	89	99	108
Other West Asia/North Africa[1]	143.2	156.0	171.5	116	125	139

Notes:
[1] Excluding Turkey.
Source: Barbier (2005, Table 1.6); adapted from Rosegrant *et al.* (2002, Table B.3).

2009; Halpern *et al.* 2008; Jackson *et al.* 2001; Lotze *et al.* 2006; Worm *et al.* 2006, 2009). The result is that coastal and marine ecosystems are under persistent threat from a variety of human-induced changes – from excessive fishing to climate change – that are altering these systems rapidly (see Figure 1.4).

The global decline of coastal and marine ecosystems is known to affect at least three critical services (Worm *et al.* 2006): the number of viable (noncollapsed) fisheries; the provision of nursery habitats such as oyster reefs, seagrass beds, and wetlands; and filtering and detoxification services provided by suspension feeders, submerged vegetation, and wetlands. Loss of filtering services is also linked to declining water quality and the increasing occurrence of harmful algal blooms, fish kills, shellfish and beach closures, and oxygen depletion. The decline in biodiversity, ecosystem functioning, and coastal vegetation may have contributed to biological invasions, declining water quality, and decreased coastal protection from flooding and storm events (Braatz *et al.* 2007, Cochard *et al.* 2008, Koch *et al.* 2009).

About 50 percent of global wetlands, which comprise not only coastal wetlands but also freshwater swamps and marshes, floodplains and peatlands, have disappeared as a result of human activities (Zedler and Kercher 2005). Much of this loss occurred in temperate regions during the first part of the twentieth century, but since the 1950s conversion of wetlands to alternative land uses has accelerated in tropical and subtropical areas. For example, in Asia about 5,000 sq. km of wetlands are vanishing annually due to drainage for agriculture, dam construction, and other uses. Estimates of the remaining global wetland range from 6–8 million sq. km (Mitsch *et al.* 2009) to 12–13 million sq. km (Finlayson *et al.* 1999). However, there is also concern that much of the remaining wetland area is degraded, as the result of hydrological alterations, salinization, eutrophication, sedimentation, filling, and exotic species invasions (Zedler and Kercher 2005).

Final remarks

The increasing evidence of global ecological scarcity has raised considerable concern over the implications for human welfare as more ecosystems are degraded or disappear. The type of tradeoff, illustrated by

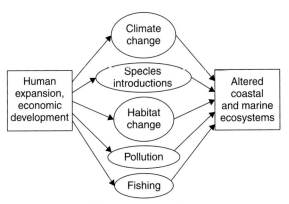

Figure 1.4 Human-induced threats to coastal and marine ecosystems
Source: Adapted from Jackson *et al.* (2001).

Figure 1.1, suggests that managing our remaining natural capital is as fundamental an economic problem as creating more wealth through accumulating human, physical, and social capital.

As argued in this chapter, we can make substantial progress in analyzing this important tradeoff only if we start implementing approaches that view the environment, and specifically ecosystems, as a form of natural capital. The remaining chapters of this book elaborate on this key theme. To set the stage, the next chapter explores further the concept of ecological services, discusses some of the important issues concerning the valuation of these services, and explores how the concept of an ecological landscape can assist the economic analysis of ecosystems as a natural asset.

However, the concept of ecosystems as natural capital is not just a convenient analytical tool. Viewing ecosystems as natural assets is also an important way of communicating to policymakers the economic importance of these valuable systems. As they provide a flow of beneficial goods and services over time, ecosystems should be considered no different from any other form of wealth in an economy. Policymakers are then confronted with a clear choice of deciding whether or not to conserve this natural capital or to convert it to another form of wealth.

By the end of the book, we will see how this concept of ecosystems as natural capital is important for thinking about sustainable economic development and policies. If an economy's endowment of natural resources and ecosystems are considered part of its overall wealth, then how one manages the economy's overall portfolio of physical, human, and natural capital becomes critical to sustaining economic welfare over time. There may be limits to how much we can substitute physical and human for natural capital. In addition, the failure to consider the economic consequences of the loss of ecological resilience – the ability of ecosystems to cope with random shocks and prolonged stress – should also make us cautious in allowing natural capital depletion. All of these considerations suggest that we should be concerned about the worsening global ecological scarcity highlighted in this chapter.

But a more fundamental problem is that we often do not know whether it is worth conserving ecosystems as natural assets simply because we do not know or bother to take into account the actual and potential benefits that they provide. As a result, development decisions will always be biased towards environmental degradation, because the prevailing assumption is that the foregone benefits provided by natural capital can be ignored. Hence, the pervasive problem of ecological scarcity results directly from our failure to treat ecosystems as economic assets. The purpose of this book is to show how economics, ecology, and other disciplines concerned with environmental management can help overcome this misperception. As the next chapter illustrates, assessing the ecological production of ecosystem goods and services and valuing their contributions to human welfare are critical steps in establishing ecosystems as natural assets.

References

Barbier, E.B. 1989. *Economics, Natural Resource Scarcity and Development: Conventional and Alternative Views*. Earthscan Publications, London.

2005. *Natural Resources and Economic Development*. Cambridge University Press.

2007. "Valuing ecosystems as productive inputs." *Economic Policy* 22:177–229.

in press. "Pricing Natures." *Annual Reviews of Resource Economics* 3.

Barbier, E.B. and G.M. Heal. 2006. "Valuing ecosystem services." *The Economists' Voice* 3(3):2. www.bepress.com/ev/vol3/iss3/art2, accessed April 4, 2011.

Beddington, J.R., D.J. Agnew, and C.W. Clark. 2007. "Current problems in the management of marine fisheries." *Science* 316:1713–1716.

Braatz, S., S. Fortuna, J. Broadhead, and R. Leslie. 2007. *Coastal Protection in the Aftermath of the Indian Ocean Tsunami: What Role for Forests and Trees?* FAO, Bangkok, pp. 157–179.

Clark, C.W. 1976. *Mathematical Bioeconomics*. Wiley Interscience, New York.

Cochard, R., S.L. Ranamukhaarachchi, G.P. Shivakotib, *et al.* 2008. "The 2004 tsunami in Aceh and Southern Thailand: A review on coastal ecosystems, wave hazards and vulnerability." *Perspectives in Plant Ecology, Evolution and Systematics* 10:3–40.

Daily, G.C., ed. 1997. *Nature's Services: Societal Dependence on Natural Ecosystems*. Island Press, Washington, DC.

Daily, G.C., T. Söderqvist, S. Aniyar *et al.* 2000. "The value of nature and the nature of value." *Science* 289:395–396.

Dasgupta, P.S. and G.M. Heal. 1979. *Economic Theory and Exhaustible Resources*. Cambridge University Press.

Dirzo, R. and P.H. Raven. 2003. "Global state of biodiversity and loss." *Annual Review of Environment and Resources* 28:137–167.

Environmental Protection Agency (EPA). 2009. *Valuing the Protection of Ecological Systems and Services*. A Report of the EPA Science Advisory Board. EPA, Washington, DC.

Finlayson, C.M., N.C. Davidson, A.G. Spiers, and N.J. Stevenson. 1999. "Global wetland inventory – current status and future priorities." *Marine Freshwater Research* 50(8):717–727.

Fischer, G. and G.K. Heilig. 1997. "Population momentum and the demand on land and water resources." *Philosophical Transactions of the Royal Society Series B* 352(1356): 869–889.

Food and Agricultural Organization (FAO) of the United Nations. 2006. *Global Forest Resources Assessment 2005, Main Report: Progress Towards Sustainable Forest Management*. FAO Forestry Paper 147. FAO, Rome.

2007. *The World's Mangroves 1980–2005*. FAO Forestry Paper 153. FAO, Rome.

2009. *The State of World Fisheries and Aquaculture 2008*. FAO, Rome.

Freeman, A.M. III, R.H. Haveman, and A.V. Kneese. 1973. *The Economics of Environmental Policy*. John Wiley, New York.

Halpern, B.S., S. Walbridge, K.A. Selkoe *et al.*, 2008. "A global map of human impacts on marine ecosystems." *Science* 319:948–952.

Herfindahl, O.C. and A.V. Kneese. 1974. *Economic Theory of Natural Resources*. Charles E. Merrill, Columbus, OH.

Howe, C.W. 1979. *Natural Resource Economics.* John Wiley, New York.

Jackson, J.B.C., M.X. Kirby, W.H. Berger *et al.* 2001. "Historical over-fishing and the recent collapse of coastal ecosystems." *Science* 293:629–638.

Koch, E.W., E.B. Barbier, B.R. Silliman *et al.* 2009. "Non-linearity in eco-system services: temporal and spatial variability in coastal protection." *Frontiers in Ecology and the Environment* 7:29–37.

Krutilla, J.V. 1967. "Conservation reconsidered." *American Economic Review* 57(4):777–786.

Krutilla, J.V. and A.C. Fisher. 1975. *The Economics of Natural Environments: Studies in the Valuation of Commodity and Amenity Resources.* Resources for the Future, Washington, DC.

Lotze, H.K., H.S. Lenihan, B.J. Bourque *et al.* 2006. "Depletion, degrad-ation and recovery potential of estuaries and coastal seas." *Science* 312:1806–1809.

McNeill, J.R. 2000. *Something New Under the Sun: An Environmental History of the 20th-century World.* W.W. Norton, New York.

2005. "Modern global environmental history." *IHDP Update* 2:1–3.

Millennium Ecosystem Assessment (MEA). 2003. *Ecosystems and Human Well-being: A Framework for Assessment.* Island Press, Washington, DC.

2005. *Ecosystems and Human Well-being: Current State and Trends.* Island Press, Washington, DC.

Mitsch, W.J., J.G. Gosselink, L. Zhang, and C.J. Anderson. 2009. *Wetland Ecosystems.* John Wiley, New York.

National Research Council (NRC). 2005. *Valuing Ecosystem Services: Toward Better Environmental Decision Making.* The National Academies Press, Washington, DC.

Orth, R.J., T.J.B. Carruthers, W.C. Dennison *et al.* 2006. "A global crisis for seagrass ecosystems." *BioScience* 56:987–996.

Pagiola, S., K. von Ritter, and J. Bishop. 2004. *How Much is an Ecosystem Worth: Assessing the Economic Value of Conservation.* The World Bank, Washington, DC.

Polasky, S. and K. Segerson. 2009. "Integrating ecology and economics in the study of ecosystem services: some lessons learned." *Annual Review of Resource Economics* 1:409–434.

Ramankutty, N. and J.A. Foley 1999. "Estimating historical changes in glo-bal land cover: croplands from 1700 to 1992." *Global Biogeochemical Cycles* 13:997–1027.

Rosegrant, M.W., X. Cai, and S.A. Cline. 2002. *World Water and Food to 2025: Dealing with Scarcity.* International Food Policy Research Institute, Washington, DC.

The Economics of Ecosystems and Biodiversity (TEEB). 2009. *TEEB for Policymakers.* TEEB–UNEP, Bonn, Germany.

United Nations Development Programme (UNDP). 2006. *Human Development Report 2006. Beyond Scarcity: Power, Poverty and the Global Water Crisis.* Palgrave Macmillan, New York.

United Nations Environment Programme (UNEP). 2006. *Marine and Coastal Ecosystems and Human Wellbeing: A Synthesis Report Based on the Findings of the Millennium Ecosystem Assessment.* UNEP, Nairobi.

2007. *Global Environmental Outlook. GEO-4: Environment for Development,* Ch. 4 Water. UNEP, Geneva.

UN-Water. 2007. *Coping with Water Scarcity: Challenge of the Twenty-First Century.* United Nations, New York, UN Water Day, March 22.

UN-Water and World Water Assessment Programme (WWAP). 2006. *Water: A Shared Responsibility.* The United Nations World Water Development Report 2. UN-Water and WWAP, New York.

Valiela, I., J.L. Bowen, and J.K. York. 2001. "Mangrove forests: one of the world's threatened major tropical environments." *BioScience* 51:807–815.

Wassenaar, T., P. Gerber, P.H. Verburg *et al.* 2007. "Projecting land use changes in the Neotropics: the geography of pasture expansion into forest." *Global Environmental Change* 17:86–104.

Waycott, M., C.M. Duarte, T.J.B. Carruthers *et al.* 2009. "Accelerating loss of seagrasses across the globe threatens coastal ecosystems." *Proceedings of the National Academy of Sciences* 106:12377–12381.

World Bank. 2008. *Word Development Indicators 2008.* The World Bank, Washington, DC.

World Resources Institute (WRI). 2001. *World Resources 2001. People and Ecosystems: The Fraying Web of Life.* WRI, Washington, DC.

Worm, B., E.B. Barbier, N. Beaumont *et al.* 2006. "Impacts of biodiversity loss on ocean ecosystem services." *Science* 314:787–790.

Worm, B., R. Hilborn, J.K. Baum *et al.* 2009. "Rebuilding global fisheries." *Science* 325:578–585.

Zedler, J.B. and S. Kercher. 2005. "Wetland resources: status, trends, ecosystem services, and restorability." *Annual Review of Environment and Resources* 20:39–74.

2 | Ecosystem services and ecological landscapes

... we have defined the environment as a kind of natural asset or non-reproducible capital good which is the source of economically valuable direct and indirect services to man. These services include residuals absorption or waste receptor services as well as life-sustaining, amenity, and materials, and materials supply services. These services are all economic goods in the sense that people are willing to pay to receive more of them or to avoid a reduction in the quantity or quality of the services that they provide.

(Freeman *et al.* 1973, p. 22)

Introduction

If we are to view ecosystems as economic assets, then it is helpful to be able to measure this form of "ecological wealth." This chapter examines further how ecosystems can be considered as economic assets. In order to do this, we develop the use of land, or ecological landscape, as the basic unit of most ecological processes and the services derived from them, and use this approach to illustrate the importance of valuing ecosystem services in land use decisions.

As noted in Chapter 1, an important contribution of natural resource economics has been to treat the natural environment as a form of capital asset.[1] The literature on ecosystem services implies that these environmental systems can also be viewed as *natural assets* that produce a flow of beneficial goods and services over time.[2] By drawing on both sets of literature, one can apply the traditional "natural capital"

---

[1] See, for example, Clark (1976); Clark and Munro (1975); Dasgupta and Heal (1974, 1979); Scott (1955); and Smith (1968).

[2] See, for example, Barbier (2007, 2011); Daily (1997); Daily *et al.* (2000); EPA (2009); MEA (2005); NRC (2005); Pagiola *et al.* (2004); Polasky and Segerson (2009); TEEB (2009); and WRI (2001).

approach of resource economics to develop the analysis of ecosystems as natural assets.

One barrier to such an approach is that, in ecology, the concept of an ecosystem has been difficult to define or to measure quantitatively (O'Neill 2001; Pickett and Cadenasso 2002). However, it is increasingly recognized that most ecological processes are influenced by the spatial extent, or landscape, that defines the boundary of the system.[3] Similarly, the various coastal and marine ecosystems that make up the land–sea interface located between watersheds, the coast, and oceans could be designated in terms of distinct *seascapes* that define the boundaries between each type of system (Moberg and Rönnbäck 2003; Shackeroff *et al.* 2009).[4]

As shown in this chapter, by adopting ecological landscape, or land area, as the basic unit, modeling the ecosystem as a natural asset is relatively straightforward. It also facilitates the examination of human transformation of an ecological landscape through land use conversion, leaving the residual land for ecological processes and habitat for species through relatively straightforward models of land use change. The next chapter will show how competing land use models in economics can be adapted and applied to modeling ecosystems as natural assets. The aim of the following chapter is to lay the foundation for this approach. We begin by exploring the relationship between ecosystems, their structure and functions, and the ecological services they generate that contribute to human welfare.

Ecosystems and ecosystem services

As pointed out by O'Neill (2001, p. 3276) "the ecosystem concept is a paradigm, an a priori intellectual structure, a specific way of looking

---

[3] See, for example, Bockstael (1996); O'Neill (2001); Perry (2002); Pickett and Cadenasso (1995, 2002); Turner (2005); and Zonneveld (1989).

[4] Thus, throughout this book, designating terrestrial ecosystems in terms of landscape, or land area, has its counterpart in defining coastal and marine ecosystems as seascapes, which could be measured in land or sea area units depending on where in the land–sea interface the ecosystems are located. For analytical convenience, many of the conceptual ideas and models developed in this book will refer to an ecological landscape, or land area, as the basic unit for analyzing an ecosystem as a natural asset. However, unless otherwise noted, it should be assumed that the same concepts and models could be applied to the various coastal and marine seascapes that define the land–sea interface.

at nature." In other words, "the ecosystem is the basic fundamental unit with which we must deal" in order to think about how the environment functions to support life, including humans (Odum 1975, p. 14). Consequently, if we want to characterize the environment as a "natural asset," then it makes sense to begin with this "basic fundamental unit" that is the ecologists' "specific way of looking at nature."

Tansley (1935) is often credited with first defining the ecosystem as a "system," in the sense that includes an assemblage of organisms interacting with its associated physical environment in a specific place (O'Neill 2001; Pickett and Cadenasso 2002). Thus, within its prescribed area or location, an ecosystem comprises its abiotic (nonliving) environment and the biotic (living) groupings of plant and animal species, or communities. The biotic and abiotic components, and the interactions between them, are often referred to as the *ecosystem structure*.

Two important *ecosystem functions* are carried out in every ecosystem: biogeochemical cycling and flow of energy. Important processes of biogeochemical cycling include primary production (photosynthesis), nutrient and water cycling, and materials decomposition. The flow, storage, and transformation of materials and energy through the system are also influenced by processes that link organisms with each other, such as the food web, which is made up of interlocking food chains. These food chains are often characterized by other important functions, such as pollination, predation, and parasitism.

The structure and functions of an ecosystem provide valuable goods and services to humans. For example, some of the living organisms found in an ecosystem might be harvested or hunted for food, collected for raw materials, or simply valued because they are aesthetically pleasing. Some of the ecosystem functions, such as nutrient and water cycling, can also benefit humans through purifying water, controlling floods, recharging aquifers, reducing pollution, or simply by providing more pleasing environments for recreation. These various benefits provided by an ecosystem via its structure and functions are now referred to as *ecosystem services*. As summarized in Box 2.1, the structure and functions of an ecosystem are not synonymous with its services. Ecosystem structure and functions describe the components of an ecosystem and its biophysical relationship regardless of whether or not humans benefit from them. Only if they contribute to human

---

Box 2.1 Ecosystem functions and services

… the term "ecosystem" describes a dynamic complex of plant, animal, and microorganism communities and their non-living environment, interacting as a system. Ecosystems encompass all organisms within a prescribed area, including humans. Ecosystem functions or processes are the characteristic physical, chemical, and biological activities that influence the flows, storage, and transformation of materials and energy within and through ecosystems. These activities include processes that link organisms with their physical environment (e.g., primary productivity and the cycling of nutrients and water) and processes that link organisms with each other, indirectly influencing flows of energy, water, and nutrients (e.g., pollination, predation, and parasitism). These processes in total describe the functioning of ecosystems … Ecosystem services are the direct or indirect contributions that ecosystems make to the well-being of human populations. Ecosystem processes and functions contribute to the provision of ecosystem services, but they are not synonymous with ecosystem services. Ecosystem processes and functions describe biophysical relationships that exist whether or not humans benefit from them. These relationships generate ecosystem services only if they contribute to human well-being, defined broadly to include both physical well-being and psychological gratification. Thus, ecosystem services cannot be defined independently of human values.

(EPA 2009, p. 12)

---

well-being do these components and relationships generate an "ecosystem service." As we shall see next, this distinction is important especially if we want to estimate the value of various ecosystem goods and services.

Assessing the value of ecosystem goods and services

The idea that ecosystems provide a range of "services" that have value to humans is an important step in characterizing these systems as "natural capital." In order to view ecosystems as a special type of capital asset – a form of "ecological wealth" – then just like any other asset or investment in the economy, ecosystems must be capable of generating current and future flows of income or benefits. It follows that, in principle, ecosystems can be valued just like any other asset in an economy. Regardless of whether or not there exists a market for the goods and services produced by ecosystems, their social value must equal the discounted net present value (NPV) of these flows.

As discussed in Chapter 1, the literature on ecological services implies that ecosystems are assets that produce a flow of beneficial goods and services over time. For example, a common practice in this literature is to adopt the broad definition of the MEA (2005) that "ecosystem services are the benefits people obtain from ecosystems." Thus the term ecosystem services is usually interpreted to imply the contribution of nature to a variety of "goods and services," which in economics would normally be classified under three different categories (Barbier 2007): 1) "goods" (e.g., products obtained from ecosystems, such as resource harvests, water, and genetic material); 2) "services" (e.g., recreational and tourism benefits or certain ecological regulatory and habitat functions, such as water purification, climate regulation, erosion control, and habitat provision); and 3) cultural benefits (e.g., spiritual and religious beliefs, heritage values).

However, for economists, the term "benefit" has a specific meaning. According to Mendelsohn and Olmstead (2009, p. 326): "The economic benefit provided by an environmental good or service is the sum of what all members of society would be willing to pay for it." Consequently, some economists argue that it is misleading to characterize all ecosystem services as "benefits." As explained by Boyd and Banzhaf (2007, p. 619), "as end-products of nature, final ecosystem services are not benefits nor are they necessarily the final product consumed. For example, recreation is often called an ecosystem service. It is more appropriately considered a benefit produced using both ecological services and conventional goods and services." To illustrate this point, they consider recreational angling. It requires certain "ecosystem services," such as "surface waters and fish populations" but also "other goods and services including tackle, boats, time allocation, and access" (Boyd and Banzhaf 2007, p. 619). But other economists still prefer the broader perspective of the MEA (2005), which equates ecosystem services with benefits. For example, Polasky and Segerson (2009, p. 412) state: "We adopt a broad definition of the term ecosystem services that includes both intermediate and final services," which they justify by explaining that "supporting services, in economic terms, are akin to the infrastructure that provides the necessary conditions under which inputs can be usefully combined to provide intermediate and final goods and services of value to society." Thus, unlike Boyd and Banzhaf (2007), Polasky and Segerson (2009) consider recreation to be an ecosystem service.

Economists do agree that, in order to determine society's willingness to pay for the benefits provided by ecosystem goods and services, one needs to measure and account for their various impacts on human welfare. Or, as Bockstael *et al.* (2000, p. 1385) state: "In economics, valuation concepts relate to human welfare. So the economic value of an ecosystem function or service relates only to the contribution it makes to human welfare, where human welfare is measured in terms of each individual's own assessment of his or her well-being." The key is determining how changes in ecosystem goods and services affect an individual's well-being, and then determining how much the individual is either willing to pay for changes that have a positive welfare impact or, conversely, how much the individual is willing to accept as compensation to avoid a negative effect.

The starting point in identifying ecosystem services and their values is the consensus economic view outlined above. As long as nature makes a contribution to human welfare, either entirely on its own or through joint use with other human inputs, then we can designate this contribution as an "ecosystem service." In other words. as stated in Box 2.1, "ecosystem services are the direct or indirect contributions that ecosystems make to the well-being of human populations." Although it is acceptable to use "the term ecosystem service to refer broadly to both intermediate and final end services," "in specific valuation contexts ... it is important to identify whether the service being valued is an intermediate or a final service" (EPA 2009, pp. 12–13).

Following this approach, for example, recreation can be considered the product of an ecosystem "service." But, as pointed out by Boyd and Banzhaf (2007, p. 619), the ecosystem provides only an "intermediate service" (along with "conventional goods and services") in the production of the final benefit of recreation and tourism. In estimating the value of this "intermediate" ecosystem service in producing recreational benefits, it is therefore important to assess only the effects of changes in the ecosystem on recreation, and not the additional influence of any human inputs. The same approach should be taken for those "final" ecosystem services, such as coastal protection, erosion control, nutrient cycling, water purification, and carbon sequestration, which may benefit human well-being with or without any additional human-provided goods and services. Valuation should show how changes in these services affect human welfare, after controlling for the influence of any additional human-provided goods and services.

Although valuing ecosystem goods and services seems straightforward, in practice there are a number of challenges to overcome. These difficulties are key to understanding why there are still a large number of ecosystem goods and services that have yet to be valued or have very unreliable valuation estimates.

The most significant problem is that very few are marketed. Some of the products provided by ecosystems, such as raw materials, food, and fish harvests, are bought and sold in markets. Given that the price and quantities of these marketed products are easy to observe, there are numerous value estimates of the contribution of the environmental input to this production. However, this valuation can be more complicated than it appears. Market conditions and regulatory policies for the commodity bought and sold will influence the values imputed to the environment input. For example, one important service of many estuarine and coastal ecosystems is that they serve as coastal breeding and nursery habitat for offshore fisheries. As many fisheries are exploited commercially, the inability to control fishing access and the presence of production subsidies and other market distortions can impact harvests, the price of fish sold and, ultimately, the estimated value of coastal habitats in supporting these fisheries (Barbier 2007, Barbier *et al.* 2002, Freeman 1991; Smith 2007).

However, the majority of ecosystem goods and services are not marketed. These include many services arising from ecosystem processes and functions that benefit human beings largely without any additional input from them, such as coastal protection, nutrient cycling, erosion control, water purification, and carbon sequestration. In recent years, substantial progress has been made by economists working with ecologists and other natural scientists in applying environmental valuation methodologies to assess the welfare contribution of these services. The various nonmarket valuation methods employed for ecosystem services are essentially the standard techniques that are available to economists.[5] Later on in this chapter, we discuss these issues further. Nevertheless, what makes applying these methods to estimate the value of a nonmarketed ecosystem service especially difficult is that it requires three important, and interrelated, steps (Barbier 1994, 2007, and in press; Freeman 2003; NRC 2005; Polasky and Segerson 2009).

The first step involves determining how best to characterize the change in ecosystem structure, functions, and processes that gives rise to the change in the ecosystem service. For example, the change could be in the spatial area or quality of a particular type of ecosystem, such as a mangrove forest, marsh vegetation, or watershed extent. It could also be a change in a key population, such as fish or main predator. Alternatively, the change could be due to variation in the flow of water, energy, or nutrients through the system, such as the variability in tidal surges due to coastal storm events or the influx of organic waste from pollution upstream from estuarine and coastal ecosystems.

The second step requires tracing how the changes in ecosystem structure, functions, and processes influence the quantities and qualities of ecosystem service flows to people. Underlying each ecosystem service is a range of important energy flow, biogeochemical, and biotic processes and functions. For example, water purification by seagrass beds is linked to the ecological processes of nutrient uptake and suspended particle deposition (Koch *et al.* 2006; Rybicki 1997). However, the key ecological process and functions that generate an ecosystem service are in turn controlled by certain abiotic and biotic components that are unique to each ecosystem's structure. The various controlling components that may affect nutrient uptake and particle deposition by seagrass ecosystems include seagrass species and density, nutrient load, water residence time, hydrodynamic conditions, and light availability. Only when these first two steps are completed is it possible to conduct the final step, which involves using existing economic valuation methods to assess the impact on human well-being that results from the change in ecosystem goods and services.

---

[5] For example, Barbier (2007); EPA (2009); Freeman (2003); Hanley and Barbier (2009); Mendelsohn and Olmstead (2009); NRC (2005); and Pagiola *et al.* (2004) discuss how these standard valuation methods are best applied to ecosystem services, emphasizing in particular both the advantages and the shortcomings of the different methods and their application.

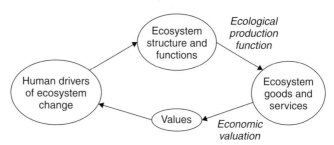

Figure 2.1 Key interrelated steps in valuing ecosystem goods and services
Source: Adapted from NRC (2005, Figure 1–3).

Figure 2.1 provides a visual summary of the key elements of this three-step approach. It indicates that "the fundamental challenge of valuing ecosystem services lies in providing an explicit description and adequate assessment of the links between the structure and functions of natural systems, the benefits (i.e., goods and services) derived by humanity, and their subsequent values" (NRC 2005, p. 2). Human drivers of ecosystem change affect important ecosystem processes and functions and their controlling components. Assessing this change is crucial yet difficult. However, as NRC (2005, pp. 2–3) points out, "making the translation from ecosystem structure and function to ecosystem goods and services (i.e., the ecological production) is even more difficult" and "probably the greatest challenge for successful valuation of ecosystem services is to integrate studies of the ecological production function with studies of the economic valuation function." Similarly, Polasky and Segerson (2009, p. 422) maintain that "among the more practical difficulties that arise in either predicting changes in service flows or estimating the associated value of ecosystem services" include the "lack of multiproduct, ecological production functions to quantitatively map ecosystem structure and function to a flow of services that can then be valued."

An example: wetland ecosystems

The Ramsar Convention on Wetlands of International Importance defines wetlands as "areas of marsh, fen, peatland, or water, whether natural or artificial, permanent of temporary, with water that is static or flowing, fresh, brackish or salt, including areas of marine water, the depth of which at low tide does not exceed six metres." This broad definition usually encompasses coastal wetlands, freshwater swamps and marshes, floodplains, and peatlands as distinct types of wetland ecosystems (Mitsch *et al.* 2009; Zedler and Kercher 2005).

Table 2.1 provides some examples of how specific wetland ecosystem services are linked to the underlying ecological structure and functions underlying each service. It also cites, where possible, economic studies that have estimated the values arising from the service. The list of studies in Table 2.1 is not inclusive; for more comprehensive summaries of the literature on economic valuation of wetlands see, e.g., Barbier *et al.* (1997), Brander *et al.* (2006), Turner *et al.* (2008) and Woodward and Wiu (2001). Nevertheless, the valuation studies are representative of the literature, and thus instructive.

For one, as the studies cited in Table 2.1 indicate, wetland valuation has tended to focus on only a few ecosystem services, such as recreation, coastal habitat-fishery linkages, raw materials and food production, and water purification. In recent years, a handful of more reliable estimates of the storm protection service of coastal wetlands have also emerged. But for a number of important wetland ecosystem services very few or no valuation studies exist. Thus, for many wetland ecosystem services, the three-step approach outlined in Figure 2.1 of tracing the ecological production function of ecosystem goods and services to their final contributions to human welfare has not been possible.

In addition, current valuation studies also illustrate the extent to which wetland ecosystem services are uniquely related to hydrological processes. As emphasized by Mitsch *et al.* (2009, p. 2), these processes are critical to the functioning and structure of wetland ecosystems: "The hydrology of the landscape influences and changes the physiochemical environment, which in turn, along with hydrology, determines the biotic communities that are found in the wetland." The consequence is that the ecosystem services provided by wetlands are driven by hydrology, and understanding how changes in hydrological processes affect the delivery of these services is crucial to determining the impact on human welfare (Brauman *et al.* 2007; Bullock and Acreman 2003; Emerton and Boss 2008; Mitsch *et al.* 2009).

If the goods and services of wetland ecosystems are influenced by "the hydrology of the landscape," then we may have a natural unit for measuring these important ecological assets. Because the structure and functions of many wetlands can be uniquely defined by

Table 2.1 *Examples of wetland ecosystem services and valuation studies*

Ecosystem structure and function	Ecosystem services	Valuation examples
Attenuates and/or dissipates waves, buffers wind	Coastal protection	Badola and Hussein (2005); Barbier (2007); Costanza *et al.* (2008); Das and Vincent (2009)
Provides sediment stabilization and soil retention	Erosion control	Sathirathai and Barbier (2001)
Water flow regulation and control	Flood protection	Brouwer and van Elk (2004)
Groundwater recharge/discharge	Water supply	Acharya and Barbier (2000, 2002)
Provides nutrient and pollution uptake, as well as retention, particle deposition	Water purification	Breaux *et al.*(1995); Byström (2000); Gren (1995); Jenkins *et al.* (2010); Yang *et al.* (2008)
Generates biogeochemical activity, sedimentation, biological productivity	Carbon sequestration	Jenkins *et al.* (2010)
Climate regulation and stabilization	Maintenance of temperature, precipitation	
Generates biological productivity and diversity	Raw materials and food	Islam and Braden (2006); Janssen and Padilla (1999); King and Lester (1995); Naylor and Drew (1998); Ruitenbeek (1994); Sathirathai and Barbier (2001)

Table 2.1 (*cont.*)

Ecosystem structure and function	Ecosystem services	Valuation examples
Provides suitable reproductive habitat and nursery grounds, sheltered living space	Maintains fishing, hunting, and foraging activities	Aburto-Oropeza *et al.* (2008); Barbier (2007); Barbier and Strand (1998); Bell (1997); Freeman (1991); Janssen and Padilla (1999); Johnston *et al.* (2002); Sanchirico and Mumby (2009); Smith (2007); Swallow (1994)
Provides unique and aesthetic landscape, suitable habitat for diverse fauna and flora	Tourism, recreation, education, and research	Bateman and Langford (1997); Bergstrom and Stoll (1993); Birol and Cox (2007); Birol *et al.* (2006); Brouwer and Bateman (2005); Carlsson *et al.* (2003); Cooper and Loomis (1993); Creel and Loomis (1992); Do and Bennett (2008); Hammitt *et al.* (2001); Jenkins *et al.* (2010); Johnston *et al.* (2002); King and Lester (1995); Othman *et al.* (2004)
Provides unique and aesthetic landscape of cultural, historic, or spiritual meaning	Culture, spiritual, and religious benefits, bequest values	Bateman and Langford (1997); Kwak *et al.* (2007); Naylor and Drew (1998)

hydrological processes, it is possible to identify the spatial unit, or ecological landscape, that is distinct to each type of wetland. Such a landscape approach is being increasingly used for assessing the cumulative effects of wetland loss and degradation, characterizing wetland boundaries and identifying restoration or mitigation opportunities (Bedford 1996, 1999; Gwin *et al.* 1999; Mitsch and Gosselink 2000; NRC 1995; Simenstad *et al.* 2006). It follows that the various goods and services provided by a wetland will also be tied to, and thus defined by, its landscape extent; i.e., "wetland values depend on the hydrogeomorphic location in which they are found" (Mitsch and Gosselink 2000, p. 27).

The example of wetlands may not be exceptional, however. If the structure and functions of most ecosystems can be delineated in terms of a well-defined ecological landscape, then the landscape could serve as the natural unit of measurement for thinking about these important systems as capital assets.

Ecosystems as ecological landscapes

If ecosystems are assets that produce a flow of beneficial goods and services over time, then we need to have a physical unit of measurement to represent this type of capital. Such physical measurement is especially important in considering a basic policy decision, such as how much of an ecosystem should be converted or developed as opposed to conserved or even restored to continue producing flows of goods and services.

But as ecologists have pointed out, the concept of an ecosystem is highly multidimensional and difficult to define or measure (O'Neill 2001; Pickett and Cadenasso 2002). The main problem, as explained by Pickett and Cadenasso (2002, p. 2) is that "the use of the ecosystem as a core idea invites a wide variety of approaches, from biodiversity, through evolutionary, to nutrient and energy processing, from instantaneous to historical, and from microbial to biospheric."

For example, an early approach to characterizing different ecosystems was in terms of its energy processing or *total energy flow*, which is defined as the portion of incoming solar radiation that is successfully converted through photosynthesis into plant matter and is thus potentially available to herbivores (Odum 1975). As Table 2.2 shows, total energy flow per annum of most solar-powered ecosystems varies from 1,000 to 40,000 kilocalories per sq. m (4.185 to 167.4 megajoules [MJ] per sq. m) This range covers both unsubsidized solar-powered ecosystems that depend largely or entirely on solar energy as the source of energy, and naturally subsidized solar-powered ecosystems that augment solar energy by auxiliary energy input of tides, waves, wind, rainfall, or water power, and possibly through the energy content of any organic matter or nutrients imported from other ecosystems. For the latter ecosystems, these

Table 2.2 *Ecosystems classified in terms of source and level of energy flow*

	Annual energy flow (kilocalories per m^2)
1. *Unsubsidized natural solar-powered ecosystems*	1,000–10,000
Examples: open oceans, upland forests.	(2,000)
Basic life-support systems found on Earth.	
2. *Naturally subsidized solar-powered ecosystems*	10,000–40,000
Examples: tidal estuary, some rainforests.	(20,000)
The naturally productive systems that not only have high life-support capacity but also produce excess organic matter that may be exported to other systems or stored.	
3. *Human-subsidized solar-powered ecosystems*	10,000–40,000
Examples: agriculture, aquaculture.	(20,000)
Food and fiber-producing systems supported by auxiliary fuel or other energy supplied by humans.	
4. *Fuel-powered urban-industrial systems*	100,000–3,000,000
Examples: cities, suburbs, industrial parks	(2,000,000)
Systems in which terrestrial energy replaces the sun as the chief energy source, yet are still dependent on the first three types of ecosystems for life support, food, fiber and fuel.	

Notes: Numbers in parentheses are estimated round-figure averages.
Source: Odum (1975, Table 2.1).

auxiliary energy sources reduce the unit cost of self-maintenance (in energy terms) by the ecosystem, which increases the amount of solar energy input converted to the chemical potential energy of plants. Hence, as indicated in Table 2.2, the mean energy flow for a naturally subsidized ecosystem, such as a tidal estuary or a rainforest, is likely to be higher than that for a purely solar-powered ecosystem, such as an upland forest or grasslands.

The ecological production of goods and services is likely to be related to the total energy flow of an ecosystem. Thus, as shown in Table 2.2, one would expect naturally subsidized ecosystems to produce more goods and services than purely solar-powered systems. For example, according to Odum (1975, p. 18),

a coastal estuary is a good example of a natural system subsidized by the energy of tides, waves, and currents. Since the back and forth flow of water does part of the necessary work of recycling mineral nutrients and transporting food and wastes, the organisms in an estuary are able to concentrate their efforts, so to speak, on more efficient conversion of sun energy to organic matter. In a very real sense, organisms in the estuary are adapted to utilize tidal power. Consequently, estuaries tend to be more fertile than, say, an adjacent land area or pond which receives the same solar input, but does not have the benefit of the tidal and other water flow energy subsidy.

Many of the valuation studies listed in Table 2.1, for example, confirm that coastal and estuarine wetlands tend to have highly valued goods and services.

However, the total energy flow of an ecosystem is not an adequate physical unit for representing it as a natural asset. For one, a flow measure, such as MJ per sq. m, has different units than an asset, which is a stock variable measured or accumulated at a specific moment in time. Second, although it is possible to compare the total energy flow of two ecosystems, such a comparison does not necessarily provide guidance as to how much to develop or conserve of one ecosystem as opposed to another. For example, as shown in Table 2.2, the energy flow for a naturally subsidized ecosystem, such as a tidal estuary or a rainforest, appears to be equivalent to human-subsidized solar-powered ecosystems, such as agriculture or aquaculture. Thus if total energy flow is the basis for determining the relative value of the two types of ecosystems, then we might be indifferent between the two. Yet, as discussed in Chapter 1, over the past fifty years, considerable land use conversion of many tropical forest and estuarine ecosystems to agriculture and aquaculture uses has occurred. Thus, it appears that the relative value of the use of the land of the two types of ecosystems, rather than their relative total energy flow, determines how humans view these two competing forms of wealth.

This suggests that the stock variable that could serve as a physical unit for depicting an ecosystem as a natural asset is its land area. Recent developments in landscape ecology, for example, suggest that the basic unit of most ecological processes is spatial and is synonymous with the land or ecological landscape that defines the boundary of the system (Bockstael 1996; O'Neill 2001; Perry 2002; Pickett and Cadenasso 1995, 2002; Turner 2005; Zonneveld 1989). As summarized by Bockstael (1996, p. 1169) the implications for economic modeling of ecosystem processes and services are clear: "because landscape pattern and ecological processes are closely linked ... land use change at one scale or another is perhaps the single greatest factor affecting ecological resources." In other words, as there are "reciprocal interactions between spatial pattern and ecological processes" (Turner 2005, p. 319), it is the spatially heterogeneous area of landscape that is fundamental to the flow of beneficial goods and services that we now recognize as ecosystem services. If for each ecosystem we can define its corresponding landscape in terms of a quantifiable "land unit," which is defined as "a tract of land that is ecologically homogeneous at the scale level concerned" (Zonneveld 1989, p. 68), then we have a representation of an ecosystem as a natural asset in the form of this unit of land, or *ecological landscape.*[6]

Allocating ecological landscapes between competing uses

If ecosystems and the services they generate can be associated with the ecological landscape defining these systems, then we can not only depict these ecosystems as natural assets but also develop ways of determining whether it is worthwhile holding on to, or conserving, these assets compared to depleting, or converting, them.

For example, let's suppose that the flow of ecosystem services in any time period t, can be quantified and that we can measure what

---

[6] Throughout this book, I will employ this term *ecological landscape* to refer to the unique natural landscape or land area associated with a single ecosystem. Such terminology is somewhat at odds with how some landscape ecologists view the term *landscape*, which is sometimes defined as an area containing two or more ecosystems in close proximity (Sanderson and Harris 2000). However, a more broad definition in landscape ecology is offered by Turner (2005, p. 320) who states: "Most generally, a landscape is an area that is spatially heterogeneous in at least one factor of interest." Similarly, Farina (2010, p. 9) suggests that "a common feature of any landscape is its heterogeneity. This heterogeneity may be scaled on structure, water, and nutrients for plants, or on suitable habitat-patches for animals." In other words, it seems perfectly appropriate to use the term "ecological landscape" to denote the land area encompassed by an ecosystem.

each individual is willing to pay for having these services provided to him or her. If we sum up, or aggregate, the willingness to pay by all the individuals benefiting in each period from the ecosystem services, we will have a monetary amount – call it B_t – which indicates the social benefits in the given time period t of those services. There will be a stream of such benefits generated by ecosystem services, from the present time and into the future. Because society is making a decision today about whether or not to preserve ecosystems, we want to consider the flow of benefits of these services, net of the costs of maintaining the natural ecosystems, in terms of their present value. To do this, any future net benefit flows are discounted into net present value (NPV) equivalents.

In essence, we are treating natural ecosystems as a special type of capital asset – a kind of "natural wealth" – which, just like any other asset or investment in an economy, is capable of generating a current and future flow of income or benefits. That is, regardless of whether or not there exists a market for the goods and services produced by ecosystems, their social value must equal the discounted NPV of these flows.

However, from the discussion so far in Chapter 1 and this chapter, compared to conventional economic or financial assets, environmental assets are subject to special measurement problems.

First, ecosystems are an unusual form of capital. As with all forms of capital, they provide a flow of services. But how this occurs in ecosystems is unique. As we have seen, ecosystems comprise the abiotic (nonliving) environment and the biotic (living) groupings of plant and animal species called communities. When these two components of ecosystems interact, they provide a flow of diverse services that benefit humans (e.g., see Table 2.1 for wetlands). Thus, it is the ecological production of ecosystem services from the structure and functions of these systems that are the key characteristic of these "natural" assets (Barbier and Heal 2006; NRC 2005; Polasky and Segerson 2009). If an ecosystem is left relatively undisturbed, then the flow services from the ecosystem's structure and functions are available in quantities that are not affected by the rate at which they are used. Although like other assets in the economy an ecosystem can be increased by investment, such as through restoration activities, ecosystems can also be depleted or degraded, e.g., through habitat destruction, land conversion, pollution impacts, and so forth.

Second, as discussed earlier in this chapter, whereas the services from most assets in an economy are marketed, the benefits arising from the regulatory and habitat functions of ecosystems generally are not. If the aggregate willingness to pay for these benefits, B_t, is not revealed through market outcomes, then efficient management of such ecosystem services requires explicit methods to measure this social value.[7] In fact, the failure to consider the values provided by key ecosystem services in current policy and management decisions is a major reason for the widespread disappearance of many ecosystems and habitats across the globe (MEA 2005). As we saw in Chapter 1, the global expansion of human populations and economic activity is an important cause of this disappearance, due to, among other things, increased demand for land, pollution, or over-exploitation of resources. The failure to measure explicitly the aggregate willingness to pay for otherwise nonmarketed ecological services exacerbates these problems, as the benefits of these services are underpriced and may lead to excessive land conversion, habitat fragmentation, harvesting, water use, and pollution caused by commercial economic activity undertaken by humans.

Figure 2.2 illustrates the difficulty that the above challenges pose for managing ecological landscapes optimally. In this figure, the example of the conversion of an area of coastal landscape to commercial development is used.

In Figure 2.2, the marginal social benefits of ecological services at any time t are represented by the line MB_t for a coastal ecosystem of given area $\bar{A}$. For the purposes of illustration, this line is assumed to be downward-sloping, which implies that for every additional square kilometer of coastal landscape area, A, preserved in its original state, more ecosystem service benefits will be generated, but at a decreasing amount. Chapter 4 provides evidence supporting this assumption that marginal ecosystem benefits tend to decline in this way across a landscape, especially for some important services of coastal landscape. Note that it is straightforward to determine the aggregate willingness to pay for the benefits of these services, B_t, from this line; it is simply

---

[7] See, for example, Barbier (2007), EPA (2009), Freeman (2003), Hanley and Barbier (2009), NRC (2005), and Pagiola *et al.* (2004), who discuss how standard economic valuation methods can be applied to nonmarket ecosystem services. Later on in this chapter, we discuss briefly some of the challenges that arise when applying these methods to valuing ecosystem services.

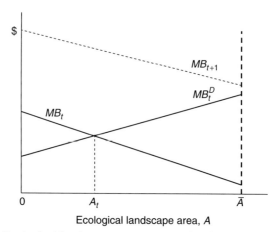

Figure 2.2 Ecological landscape conversion to development

the area under the MB_t line. If there is no other use for the ecological landscape, then the opportunity costs of maintaining it are zero, and B_t is at its maximum size when the entire coastal ecosystem is maintained at its original land area size $\bar{A}$. The ecosystem management decision is therefore simple; the coastal landscape should be completely preserved and allowed to provide its full flow of services in perpetuity.

However, population and economic development pressures in many areas of the world usually mean that the opportunity cost of maintaining coastal landscape is not zero. The ecosystem management decision needs to consider these alternative development uses of coastal landscape, which should be included in Figure 2.2. For example, suppose that the marginal social benefits of converting ecosystem land for these development options is now represented by a new line MB_t^D in the figure. Efficient land use now requires that $\bar{A} - A_t$ of coastal landscape should be converted for development leaving A_t of the original ecosystem undisturbed.

Both of the outcomes discussed so far assume that the willingness to pay for the marginal benefits arising from coastal ecosystem services, MB_t, is explicitly measured, or valued. But if this is not the case, then these nonmarketed flows are likely to be ignored in the land use decision. Only the marginal benefits of the MB_t^D marketed outputs arising from coastal economic development activities will be taken into account and, as indicated in the figure, this implies that the entire ecosystem area $\bar{A}$ will be converted for development.

A further problem is the uncertainty over the future values of coastal landscape. It is possible, for example, that the benefits of eco-system services are larger in the future as more scientific information becomes available over time. For example, suppose that in the sub-sequent period t+1 it is discovered that the value of coastal ecosys-tem services is actually much larger, so that the marginal benefits of these services, MB_{t+1}, in present value terms is now represented by the dotted line in Figure 2.2. If the present value marginal benefits from coastal zone development in the future are largely unchanged, i.e., $MB_t^D \approx M_{t+1}^D$, then, as the figure indicates, the future benefits of ecosystem services exceed these costs, and the ecological land-scape should be restored to its original area $\bar{A}$, assuming of course that it is technically feasible and not excessively expensive to do so. Unfortunately, in making development decisions today we often do not know that, in the future, the value of ecosystem services will turn out to exceed development benefits. Our simple example shows that, if we have already made the decision today to convert $\bar{A} - A_t$ area of the ecological landscape, then we will have to reverse this decision in the future period and restore the original coastal ecosystem.

Taking into account future ecosystem service values is further com-plicated if development today leads to irreversible loss of ecological landscape or, equivalently, ecological restoration of the landscape is prohibitively expensive. As pointed out by Krutilla and Fisher (1985), if environmental assets are irreversibly depleted, their value will rise relative to the value of other reproducible and accumulating economic assets. Such a scenario is likely for unique ecosystems and their land-scapes that are in fixed supply and are difficult to substitute for or restore, which implies that the beneficial services provided by their regulatory and habitat functions will decline over time as these assets are converted or degraded. Any decision today that leads to irrevers-ible conversion therefore imposes a *user cost* on individuals who face a rising scarcity value of future ecosystem benefits as a consequence. This user cost should be part of a cost–benefit analysis of a develop-ment proposal – but rarely is considered in actual ecological land-scape development decisions.

Figure 2.3 illustrates the additional measurement problem arising from irreversible conversion of fixed ecosystem assets. As in the ori-ginal example of Figure 2.2, if only the current benefits, MB_t, and opportunity costs, MB_t^D, of maintaining the original ecosystem are

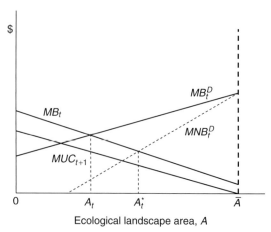

Figure 2.3 Irreversible ecological landscape conversion to development

considered, then an amount $\bar{A} - A_t$ of ecological landscape area would be converted today. But suppose that the loss of coastal ecosystem services arising from converting $\bar{A} - A_t$ causes the value of these services to rise. However, if ecosystem conversion is irreversible, then ecological landscape area remains at A_t in time period $t + 1$. The resulting decline in welfare for individuals in the future is the user cost of irreversible loss of coastal and marine ecosystem services due to conversion today.[8] In Figure 2.3, the marginal user cost of development, measured in present value terms, is represented as the straight line MUC_{t+1}, which is zero when all the ecological landscape is preserved but rises as more coastal land is converted. The correct land use decision should take into account this additional cost of irreversible ecosystem conversion due to expansion of coastal zone development today. Deducting the marginal user cost from MB_t^D yields the net marginal benefits of the development option, MNB_t^D. The latter is the appropriate measure of the opportunity costs of maintaining the ecological landscape, and equating it with the marginal social benefits of ecosystem services

---

[8] Formally, let the change in natural landscape area over time be denoted as $A_{t+1} - A_t = f(d_t)$ where d_t represents the influence of development activities (e.g., conversion, degradation, etc.) in time t on the landscape area. If the "shadow value" that an increment of A_{t+1} would have over the remainder of the time horizon $(t + 1,...,T)$ is defined as λ_{t+1}, then the expression $\lambda_{t+1} \, \partial f / \partial d_t$ explicitly reflects the influence of d_t on the value of the change in landscape area over time. If an increase in d_t reduces natural landscape area, then the latter expression indicates the user cost of landscape conversion.

determines the intertemporally optimal landscape allocation. Only $\bar{A} - A_t^*$ of coastal ecosystem area should be converted for development, leaving A_t^* of the original coastal ecosystem undisturbed.

Another problem of irreversible ecological landscape conversion is that it can increase the risk of ecological collapse. Ecosystems tend to display nonconvexities manifested through positive feedback interactions, which imply the presence of ecological thresholds.[9] That is, large shocks or sustained disturbances to ecosystems can set in motion a series of interactions that can breach ecological thresholds that cause the systems to "flip" from one functioning state to another. Although it is possible under certain conditions for the system to recover to its original state, under other conditions the change might be permanent. Thus, as Dasgupta and Mäler (2003, p. 501) remark, "if a large damage were to be inflicted on an ecosystem whose ability to function is conditional on it being above some threshold level (in size, composition, or whatever), the consequence would be irreversible." The inability of an ecosystem to recover, or return, to its original state is essentially what is implied by an ecological collapse. Increasingly, ecologists have identified ecological landscape conversion as one type of irreversible "large damage" that can increase the threat of ecosystem collapse (Busing and White 1993; Dobson *et al.* 2006; Lotze *et al.* 2006; Peterson *et al.* 1998; Turner *et al.* 1993).

Throughout this book, we will be exploring in more detail the issues raised with Figures 2.2 and 2.3. In Chapter 3 we incorporate many of the above characteristics of ecosystems as natural assets to develop a basic model of ecological landscape allocation. Chapters 4 and 5 extend the basic model to allow for spatial variation in the provision of an ecological function and open economy conditions, respectively. Chapter 6 addresses the issue of the risk of collapse from irreversible landscape conversion. Finally, Chapter 7 discusses the various areas of further research, especially interdisciplinary collaboration between economists, ecologists, and environmental scientists, which will be required to make further progress in developing the analysis of ecosystems as natural assets.

The remainder of this chapter examines some key issues that arise in valuing ecosystem services and illustrates the importance of valuing

---

[9] See, for example, Batabayal *et al.* (2003); Dasgupta and Mäler (2003); Elmqvist *et al.* (2003); Holling (1973); Levin (1999); May (1975); Murray (1993); Perrings (1998); Pimm (1984); and Scheffer *et al.* (2001).

these services in landscape conversion and restoration decisions with several case study examples.

Valuing nonmarket ecosystem services

Uncertainty, irreversible loss, and resilience costs are important issues to consider in valuing ecosystem service tradeoffs affected by economic development and population growth. However, even before we tackle these "second-order" valuation issues, we are faced with a more basic problem of how to go about valuing the various services of ecosystems. As emphasized by NRC (2005), the "fundamental challenge" in valuing these flows is that ecosystem services are largely not marketed. In other words, returning to Figure 2.2, unless some attempt is made to value the aggregate willingness to pay for these services, B_t, then it will be difficult to succeed at effective land use management to balance development and conservation tradeoffs.

Earlier in this chapter, we discussed the three-step approach that is required to integrate the "ecological production" of ecosystem goods and services with "economic valuation" of these benefits, which was summarized visually by Figure 2.1. In recent years substantial progress has been made by economists working with ecologists and other natural scientists on this "fundamental challenge" to improve the application of environmental valuation methodologies to nonmarket ecosystem services. Nevertheless, a number of important challenges arise in applying these methods. To help our subsequent discussion of valuation issues, it is useful to look at a more detailed version of Figure 2.1 that emphasizes the economic valuation component of the latter diagram (see Figure 2.4).

As indicated in Figure 2.4, there are a number of different ways in which humans benefit from, or value, ecosystem goods and services. The first distinction is between the *use values* as opposed to *nonuse values* arising from these goods and services. Typically, use values involve some human "interaction" with the environment whereas nonuse values do not, as they represent an individual valuing the pure "existence" of a natural habitat or ecosystem or wanting to "bequest" it to future generations. Direct use values refer to both consumptive and nonconsumptive uses that involve some form of direct physical interaction with environmental goods and services, such as recreational activities, resource harvesting, drinking clean water,

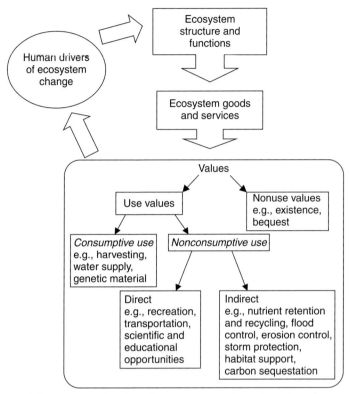

Figure 2.4 Economic valuation of ecosystem goods and services
Source: Adapted from NRC (2005, Figure 7–1).

breathing unpolluted air, and so forth. Indirect use values refer to those ecosystem services whose values can only be measured indirectly, since they are derived from supporting and protecting activities that have directly measurable values. For example, for wetlands, the indirect use values associated with ecosystems services include coastal protection, erosion control, flood protection, water purification, carbon sequestration, maintenance of temperature and precipitation, and habitat support for fishing, hunting, and foraging activities outside the wetlands (see Table 2.1).[10]

---

[10] Another component of value, *option value*, is commonly referred to as a nonuse value in the literature. However, option value arises from the difference between valuation under conditions of certainty and uncertainty, and is a numerical calculation, not a value held by people per se. See NRC (2005, ch. 6) for further discussion.

Table 2.3 indicates the various nonmarket methods that can be used for valuing ecosystem goods and services. As shown in the table, the methods employed are essentially the standard nonmarket valuation techniques that are available to economists. For example, each of the studies of wetland ecosystem goods and services listed in Table 2.1 employ one or more of the valuation techniques indicated in Table 2.3. However, the application of nonmarket valuation to ecosystem goods and services is not without difficulties. Barbier (2007), EPA (2009), Freeman (2003), Hanley and Barbier (2009), Mendelsohn and Olmstead (2009), NRC (2005), and Pagiola *et al.* (2004) discuss in some detail how these standard valuation methods are best applied to various ecosystem services, emphasizing in particular both the advantages and the shortcomings of the different methods and their application. Here, we simply summarize some of the key issues.

First, the application of some of the valuation methods listed in Table 2.3 is often limited to specific types of ecological goods and services. For example, the travel cost method is used principally for those environmental values that enhance individuals' enjoyment of recreation and tourism; averting behavior models are best applied to the health effects arising from environmental pollution. Similarly, hedonic wage and property models are used primarily for assessing work-related environmental hazards and environmental impacts on property values, respectively.

In contrast, stated preference methods, which include contingent valuation methods and choice modeling, have the potential to be used widely in valuing ecosystem goods and services. These valuation methods share the common approach of surveying individuals who benefit from an ecological service or range of services, in the hope that analysis of these responses will provide an accurate measure of the individuals' willingness to pay for the service or services. In addition, stated preference methods can go beyond estimating the value to individuals of single and even multiple benefits of ecosystems and in some cases elicit nonuse values that individuals attach to ensuring that a preserved and well-functioning system will be around for future generations to enjoy. For example, a study of mangrove-dependent coastal communities in Micronesia demonstrated through the use of contingent valuation techniques that the communities "place some value on the existence and ecosystem functions of mangroves over and above the value of mangroves' marketable products" (Naylor and

Table 2.3 *Various nonmarket valuation methods applied to ecosystem services*

Valuation method[1]	Types of value estimated	Common types of applications	Ecosystem services valued
Travel cost	Direct use	Recreation	Maintenance of beneficial species, productive ecosystems, and biodiversity
Averting behavior	Direct use	Environmental impacts on human health	Pollution control and detoxification
Hedonic price	Direct and indirect use	Environmental impacts on residential property and human morbidity and mortality	Storm protection; flood mitigation; maintenance of air quality
Production function	Indirect use	Commercial and recreational fishing; agricultural systems; control of invasive species; watershed protection; damage costs avoided	Maintenance of beneficial species; maintenance of arable land and agricultural productivity; prevention of damage from erosion and siltation; groundwater recharge; drainage and natural irrigation; storm protection; flood mitigation
Replacement cost	Indirect use	Damage costs avoided; freshwater supply	Drainage and natural irrigation; storm protection; flood mitigation
Stated preference	Use and nonuse	Recreation; environmental impacts on human health and residential property; damage costs avoided; existence and bequest values of preserving ecosystems	All of the above

Notes:

[1] See Barbier (2007); EPA (2009); Freeman (2003); Hanley and Barbier (2009); Mendelsohn and Olmstead (2009); NRC (2005); and Pagiola *et al.* (2004) for more discussion of these various nonmarket valuation methods and their application to valuing ecosystem goods and services.

Source: Adapted from NRC (2005), Table 4–2.

Box 2.2 Valuing water supply to New York City by the Catskills watershed

The policy decision of whether or not to protect the Catskills watershed in upstate New York in order to provide clean drinking water to New York City is a good example of valuing a single eco-system service through the replacement cost method (Chichilinsky and Heal 1998; NRC 2005).

Historically, the Catskills watersheds have supplied New York City "freely" with high-quality water with little contamination as part of the "natural filtration" process of the rich and diverse ecosystems on the banks of streams, rivers, lakes, and reservoirs comprising these watersheds. However, increasing housing develop-ments and pollution from vehicles and agriculture have threatened water quality in the region. By 1996, New York City faced a choice: either it could build water filtration systems to clean its water sup-ply or the city could protect the Catskill watersheds to ensure high-quality drinking water. In retrospect, the decision was an easy one for New York City. It was not necessary to value all the services of the Catskills watershed ecosystems; instead, it was sufficient simply to demonstrate that protecting and restoring the ecological integrity of the Catskills was less costly than replacing this ecosystem service with a human-constructed water filtration system. It was estimated that the total costs of building and operating the filtration system were in the range of $6–8 billion. In comparison, to protect the water provision service of the Catskills, New York is obligated to spend $250 million during a ten-year period to purchase and set aside over 140,000 hectares in the watershed. In addition, a series of land regulations were implemented to control development and land use in other parts of the watershed. Overall, New York City estimated that it would cost $1–1.5 billion to protect and restore the natural ecosystem processes in the watershed, thus preserving the clean drinking water service provided by the Catskills.

In addition, the wetlands are a unique migratory habitat for many wildfowl and wader species from Palaearctic regions, and contain a number of forestry reserves (Hollis *et al.* 1993; Lemley *et al.* 2000; Thompson and Polet 2000).

However, the Hadejia–Jama'are floodplain has come under increasing pressure from drought and upstream water developments. Due to past water diversion, the maximum extent of flooding declined from between 250,000 to 300,000 ha in the 1960s and 1970s to around 70,000–100,000 ha in the 1990s (Goes 2002; Thompson and Hollis 1995; Thompson and Polet 2000), which is about the present level of flooding. Drought is a persistent, stochastic environmental problem facing all Sub-Saharan arid and semi-arid zones, and the main cause of unexpected reductions in flooding in drought years. But the main long-term threat to the floodplain is water diversion through large-scale water projects on the Hadejia and Jama'are Rivers. Upstream developments are affecting incoming water, either through dams altering the timing and size of flood flows or through diverting surface or groundwater for irrigation. These developments have been taking place without consideration of their impacts on the Hadejia–Jama'are floodplain or any subsequent loss of economic benefits that are currently provided by use of the floodplain.

The largest upstream irrigation scheme at present is the Kano River Irrigation Project (KRIP), which currently amounts to 22,000 ha (Sangari 2006). Water supplies for the project are provided by Tiga Dam, the biggest dam in the basin, which was completed in 1974. Water is also released from this dam to supply Kano City. The second major irrigation scheme within the river basin is the Hadejia Valley Irrigation Project (HVIP), which irrigates 8,000 ha (Balmisse *et al.* 2003). The HVIP is supplied by Challawa Gorge Dam on the Challawa River, upstream of Kano, which was finished in 1992. Challawa Gorge also provides water for the Kano City water supply. A number of small dams and associated irrigation schemes have also been constructed or are planned for minor tributaries of the Hadejia River. In comparison, the Jama'are River is relatively uncontrolled with only one small dam across one of its tributaries. However, plans for a major dam on the Jama'are at Kafin Zaki have been in existence for many years, which would provide water for an irrigated area totalling 84,000 ha. Work on Kafin Zaki Dam has been started and then stopped a number of times. In 2008, the Bauchi state government announced plans to proceed again with construction of the dam, although work has yet to start.

The current and planned water diversions in the Hadejia–Jama'are River Basin are, unfortunately, an example of the classic case of ignoring the benefits provided by a natural asset, which in this case is the downstream floodplain landscape. As shown in Figure 2.2, against the benefits of these upstream water developments must be weighed the opportunity cost of the downstream floodplain losses. Otherwise, too much water is diverted upstream, and the floodplain landscape will diminish excessively.

For example, economic valuation studies have focused on three types of floodplain benefits that are affected by the impacts of upstream water diversion on the floodplain:

- Flood-recession agriculture, fuelwood, and fishing in the floodplain (Barbier *et al.* 1993).
- Groundwater recharge of domestic water supply for household use (Acharya and Barbier 2002).
- Groundwater recharge that supports dry season irrigated agricultural production (Acharya and Barbier 2000).

Barbier and Thompson (1998) simulated the impacts of various upstream water diversion scenarios in the Hadejia–Jama'are River Basin on the flood extent that determines the downstream floodplain area. The economic gains of the upstream water projects were then compared to the resulting economic losses to downstream agricultural, fuelwood, and fishing benefits. All scenarios were compared to a baseline simulation without any of the large-scale water resource schemes in place within the river basin.

Table 2.4 summarizes the estimated gains in irrigation benefits upstream with the downstream losses from agricultural, fuelwood, and fish production in the floodplain for the different upstream dam and water release scenarios. Given the high productivity of the floodplain, the losses in economic benefits due to changes in flood extent for all scenarios are large, ranging from $4 million to $23 million. As expected, there is a direct tradeoff between increasing irrigation and dam developments upstream and impacts on the wetland benefits downstream. Scenario 2, which yields the lowest upstream irrigation gains, also has the least impact in terms of floodplain losses, whereas Scenario 4 has both the highest irrigation gains and floodplain losses.

Although Scenario 2 is the preferred outcome, as it produces the lowest net loss overall, it is clearly unrealistic. Challawa Gorge was completed in 1992, small dams have been built on the Hadejia's tributaries, and the HVIP has been implemented. In fact, Scenario 4 is

Table 2.4 *Losses in floodplain benefits versus gains in irrigated production, net present value ($ 1989/90 prices), Nigeria*

	Irrigation value [1][a]	Floodplain loss [2][b]	Net loss [2] – [1]	[1] as % of [2]
Scenario 1	682,983	–4,045,024	–3,362,041	16.88
Scenario 2	354,139	–2,558,051	–2,203,912	13.84
Scenario 3	682,963	–7,117,291	–6,434,328	9.60
Scenario 4	3,124,015	–23,377,302	–20,253,287	13.36
Scenario 5	556,505	–15,432,952	–14,876,447	3.61

Notes:
[a] Based on the mean of the net present values of per ha production benefits for the Kano River Irrigation Project (KRIP), and applied to the gains in total irrigation area for each scenario.
[b] Based on the mean of the net present values of total agricultural, fuelwood, and fishing benefits for the Hadejia–Jama'are floodplain, averaged over the actual peak flood extent for the wetlands of 112,817 ha in 1989/90 and applied to the declines in mean peak flood extent associated with each scenario.
Scenario 1: Tiga Dam only. KRIP at 27,000 ha. No regulated water releases.
Scenario 2: Tiga Dam only. KRIP at 14,000 ha. Regulated water release of 400 $10^6 m^3$ in August.
Scenario 3: Tiga Dam, Challawa Gorge, and small dams on Hadejia tributaries. KRIP at 27,000 ha. Regulated water release from Challawa Gorge of 348 10^6 m³/yr.
Scenario 4: Tiga Dam, Challawa Gorge, small dams on Hadejia tributaries, Hadejia Valley Irrigation Project (HVIP), Kafin Zaki Dam. KRIP at 27,000 ha; 84,000 ha of irrigated agriculture from Kafin Zaki; HVIP at 12,500 ha. Regulated water release from Challawa Gorge of 348 10^6 m³/yr.
Scenario 5: Tiga Dam, Challawa Gorge, small dams on Hadejia tributaries, HVIP, Kafin Zaki Dam. KRIP at 14,000 ha; HVIP at 8,000 ha. Regulated water releases of 350 $10^6 m^3$ in August from Tiga Dam, 348 10^6 M³/yr and 100 $10^6 m^3$ in July from Challawa Gorge, 100 $10^6 m^3$/month in October to March and 500 $10^6 m^3$ in August from Kafin Zaki, and Hadejia Barrage open in August.
Source: Barbier and Thompson (1998).

already on the way to being implemented – although when the construction of Kafin Zaki Dam might occur is presently uncertain. The only alternative to Scenario 4, which assumes full implementation of all upstream water projects and dams without any releases for the downstream floodplain, is Scenario 5, which also assumes full upstream development but with less irrigation to allow regulated water releases from the dams to sustain inundation of the down-stream floodplain.

The results confirm that, in all the scenarios simulated, the additional value of production from large-scale irrigation schemes does not replace the lost production attributed to the wetlands downstream. Gains in irrigation values account for at most 17 percent of the losses in floodplain benefits. Interestingly, even in Scenario 4 that allows for full development of all planned upstream dam and irrigation projects, the losses to floodplain agriculture, fishing, and fuelwood benefits are so large that the additional irrigation values gained compensate for only 13 percent of the losses. Further expansion of the KRIP and HVIP, as well as the construction of Kafin Zaki Dam and additional upstream irrigation schemes, are not appropriate developments in the river basin. Further upstream water diversion for irrigation is also questionable, given the serious concerns about the inefficient use of water by farmers in the KRIP and HVIP (Balmisse *et al.* 2003; Sangari 2006). However, as an alternative, if Kafin Zaki Dam were to be constructed and formal irrigation within the basin limited to its current extent, the introduction of a regulated flooding regime (Scenario 5) would reduce the net losses from around $20 million to just under $15 million. Scenario 5 may therefore be the most efficient outcome for allocating water between the floodplain and upstream dam develoments.

Such a regulated flooding regime could also produce additional economic benefits that are not captured in our analysis. Greater certainty over the timing and magnitude of the floods may enable farmers to adjust to the resulting reduction in the risks normally associated with floodplain farming. Enhanced dry season flows provided by the releases from Challawa Gorge and Kafin Zaki dams in Scenario 5 would also benefit farmers along the Hadejia and Jama'are Rivers while the floodplain's fisheries may also experience beneficial impacts from the greater extent of inundation remaining throughout the dry season (Neiland *et al.* 2005). Thus, the introduction of a regulated flooding regime in conjunction with upstream water developments may be the only realistic hope of minimizing floodplain losses.

Some of the upstream water developments are being used or have the potential to supply water to Kano City. Although these releases were included in the hydrological simulations by Barbier and Thompson (1998), the economic analysis was unable to calculate the benefits to

Kano City of these water supplies. However, the hydrological analysis shows that the proposed regulated water release from Tiga Dam to reduce downstream floodplain losses would not affect the ability of Tiga Dam to supply water to Kano. Although the potential exists for Challawa Gorge to supply additional water to Kano, it is unclear how much water could be used for this purpose. The resulting economic benefits are unlikely to be large enough to compensate for the substantial floodplain losses incurred by the Gorge and the additional upstream developments in the Hadejia Valley. Currently, there are no plans for Kafin Zaki Dam to be used to supply water to Kano.

In addition, Barbier and Thompson (1998) were unable to calculate other important floodplain benefits, such as the role of the wetlands in supporting pastoral grazing and in recharging groundwater both within the floodplain and in surrounding areas.

For example, one of the concerns is that disruptions to flood extent will affect the annual recharge of the underlying aquifers, which will in turn impact the welfare of local populations dependent on this groundwater for drinking water and other household uses (Thompson and Goes 1997; Thompson and Hollis 1995). In a separate study, Acharya and Barbier (2002) estimate the value placed on groundwater either purchased or collected from village wells by households in the floodplain region. Three villages in the Madachi region of the Hadejia–Jama'are floodplain and one village in the Sugum region were chosen for the economic valuation study, based on the hydrological evidence that the villages in these areas rely on groundwater recharged mainly by wetlands (Thompson and Goes 1997). The flooding in Madachi is caused by the floodwaters of the Hadejia River. The Sugum region is located in the eastern part of the wetlands and is influenced by the flooding of the Jama'are River.

The results of the analysis by Acharya and Barbier (2002) suggest that the value of the recharge function is $13,209 per day for the floodplain. The average welfare loss for a 1 meter drop in groundwater levels is approximately $0.12 per household per day. This average suggests a daily loss of approximately 0.23 percent of monthly income for households that purchase their water, 0.4 percent of monthly income for households that collect their water, and 0.14 percent for households that do both.

If upstream water diversion is causing less flooding and standing water downstream, then the resulting reduction in groundwater recharge could have important implications for dry season irrigated agricultural production downstream (Thompson and Goes 1997; Thompson and Hollis 1995). Acharya and Barbier (2000) also conducted an economic analysis of the impact of a decline in groundwater levels on dry season vegetable and wheat irrigated agricultural production in the floodplain region. They surveyed a sample of thirty-seven farms in the Madachi area, out of a total 309 dry season farmers on 6,600 ha of cropland irrigated through tubewell abstraction from shallow aquifers. Wheat, tomato, onions, spring onions, sweet potatoes, and pepper are the main cash crops grown by the farmers, although okra and eggplant are more minor crops grown principally for home consumption. On average, irrigated dry season agriculture in the Madachi area is worth $412.5 per ha, with a total estimated annual value of $2.72 million over the entire 6,600 ha.

Acharya and Barbier (2000) estimate that a fall in groundwater levels from 6 to 7 meters depth results in losses of $32.5 per vegetable farmer – approximately 7.65 percent of yearly income – and $331 for vegetable and wheat farmers, or around 77 percent of annual income. The total loss associated with the 1 meter change in groundwater was estimated to be $62,249 for all 6,600 ha of dryland farming in the Madachi area.

Mangrove land use, Thailand

In Thailand, aquaculture expansion has been associated with mangrove wetlands destruction. Since 1961 Thailand has lost 1,500–2,000 sq. km of coastal mangroves, or about 50–60 percent of the original area (FAO 2003). Over 1975–1996, 50–65 percent of Thailand's mangroves was lost to shrimp farm conversion alone (Aksornkoae and Tokrisna 2004).

Mangrove deforestation in Thailand has focused attention on the two principle services provided by mangrove ecosystems, their role as nursery and breeding habitats for offshore fisheries; and their role as natural "storm barriers" to periodic coastal storm events, such as wind storms, tsunamis, storm surges, and typhoons. In addition, many coastal communities exploit mangroves directly for a variety of products, such as fuelwood, timber, raw materials, honey and resins, and crabs and shellfish. Various studies have suggested that these three benefits of mangroves are significant in Thailand (Barbier 2003, 2007; Sathirathai and Barbier 2001).

Valuation of the ecosystem services provided by mangroves is therefore important for two land use policy decisions in Thailand. First, although declining in recent years, conversion of mangroves to shrimp farm ponds and other commercial coastal developments continues to be a major threat to Thailand's remaining mangrove areas. Second, since the December 2004 tsunami disaster, there is now considerable interest in rehabilitating and restoring mangrove ecosystems as "natural barriers" to future coastal storm events. Thus valuing the goods and services of mangrove ecosystems can help to address two important policy questions: Do the net economic returns to shrimp farming justify further mangrove conversion to this economic activity, and is it worth investing in mangrove replanting and ecosystem rehabilitation in abandoned shrimp farm areas?

To illustrate how improved and more accurate valuation of ecosystems can help inform these two policy decisions, Table 2.5 compares the per hectare (ha) net returns to shrimp farming, the costs of mangrove rehabilitation, and the value of mangrove services. All land uses are assumed to be instigated over 1996–2004 and are valued in 1996 $ per ha.

Several analyses have demonstrated that the overall commercial profitability of shrimp aquaculture in Thailand provides a substantial incentive for private landowners to invest in such operations (Barbier 2003; Sathirathai and Barbier 2001; Tokrisna 1998). However, many of the conventional inputs used in shrimp pond operations are subsidized, below border-equivalent prices, thus increasing artificially the private returns to shrimp farming. In Table 2.5 the net economic returns to shrimp farming, which are calculated once the estimated subsidies are removed, are based on nondeclining yields over a five-year period of investment (Sathirathai and Barbier 2001). After this period, there tends to be problems of drastic yield decline and disease; shrimp farmers then usually abandon their ponds and find a new location. In Table 2.5 the annual economic returns to shrimp aquaculture are estimated to be $322 per ha, and when discounted over the five-year period at a 10–15 percent rate yield a net present value of $1,078–1,220 per ha.

There is also the problem of the highly degraded state of abandoned shrimp ponds after the five-year period of their productive life.

Table 2.5 *Comparison of land use values per ha, Thailand, 1996–2004 ($)*

Land use	Net present value per ha (10–15% discount rate)
Shrimp farming	
Net economic returns[1]	1,078–1,220
Mangrove ecosystem rehabilitation	
Total cost[2]	8,812–9,318
Ecosystem goods and services	
Net income from collected forest products[3]	484–584
Habitat-fishery linkage[4]	708–987
Storm protection service[5]	8,966–10,821
Total	**10,158–12,392**

Notes:

[1] Based on annual net average economic returns $322 per ha for five years. From Sathirathai and Barbier (2001), updated to 1996 $.

[2] Based on costs of rehabilitating abandoned shrimp farm site, replanting mangrove forests, and maintaining and protecting mangrove seedlings. From Sathirathai and Barbier (2001), updated to 1996 $.

[3] Based on annual average value of $101 per ha over 1996–2004. From Sathirathai and Barbier (2001), updated to 1996 $.

[4] Based on a dynamic analysis of mangrove-fishery linkages over 1996–2004 and assuming the estimated Thailand deforestation rate of 3.44 sq. km per year (see Barbier 2007).

[5] Based on marginal value per ha of expected damage function approach of Barbier (2007).

Across Thailand those areas with abandoned shrimp ponds degenerate rapidly into wasteland, since the soil becomes very acidic, compacted, and too poor in quality to be used for any other productive use, such as agriculture. To rehabilitate the abandoned shrimp farm site requires treating and detoxifying the soil, replanting mangrove forests, and maintaining and protecting mangrove seedlings for several years. As shown in Table 2.5, these restoration costs are considerable: $8,812–9,318 per ha in net present value terms. This reflects the fact that converting mangroves to establish shrimp farms is almost an "irreversible" land use, and without considerable additional investment in restoration, these areas do not regenerate into mangrove forests. What should happen is that, before the decision to allow shrimp farming to take place, the restoration costs could be treated as one measure of the "user cost" of converting mangroves irreversibly, and this cost should be deducted from the estimation of the net returns to shrimp aquaculture. As the restoration costs exceed the net economic returns per ha, the decision should be to prevent the shrimp aquaculture operation from occurring.

Unfortunately, past land use policy in Thailand has ignored the user costs of shrimp farming, and as a result many coastal areas have been deforested of mangroves. Many short-lived shrimp farms in these areas have also long since fallen unproductive and are now abandoned. Thus, an important issue today is whether it is worth restoring mangroves in these abandoned areas. If the foregone benefits of the ecological services of mangroves are not large, then mangrove restoration may not be a reasonable option. Table 2.5 therefore indicates the value of three of these benefits: the net income from local mangrove forest products, habitat-fishery linkages, and storm protection.

Sathirathai and Barbier (2001) estimate the value to local communities of using mangrove resources in terms of the net income generated from the forests in terms of various wood and nonwood products. If the extracted products were sold, market prices were used to calculate the net income generated (gross income is minus the cost of extraction). If the products were used only for subsistence, the gross income was estimated based on surrogate prices, i.e., the market prices of the closest substitute. Based on surveys of local villagers in Surat Thani Province, the major products collected by the households were various fishery products, honey, and wood for fishing gear and fuelwood. As shown in Table 2.5, the net annual income from these products is $101 per ha, or a net present value of $484–584 per ha.

The coastal habitat-fishery service of mangroves in Thailand may also be modeled through incorporating the change in wetland area within a multi-period harvesting model of the fishery (Barbier 2007). The key to this approach is to model a coastal wetland that serves as a breeding and nursery habitat for fisheries as affecting the growth function of the fish stock. As a result, the value of a change in this habitat-support function is determined in terms of the impact of any change in mangrove area on the dynamic path of the returns earned from the fishery. As Table 2.5 indicates, the net present value of this service ranges from $708 to $987 per ha.

The value of the coastal protection service of mangroves in Table 2.5 is derived by employing the expected damage function (EDF) valuation methodology for estimating the expected damage costs avoided through increased provision of the storm protection service of coastal wetlands (Barbier 2007). By applying this EDF approach, Table 2.5 estimates the benefits from the storm protection service of mangroves in Thailand to be $1,879 per ha, or $8,966–10,821 per ha in net present value terms.

Table 2.5 indicates that the net present value of all three mangrove ecosystem benefits ranges from $10,158 to $12,392 per ha. These ecosystem service values clearly exceed the net economic returns to shrimp farming. In fact, the net income to local coastal communities from collected forest products and the value of habitat-fishery linkages total $1,192–1,571 per ha, which are greater than the net economic returns to shrimp farming. However, the value of the storm protection is critical to the decision as to whether or not to replant and rehabilitate mangrove ecosystems in abandoned pond areas. As shown in Table 2.5, the storm protection benefit makes mangrove restoration an economically feasible land use option.

To summarize, this case study has shown the importance of valuing the ecological services in wetland conversion and restoration decisions, as outlined in Figure 2.2. The irreversible conversion of mangroves for aquaculture results in the loss of ecological services that generate significantly large economic benefits. This loss of benefits should be taken into account in land use decisions that lead to the widespread conversion of mangroves, but typically are ignored in private sector calculations. The high restoration costs also reflect the fact that "reversing" mangrove conversion is difficult, and should not always be considered *ex post*. Instead, before the decision to allow shrimp farming to take place, the restoration costs could be treated as one measure of the "user cost" of converting mangroves irreversibly, and this cost should be deducted from the estimation of the net returns to shrimp aquaculture.

Willamette Basin, Oregon, United States

The Natural Capital Project, a partnership between Stanford University, the Nature Conservancy, and World Wildlife Fund, has the aim of developing decision tools for quantifying and modeling ecosystem services to analyze different scenarios of ecological land-scape management. One of these tools, based on ecological produc-tion functions and economic valuation methods, is called Integrated Valuation of Ecosystem Services and Tradeoffs (InVEST), which has been applied to analyze various landscape conservation and develop-ment scenarios in the Willamette Basin, Oregon (Daily *et al.* 2009; Nelson *et al.* 2008, 2009; Polasky *et al.* 2005, 2008). Such applica-tions are a good example of the type of landscape tradeoffs depicted in Figure 2.2.

The Willamette Basin is essentially the Willamette River watershed in central Oregon, which covers nearly 30,000 sq. km and is bor-dered on the east by the crest of the Cascade Mountain Range and on the west by the crest of the Coast Mountain Range. The main eco-regions of the Basin are the Coast Range, the Willamette Valley, and the Cascades Range. The Coast Range is a low mountain range that extends along the entire Oregon coast and is dominated by high rain-fall and conifer forests. The Willamette Valley contains terraces and the floodplain of the Willamette River system, which includes most of the agricultural and urban land use of the Basin. The Cascades Range has sparsely populated, steep, and mountainous ecosystems.

Using the InVEST model, Nelson *et al.* (2009) analyze how three dif-ferent land use scenarios for the Willamette Basin affect hydrological services (water quality and storm peak mitigation), soil conservation, carbon sequestration, biodiversity conservation, and the value of sev-eral marketed commodities (agricultural crop products, timber harvest, and rural residential housing). Each of the scenarios includes a set of spatially referenced landscape use predictions of the Basin at ten-year intervals from 1990 to 2050. The three land use scenarios are:

- *Plan Trend*: This is essentially the baseline scenario, which predicts future landscape uses in the Basin given current land use policies and the continuation of recent trends from 1990 to 2050.
- *Development*: Future landscape uses in the Basin assuming less conservation and more commercial development in response to market forces compared to current land use policies and trends, leading in particular to greater rural residential development and timber production by 2050.
- *Conservation*: Future landscape uses in the Basin assuming more conservation and less commercial development compared to current

land use policies and trends, leading in particular to more forest protection, less rural residential housing, and less agricultural production by 2050.

All three scenarios assume that human population in the Willamette Basin will increase from 2 million inhabitants in 1990 to 3.9 million in 2050.

The results of the model's land use predictions suggest that the two main conservation outcomes, biodiversity conservation and the provision of ecosystem services, are complementary. That is, any land use in the Willamette Basin that enhances biodiversity conservation also enhances the provision of hydrological services, soil conservation, and carbon sequestration. However, there is a clear tradeoff between land uses that promote marketed commodities, such as agricultural crop products, timber harvest, and rural residential housing, as opposed to biodiversity conservation and ecosystem services. As the authors conclude: "These results indicate that when landowner decisions are based solely on market returns (without payments for ecosystem services), they will tend to generate [land use] patterns with lower provision of ecosystem services and biodiversity conservation" (Nelson *et al.* 2009, p. 10).

As for the different overall land use scenarios analyzed, the Conservation scenario produced the largest gains (or smallest losses) in ecosystem services and biodiversity conservation from 1990 to 2050 across the Willamette Basin. For example, water quality and soil conservation improved significantly, storm peak mitigation declined the least, and the estimated value of carbon sequestration is the highest under the Conservation scenario compared to the other two land use scenarios. Although the value of marketed commodities declined in the majority of locations in the Basin under the Conservation scenario, the aggregate market value of these commodities for the whole region still increases by 2050, because the high value of rural residential development near cities more than compensates for the losses elsewhere. However, the value of marketed commodities increased even more under the Plan Trend and Development scenarios, which saw many more areas expand rural residential development and intensive timber harvesting by 2050.

These potential tradeoffs between conservation versus development land use options under the three different landscape scenarios for the Willamette Basin are reflected in Table 2.6. For each of the

Table 2.6 *Tradeoffs in landscape use scenarios,* Willamette Basin, Oregon, *1990–2050*

Scenarios	Net present market value of 1990–2050 commodities ($ billion)	Net present value of 1990–2050 carbon capture ($ billion)	Total of 1990–2050 net present values ($ billion)	Countryside species–area relationship score in 2050
Plan Trend	15.26	0.9	16.16	0.558
Development	15.27	0.8	16.07	0.560
Conservation	14.78	1.6	16.38	0.586

Source: Nelson *et al.* (2009).

three scenarios over 1990 to 2050, the table shows the net present value of all the commodities produced, the net present value of carbon sequestration of the landscape, and a measure of biodiversity conservation in terms of a twenty-four-species countryside species–area relationship index. Although carbon sequestration was the only ecosystem service that could be valued, recall that Nelson *et al.* (2009) found that the provision of all ecosystem services and biodiversity conversion is highly correlated across land uses. As the table indicates, there is a clear tradeoff between the value of marketed commodities generated by the different scenarios and biodiversity conservation.

For example, both the Plan Trend and Development scenarios generate higher net present value (NPV) over 1990 to 2050 in terms of rural residential housing, timber production, and agricultural crops ($15.26 billion and $15.27 billion, respectively) than the Conservation scenario ($14.78 billion). However, by 2050 the Conservation scenario clearly conserves more biodiversity, and thus provides more ecosystem services, than the other two landscape scenarios. As indicated in Table 2.6, the net present value of carbon sequestration from 1990 to 2050 is especially large under the Conservation scenario ($1.6 billion) compared to the Plan Trend and Development scenarios ($0.9 billion and $0.8 billion respectively). In fact, if these carbon sequestration values are added to the NPV of marketed commodities, then the Conservation scenario generates more monetary value over 1990 to 2050 than either the Plan Trend or Development scenarios. This leads Nelson *et al.*

(2009, p. 10) to conclude that "if markets for carbon sequestration emerge, payments for sequestered carbon may make it more profitable for landowners to choose [land uses] favoring conservation."

Estimating recreational benefits from past studies, Europe

One of the more important nonmarket ecosystem services associated with ecological landscapes is recreation. For several ecosystems, such as wetlands, forests, and coral reefs, enough recreational values have been estimated to allow meta-analysis of the various studies (Brander *et al.* 2006, 2007; Zandersen and Tol 2009).

Because of the long history of estimating the willingness to pay (WTP) for recreation, some economic studies have tried to find ways to utilize this information. For example, in Europe there have been more valuation studies of woodland recreation than any other nonmarket ecosystem service of forests (Bateman *et al.* 2005; Willis *et al.* 2003; Zandersen *et al.* 2007). This is not surprising; as Table 2.7 shows, recreation is the highest value of all forest ecosystem services in Great Britain.[11] Estimating the nonmarket recreation values of the remaining forest landscapes in Europe could therefore prove important for assessing the type of conservation versus development tradeoffs depicted in Figure 2.2.

---

[11] Note that Table 2.7 also indicates a high value for the biodiversity of remaining non-coniferous forests in Great Britain. However, this estimated biodiversity value for forests in Britain should be treated with caution. According to Willis *et al.* (2003, pp. 14–15), "non-use biodiversity values are particularly difficult to capture. Both CV and stated choice (SC) experiments encounter difficulties in deriving biodiversity values. These problems arise for a number of reasons. First, people have widely different preferences for wildlife, so the variance of the mean WTP value is large. Second, people's WTP for biodiversity in different types of British woodland is a very small fraction of income; whilst WTP variation between individuals is mainly driven by taste for different forms of wildlife, vis a vis other goods, rather than by income. Because taste is difficult to measure, the variation in WTP between individuals is difficult to explain. Third, biodiversity is a difficult concept for people to grasp, and people find it difficult to trade off species importance within fungi, plants, invertebrates, birds, and mammals, and to tradeoff species importance between these groups. They also find it difficult to tradeoff changes in numbers in a particular species against changes in the number of species represented in a habitat. Thus biodiversity is a complex issue over which many people struggle to form preferences. These preferences, once formed, seem to vary widely."

Table 2.7 *Forest ecosystem service values, Great Britain*

Environmental benefit	Annual value (£m, 2002 prices)	Capitalized value (£m, 2002 prices)
Recreation	392.65	11,218
Biodiversity[1]	386.00	11,029
Landscape[2]	150.22	4,292
Carbon sequestration	93.66	2,676
Air pollution absorption	0.39	11
Total	1,022.92	29,226

Notes:
[1] Public preferences and willingness to pay for the nonuse biodiversity value of the remaining forest area in Great Britain, which has different biodiversity characteristics from remote coniferous forests.
[2] Public preferences and willingness to pay for forested landscapes, seen either from home or during regular journeys to and from home.
Source: Willis *et al.* (2003).

However, valuing forest recreation through stated preference and travel cost methods is an expensive undertaking. Thus economists have sought to find ways of avoiding or reducing the costs of estimating nonmarket recreation values of various forested landscapes by employing previous valuation studies of recreation as potentially useful sources of information for new studies.

One approach is to conduct a meta-analysis of past recreation values and see if they can transfer to the new landscape site. But this approach has its limitations, even in Europe where there are numerous past forest recreation value studies. For example, a meta-analysis of forest recreation in Europe based on studies that have applied the travel cost method covering twenty-six studies in nine countries since 1979 found large variation in values across these studies (Zandersen and Tol 2009). The analysis showed that consumer surplus ranges between €0.66 and €112 per trip, with a median of €4.52 per trip. Including exogenous variables shows that site attributes, GDP per capita, and population density play a significant role in the variation in consumer surplus estimates. But how to control for these exogenous influences to make reliable transfers of such varying recreational benefits to very different forest landscapes across Europe seems to be a formidable obstacle.

One approach to overcoming these difficulties, taken by Bateman *et al.* (2005, ch. 2–4), was to review all stated preference studies of recreation in the United Kingdom and conduct a meta-analysis on a selected number. They concluded that the results of such studies are subject to design effects, but could be usefully employed to quantify the limits of such effects. In addition, the authors concluded that previous studies suggest that there is scope for combining geographical information systems (GIS) techniques within a travel cost model of recreational demand. An important advantage of using GIS techniques in travel cost studies is that it allows standardization and improvement in the accuracy of measuring travel distance and duration variables, which are key determinants in estimating travel time and expenditure by individuals. Bateman *et al.* apply this methodology to a follow-up study of visitors to Lynford Stag, a major woodland recreation site near Thetford, East Anglia. They found that the use of GIS-based measures of travel offered substantial improvement in the robustness of benefit estimates compared either to conventional straight-line or road-fitted measures, and were more reliable compared to the highly variable recreational values produced by previous stated preference studies of recreation at Thetford. In particular, the use of GIS allowed better measurement of journey outset location, modeling journey routing, and conducting sensitivity analysis on journey outset locations. In addition, the GIS information could be used effectively to model the predicted number of visitors to a particular woodland site and to test the efficiency of the resultant arrivals function in estimating visits to other sites. Again, Bateman *et al.* employ their Thetford study to use GIS information to predict future visits, both to Thetford and to similar recreational forests found in Wales.

There are other ways that past recreation information can be used to improve current valuation estimates. For example, Zandersen *et al.* (2007) evaluate two separate random utility model estimations based on 1977 and 1997 national visitor surveys of recreation in fifty-two forests in Denmark for possible changes in preferences towards forest characteristics and travel over the twenty-year period. GIS techniques were also employed to account for site heterogeneity and the spatial pattern of population density and other demographic characteristics. The authors then combine the 1997 random utility model with a count data model to determine total demand for visits at each forest site, and controlling for changes in trip demand, they conduct a value transfer from 1977 to 1997. Finally, Zandersen *et al.* use sensitivity analysis to determine whether the twenty-year benefits transfer improves the estimation of the present total demand for recreation. They find that the error margins improve by 282 percent, although the average errors of the best transfer model remain at 25 percent.

Overall, these studies from Europe suggest that careful meta-analysis and transfer of recreational values estimated from past studies is most likely to be successful if confined to transferring these benefit estimates within a specific country (e.g., Denmark) or region (e.g., southern Britain) and where important forest and socio-economic characteristics are carefully accounted for. Estimating recreational benefits based on past valuation studies, and then attempting to apply the median and average value estimates to different European forest landscapes and countries, is likely to be much less reliable.

Final remarks

This chapter has sought to show how the concept of an ecological landscape facilitates our characterization of ecosystems as natural assets. That is, if ecosystems and the goods and services they generate can be associated with the ecological landscape defining these systems, then we have a way of depicting these ecosystems as natural assets that is amenable to economic analysis. Viewing ecosystems as natural assets is also an important way of communicating to policymakers the economic importance of these valuable systems. As they provide a flow of beneficial goods and services over time, ecosystems should be considered no different from any other form of wealth in an economy. Policymakers are then confronted with a clear choice of deciding whether or not to conserve this natural capital or to convert it to another form of wealth. As illustrated by Figure 2.2, if the goods and services of ecosystems are related to their landscape extent, then characterizing ecosystems as natural assets and analyzing the tradeoff between conservation versus conversion are straightforward decisions.

Assessing the nonmarket value of ecosystem goods and services is essential to getting the conservation versus development tradeoff right. However, as we have seen in this chapter, the majority of ecosystem services are not marketed. These include many important services arising from ecosystem processes and functions, such as coastal protection, nutrient cycling, erosion control, water purification, and carbon sequestration. In recent years, substantial progress has been made by economists working with ecologists and other natural scientists in applying environmental valuation methodologies to assess the welfare contribution of these and other important ecosystem benefits. As shown in the various case studies and examples discussed throughout this chapter, valuing nonmarket ecosystem goods and services is critical to the management of key ecological landscapes.

As we gain familiarity with the ecological and economic steps needed for valuing ecosystems, and we begin applying such methods to more ecological goods and services, we start to appreciate the role of economic valuation in assisting the management of ecological landscapes. This has certainly become the case for some ecosystems, such as wetlands, as reflected in the increasing number of studies that are evaluating different conservation versus development scenarios at the landscape level. Various examples include: balancing agricultural conversion with riverine wetland conservation in South Africa (Jogo and Hassan 2010); managing environmental change in the Norfolk and Suffolk Broads of the UK (Turner *et al.* 2004); comparing flood control regimes to natural floodplain production in Bangladesh (Islam and Braden 2006); examining rural land use changes and floodplain management scenarios in the UK (Posthumus *et al.* 2010); valuing changes in ecosystem services from various wetland management regimes in Greece (Birol *et al.* 2006); evaluating preferences for alternative restoration options for the Greater Everglades ecosystem in the US (Milon and Scrogin 2006); valuing ecosystem services from wetlands restoration in the Mississippi Valley, US (Jenkins *et al.* 2010); and assessing different mangrove management options in Malaysia (Othman *et al.* 2004).

Progress will continue to be made for other ecosystems and their goods and services, too, which is an important area for future research that will be discussed later in this book. Meanwhile, the aim of the next chapter is to explore further how competing land use models can be adapted and applied to modeling ecosystems as natural assets.

References

Aburto-Oropeza, O., E. Ezcurra, G. Danemann *et al.* 2008. "Mangroves in the Gulf of California increase fishery yields." *Proceedings of the National Academy of Sciences* 105:10456–10459.

Acharya, G. and E.B. Barbier. 2000. "Valuing groundwater recharge through agricultural production in the Hadejia-Jama'are wetlands in Northern Nigeria." *Agricultural Economics* 22:247–259.

2002. "Using domestic water analysis to value groundwater recharge in the Hadejia-Jama'are floodplain." *American Journal of Agricultural Economics* 84(2):415–426.

Aksornkoae, S. and R. Tokrisna. 2004. "Overview of shrimp farming and mangrove loss in Thailand." In E.B. Barbier and S. Sathirathai, eds. *Shrimp Farming and Mangrove Loss in Thailand.* Edward Elgar, London.

Badola, R. and S.A. Hussain. 2005. "Valuing ecosystems functions: an empirical study on the storm protection function of Bhitarkanika mangrove ecosystem, India." *Environmental Conservation* 32:85–92.

Balmisse, S., G. Faure and I.Y. Ilu. 2003. "Integration of existing farming systems in Hadejia Valley Irrigation Project." In J.Y. Jamin, L. Seiny Boukar, and C. Floret, eds. *Savanes Africaines: Des Espaces en Mutation, Des Acteurs Face á de Nouveaux Défis.* CIRAD, Montpellier, France.

Barbier, E.B. 1994. "Valuing environmental functions: tropical wetlands." *Land Economics* 70:155–173.

2000. "Valuing the environment as input: applications to mangrove-fishery linkages." *Ecological Economics* 35:47–61.

2003. "Habitat-fishery linkages and mangrove loss in Thailand." *Contemporary Economic Policy* 21:59–77.

2007. "Valuing ecosystems as productive inputs." *Economic Policy* 22:177–229.

in press. "Pricing nature." *Annual Review of Resource Economics* 3.

Barbier, E.B. and G.M. Heal. 2006. "Valuing ecosystem services." *The Economists' Voice* 3(3):2. www.bepress.com/ev/iss3/art2, accessed April 4, 2011.

Barbier, E.B. and I. Strand. 1998. "Valuing mangrove-fishery linkages: a case study of Campeche, Mexico." *Environmental and Resource Economics* 12:151–166.

Barbier, E.B. and J.R. Thompson. 1998. "The value of water: floodplain versus large-scale irrigation benefits in Northern Nigeria." *Ambio* 27(6):434–440.

Barbier, E.B., W.M. Adams, and K. Kimmage. 1993. "An economic valuation of wetland benefits." In G.E. Hollis, W.M. Adams, and M. Aminu-Kano, eds. *The Hadejia-Nguru Wetlands: Environment,*

Economy and Sustainable Development of a Sahelian Floodplain Wetland. IUCN, Geneva.

Barbier, E.B., M. Acreman, and D.J. Knowler. 1997. *Economic Valuation of Wetlands: A Guide for Policymakers and Planners*. Ramsar Convention Bureau, Gland, Switzerland.

Barbier, E.B., I. Strand, and S. Sathirathai. 2002. "Do open access conditions affect the valuation of an externality? Estimating the welfare effects of mangrove-fishery linkages in Thailand." *Environmental and Resource Economics* 21:343–367.

Batabayal, A.A., J.R. Kahn, and R.V. O'Neil. 2003. "On the scarcity value of ecosystem services." *Journal of Environmental Economics and Management* 46:334–352.

Bateman, I.J. and I.H. Langford. 1997. "Non-users willingness to pay for a national park: an application of the contingent valuation method." *Regional Studies* 31:571–582.

Bateman, I.J., A.A. Lovett, and J.S. Brainard. 2005. *Applied Environmental Economics: A GIS Approach to Cost-Benefit Analysis*. Cambridge University Press.

Bateman, I.J., B.H. Day, A.P Jones, and S. Jude. 2009. "Reducing gain-loss asymmetry: a virtual reality choice experiment valuing land use change." *Journal of Environmental Economics and Management* 58:106–118.

Bedford, B.L. 1996. "The need to define hydrological equivalence at the landscape scale for freshwater wetland mitigation." *Ecological Applications* 6(1):57–68.

———— 1999. "Cumulative effects on wetland landscapes: links to wetland restoration in the United States and Southern Canada." *WETLANDS* 19(4):775–788.

Bell, F.W. 1997. "The economic valuation of saltwater marsh supporting marine recreational fishing in the southeastern United States." *Ecological Economics* 21(3):243–254.

Bergstrom, J.C. and J.R. Stoll. 1993. "Value estimator models for wetlands-based recreational use values." *Land Economics* 69:132–137.

Birol, E. and V. Cox. 2007. "Using choice experiments to design wetland management programmes: the case of the Severn Estuary Wetland, UK." *Journal of Environmental Planning and Management* 50(3):363–380.

Birol, E., K. Karousakis, and P. Koundouri. 2006. "Using a choice experiment to account for preference heterogeneity in wetland attributes: the case of Cheimaditida wetland in Greece." *Ecological Economics* 60:145–156.

Bockstael, N.E. 1996. "Modeling economics and ecology: the importance of a spatial perspective." *American Journal of Agricultural Economics* 78:1168–1180.

Bockstael, N.E., A.M. Freeman III, R.J. Kopp, P.R. Portney, and V.K. Smith. 2000. "On measuring economic values for nature." *Environmental Science and Technology* 34:1384–1389.

Boyd, J. and S. Banzhaf. 2007. "What are ecosystem services? The need for standardized environmental accounting units." *Ecological Economics* 63:616–626.

Brander, L.M., R.J.G.M. Florax, and J.E. Vermaat. 2006. "The empirics of wetland valuation: a comprehensive summary and a meta-analysis of the literature." *Environmental and Resource Economics* 33:223–250.

Brander, L.M., P. van Beukering, and H.S.J. Cesar. 2007. "The recreational value of coral reefs: a meta-analysis." *Ecological Economics* 63: 209–218.

Brauman, K.A., G.C. Daily, T.K. Duarte, and H.A. Mooney. 2007. "The nature and value of ecosystem services: an overview highlighting hydrologic services." *Annual Review of Environment and Resources* 32:67–98.

Breaux, A., S. Farber, and J. Day. 1995. "Using natural coastal wetlands systems for wastewater treatment: an economic benefit analysis." *Journal of Environmental Management* 44(3):285–291.

Brouwer, R. and I.J. Bateman. 2005. "Temporal stability and transferability of models of willingness to pay for flood control and wetland conservation." *Water Resources Research* 41:1–6.

Brouwer, R. and R. van Elk. 2004. "Integrated ecological, economics and social impact assessment of alternative flood control policies in the Netherlands." *Ecological Economics* 50:1–21.

Bullock, A. and M.C. Acreman. 2003. "The role of wetlands in the hydrological cycle." *Hydrology and Earth System Sciences* 7(3):75–86.

Busing, R.T. and P.S. White. 1993. "Effects of area on old-growth forest attributes: implications for equilibrium landscape concept." *Landscape Ecology* 8:119–126.

Byström, O. 2000. "The replacement value of wetlands in Sweden." *Environmental and Resource Economics* 16:347–362.

Carlsson, F., P. Frykblom, and C. Lilijenstolpe. 2003. "Valuing wetland attributes: an application of choice experiments." *Ecological Economics* 47:95–103.

Chichilnisky, G. and G.M. Heal. 1998. "Economic returns from the biosphere." *Nature* 391:629–630.

Chong, J. 2005. *Protective Values of Mangrove and Coral Ecosystems: A Review of Methods and Evidence*. IUCN, Gland, Switzerland.

Christie, M., N. Hanley, J. Warren *et al.* 2006. "Valuing the diversity of biodiversity." *Ecological Economics* 58(2):304–317.

Clark, C.W. 1976. *Mathematical Bioeconomics*. 1st edn. John Wiley, New York.

Clark, C.W. and G. Munro. 1975. "The economics of fishing and modern capital theory: a simplified approach." *Journal of Environmental Economics and Management* 2:92–106.

Cooper, J. and J. Loomis. 1993. "Testing whether waterfowl hunting benefits increase with greater water deliveries to wetlands." *Environmental and Resource Economics* 3:545–561.

Costanza, R., O. Pérez-Maqueo, M.L. Martinez *et al.* 2008. "The value of coastal wetlands for hurricane protection." *Ambio* 37:241–248.

Creel, M. and J. Loomis. 1992. "Recreation value of water to wetlands in the San Joaquin Valley: linked multinomial logit and count data trip frequency models." *Water Resources Research* 28:2597–2606.

Daily, G.C., ed. 1997. *Nature's Services: Societal Dependence on Natural Ecosystems*. Island Press, Washington, DC.

Daily, G.C., T. Söderqvist, S. Aniyar *et al.* 2000. "The value of nature and the nature of value." *Science* 289:395–396.

Daily, G.C., S. Polasky, J. Goldstein *et al.* 2009. "Ecosystem services in decision making: time to deliver." *Frontiers in Ecology and the Environment* 7(1):21–28.

Das, S. and J.R. Vincent. 2009. "Mangroves protected villages and reduced death toll during Indian super cyclone." *Proceedings of the National Academy of Sciences* 106:7357–7360.

Dasgupta, P.S. and G.M. Heal. 1974. "The optimal depletion of exhaustible resources." *Review of Economic Studies*, Symposium on the Economics of Exhaustible Resources, 3–28.

1979. *Economic Theory and Exhaustible Resources*. Cambridge University Press.

Dasgupta, P.S. and K.-G. Mäler. 2003. "The economics of non-convex ecosystems: an introduction." *Environmental and Resource Economics* 26:499–525.

Do, T.N. and J. Bennett. 2008. "Estimating wetland biodiversity values: a choice modelling application in Vietnam's Mekong River Delta." *Environment and Development Economics* 14:163–186.

Dobson, A., D. Lodge, J. Alder *et al.* 2006. "Habitat loss, trophic collapse, and the decline of ecosystem services." *Ecology* 87:1915–1924.

Ellis, G.M. and A.C. Fisher. 1987. "Valuing the environment as input." *Journal of Environmental Management* 25:149–156.

Elmqvist, T., C. Folke, M. Nyström *et al.* 2003. "Response diversity, ecosystem change, and resilience." *Frontiers in Ecology and the Environment* 1:488–494.

Emerton, L. and L. Boss. 2008. *Value: Counting ecoservices as water infrastructure.* IUCN, Gland, Switzerland.

Environmental Protection Agency (EPA). 2009. *Valuing the Protection of Ecological Systems and Services.* A Report of the EPA Science Advisory Board. EPA, Washington, DC.

Farina, A. 2010. *Ecology, Cognition and Landscape: Linking Natural and Social Systems.* Springer, Dordrecht, the Netherlands.

Fisher, A.C., J.V. Krutilla, and C.J. Cicchetti. 1972. "The economics of environmental preservation: a theoretical and empirical analysis." *American Economic Review* 62(4):605–619.

Food and Agricultural Organization of the United Nations (FAO). 2003. "Status and trends in mangrove area extent worldwide" (by M.L.Wilkie and S. Fortuna), *Forest Resources Assessment Working Paper* No. 63. Forest Resources Division, FAO, Rome.

Freeman, A.M. III. 1991. "Valuing environmental resources under alternative management regimes." *Ecological Economics* 3:247–256.

2003. *The Measurement of Environmental and Resource Values: Theory and Methods*, 2nd edn. Resources for the Future, Washington, DC.

Freeman, A.M. III, R.H. Haveman, and A.V. Kneese. 1973. *The Economics of Environmental Policy.* John Wiley, New York.

Goes, B.J.M. 2002. "Effects of river regulation on aquatic macrophyte growth and floods in the Hadejia-Nguru Wetlands and flow in the Yobe River, northern Nigeria; implications for future water management." *River Research and Applications* 18:81–95.

Gren, I.-M. 1995. "The value of investing in wetlands for nitrogen abatement." *European Review of Agricultural Economics* 22:157–172.

Gwin, S.E., M.E. Kentula, and P.W. Shaffer. 1999. "Evaluating the effect of wetland regulation through hydrogeomorphic classification and landscape profiles." *WETLANDS* 19(3):477–489.

Hammitt, J.K., J.-T. Liu, and J.-L. Liu. 2001. "Contingent valuation of a Taiwanese wetland." *Environment and Development Economics* 6:259–268.

Hanley, N. and E.B. Barbier. 2009. *Pricing Nature: Cost-Benefit Analysis and Environmental Policy.* Edward Elgar, London.

Holling, C.S. 1973. "Resilience and stability of ecological systems." *Annual Review of Ecological Systems* 4:1–23.

Hollis, G.E., W.M. Adams, and M. Aminu-Kano, eds. 1993. *The Hadejia-Nguru Wetlands: Environment, Economy and Sustainable Development of a Sahelian Floodplain Wetland.* IUCN, Geneva.

Islam, M. and J.B. Braden. 2006. "Bio-economic development of flood-plains: farming versus fishing in Bangladesh." *Environment and Development Economics* 11:95–126.

Janssen, R. and J.E. Padilla. 1999. "Preservation or conservation? Valuation and evaluation of a mangrove forest in the Philippines." *Environmental and Resource Economics* 14:297–331.

Jenkins, W.A., B.C. Murray, R.A. Kramer, and S.P. Faulkner. 2010. "Valuing ecosystem services from wetlands restoration in the Mississippi Alluvial Valley." *Ecological Economics* 69:1051–1061.

Jogo, W. and R. Hassan. 2010. "Balancing the use of wetlands for economic well-being and ecological security: the case of the Limpopo wetland in southern Africa." *Ecological Economics* 69:1569–1579.

Johnston, R.J., T.A. Grigalunas, J.J. Opaluch, M. Mazzotta, and J. Diamantedes. 2002. "Valuing estuarine resource services using economic and ecological models: the Peconic Estuary system." *Coastal Management* 30(1):47–65.

King, S.E. and J.N. Lester. 1995. "The value of salt marsh as a sea defence." *Marine Pollution Bulletin* 30(3):180–189.

Koch, E.W., J. Ackerman, M. van Keulen, and J. Verduin. 2006. "Fluid dynamics in seagrass ecology: from molecules to ecosystems." In A.W.D. Larkum, R.J. Orth, and C.M. Duarte, eds. *Seagrasses: Biology, Ecology and Conservation*. Springer Verlag, Dordrecht, the Netherlands, pp. 193–225.

Krutilla, J.V. and A.C. Fisher. 1985. *The Economics of Natural Environments: Studies in the Valuation of Commodity and Amenity Resources*, 2nd edn. Resources for the Future, Washington, DC.

Kwak, S-J., S.-H. Yoo, and C.-K. Lee. 2007. "Valuation of the Woopo Wetland in Korea: a contingent valuation study." *Environment and Development Economics* 12:323–328.

Lemley, A.D., R.T. Kingsford, and J.R. Thompson. 2000. "Irrigated agriculture and wildlife conservation: conflict on a global scale." *Environmental Management* 25(5):485–512.

Levin, S. 1999. *Fragile Dominion: Complexity and the Commons*. Perseus Books, Reading, MA.

Lotze, H.K., H.S. Lenihan, B.J. Bourque *et al.* 2006. "Depletion, degradation and recovery potential of estuaries and coastal seas." *Science* 312:1806–1809.

May, R.M. 1975. *Stability and Complexity in Model Ecosystems*. 2nd edn. Princeton University Press, NJ.

McConnell, K.E. and N.E. Bockstael. 2005. "Valuing the environment as a factor of production." Chapter 14 in K.-G. Mäler and J.R. Vincent, eds. *Handbook of Environmental Economics, Vol. II*. Elsevier, Amsterdam, pp. 621–669.

Mendelsohn, R. and S. Olmstead. 2009. "The economic valuation of environmental amenities and disamenities: methods and applications." *Annual Review of Environment and Resources* 34:325–347.

Millennium Ecosystem Assessment (MEA). 2005. *Ecosystems and Human Well-being: Current State and Trends.* Island Press, Washington, DC.

Milon, J.W. and D. Scrogin. 2006. "Latent preferences and valuation of wetland ecosystem restoration." *Ecological Economics* 56:152–175.

Mitsch, W.J. and J.G. Gosselink. 2000. "The value of wetlands: importance of scale and landscape setting." *Ecological Economics* 35:25–33.

Mitsch, W.J., J.G. Gosselink, L. Zhang, and C.J. Anderson. 2009. *Wetland Ecosystems.* John Wiley, New York.

Moberg, F. and P. Rönnbäck. 2003. "Ecosystem services of the tropical seascape: interactions, substitutions and restoration." *Ocean and Coastal Management* 46:27–46.

Murray, J.D. 1993. *Mathematical Biology,* Springer-Verlag, Berlin.

National Research Council (NRC). 1995. *Wetlands: Characteristics and Boundaries.* The National Academies Press, Washington, DC.
    2005. *Valuing Ecosystem Services: Toward Better Environmental Decision Making.* The National Academies Press, Washington, DC.

Naylor, R. and M. Drew. 1998. "Valuing mangrove resources in Kosrae, Micronesia." *Environment and Development Economics* 3:471–490.

Neiland, A.R., S.P. Mandakan, and C. Béné. 2005. "Traditional management systems, poverty and change in the arid zone fisheries of Northern Nigeria." *Journal of Agrarian Change* 5(1):117–148.

Nelson, E., S. Polasky, D.J. Lewis *et al.* 2008. "Efficiency of incentives to jointly increase carbon sequestration and species conservation on a landscape." *Proceedings of the National Academy of Sciences* 105(28):9471–9476.

Nelson, E., G. Mendoza, J. Regetz *et al.* 2009. "Modeling multiple ecosystem services, biodiversity conservation, commodity production, and tradeoffs at landscape scales." *Frontiers in Ecology and the Environment* 7(1):4–11.

Odum, E.P. 1975. *Ecology,* 2nd edn. Holt Rinehart and Winston, New York.

O'Neill, R.V. 2001. "Is it time to bury the ecosystem concept? (With full military honors, of course!)" *Ecology* 82: 3275–3284.

Othman, J., J. Bennett, and R. Blamey. 2004. "Environmental management and resource management options: a choice modelling experience in Malaysia." *Environment and Development Economics* 9:803–824.

Pagiola, S., K. von Ritter, and J. Bishop. 2004. *How Much is an Ecosystem Worth? Assessing the Economic Value of Conservation.* The World Bank, Washington, DC.

Perrings, C. 1998. "Resilience in the dynamics of economic-environmental systems." *Environmental and Resource Economics* 11:503–520.

Perry, G.L.W. 2002. "Landscapes, space and equilibrium: shifting viewpoints." *Progress in Physical Geography* 26:339–359.

Peterson, G., C.R. Allen, and C.S. Holling. 1998. "Ecological resilience, biodiversity and scale." *Ecosystems* 1:6–18.

Pickett, S.T.A. and M.L. Cadenasso. 1995. "Landscape ecology: spatial heterogeneity in ecological systems." *Science* 269: 331–334.

2002. "The ecosystem as a multidimensional concept: meaning, model, and metaphor." *Ecosystems* 5:1–10.

Pimm, S.L. 1984. "The complexity and stability of ecosystems." *Nature* 307:321–326.

Polasky, S. and K. Segerson. 2009. "Integrating ecology and economics in the study of ecosystem services: some lessons learned." *Annual Review of Resource Economics* 1:409–434.

Polasky, S., E. Nelson, E. Lonsdorf, P. Fackler, and A. Starfield. 2005. "Conserving species in a working landscape: land use with biological and economic objectives." *Ecological Applications* 15(4): 1387–1401.

Polasky, S., E. Nelson, J. Camm *et al.* 2008. "Where to put things? Spatial land management to sustain biodiversity and economic returns." *Biological Conservation* 141:1505–1524.

Posthumus, H., J.R. Rouquette, J. Morris, D.J.G. Gowing, and T.M. Hess. 2010. "A framework for the assessment of ecosystem goods and services: a case study on lowland floodplains in England." *Ecological Economics* 69:1510–1523.

Ruitenbeek, H.J. 1994. "Modeling economy-ecology linkages in mangroves: economic evidence for promoting conservation in Bintuni Bay, Indonesia." *Ecological Economics* 10:233–247.

Rybicki, N.B. 1997. "Observations of tidal flux between a submersed aquatic plant stand and the adjacent channel in the Potomac River near Washington, DC." *Limnology and Oceanography* (0024–3590), 42(2): 307.

Sanchirico, J.N. and P. Mumby. 2009. "Mapping ecosystem functions to the valuation of ecosystem services: implications of species-habitat associations for coastal land-use decisions." *Theoretical Ecology* 2:67–77.

Sanderson, J. and L.D. Harris, eds. 2000. *Landscape Ecology: A Top-Down Approach.* Lewis Publishers, Boca Raton, FL.

Sangari, D.U. 2006. "An evaluation of water and land uses in the Kano River Project, Phase I, Kano State." *Journal of Applied Science and Environmental Management* 11(2):105–111.

Sathirathai, S. and E.B. Barbier. 2001. "Valuing mangrove conservation, Southern Thailand." *Contemporary Economic Policy* 19:109–122.

Scheffer, M., S. Carpenter, J.A. Foley, C. Folke, and B. Walker. 2001. "Catastrophic shifts in ecosystems." *Nature* 413:591–596.

Scott, A. 1955. "The fishery: the objectives of sole ownership." *Journal of Political Economy* 63:116–124.

Shabman, L.A. and S.S. Batie. 1978. "Economic value of natural coastal wetlands: a critique." *Coastal Zone Management Journal* 4(3):231–247.

Shackeroff, J.M., E.L. Hazen, and L.B. Crowder. 2009. "The oceans as peopled seascapes." In K. McLeod and H. Leslie, eds. *Ecosystem-based management for the oceans*, Island Press, Washington, DC, pp. 33–54.

Simenstad, C., D. Reed, and M. Ford. 2006. "When is restoration not? Incorporating landscape-scale processes to restore self-sustaining ecosystems in coastal wetland restoration." *Ecological Engineering* 26:27–39.

Smith, M.D. 2007. "Generating value in habitat-dependent fisheries: the importance of fishery management institutions." *Land Economics* 83:59–73.

Smith, V.L. 1968. "Economics of production from natural resources." *American Economic Review* 58(3):409–431.

Swallow, S.K. 1994. "Renewable and nonrenewable resource theory applied to coastal agriculture, forest, wetland and fishery linkages." *Marine Resource Economics* 9:291–310.

Tansley, T.G. 1935. "The use and abuse of vegetational concepts and terms." *Ecology* 16:284–307.

The Economics of Ecosystems and Biodiversity (TEEB). 2009. *TEEB for Policymakers*. TEEB–UNEP, Bonn, Germany.

Thomas, D.H.L. and W.M. Adams. 1999. "Adapting to dams: agrarian change downstream of the Tiga Dam, Northern Nigeria." *World Development* 26(6):919–935.

Thompson, J.R. and B. Goes. 1997. "Inundation and groundwater recharge in the Hadejia-Nguru wetlands, northeast Nigeria: hydrological analysis." Report for the Hadejia-Nguru Wetlands Conservation Project, Kano, Nigeria and the Wetland Research Unit, University College London.

Thompson, J.R. and G.E. Hollis. 1995. "Hydrological modelling and the sustainable development of the Hadejia-Nguru wetlands, Nigeria." *Hydrological Science Journal* 40:97–116.

Thompson, J.R. and G. Polet. 2000. "Hydrology and land use in a Sahelian floodplain wetland." *WETLANDS* 20(4):639–659.

Tokrisna, R. 1998. "The use of economic analysis in support of development and investment decision in Thai aquaculture: with particular reference to marine shrimp culture." A paper submitted to the Food and Agriculture Organization of the United Nations.

Turner, M.G. 2005. "Landscape ecology: what is the state of the science?" *Annual Reviews of Ecological and Evolutionary Systems* 36:319–344.

Turner, M.G., W.H. Romme, R.H. Gardner, R.V. O' Neill, and T.K. Kratz. 1993. "A revised concept of landscape equilibrium: disturbance and stability on scaled landscapes." *Landscape Ecology* 8:213–227.

Turner, R.K., I.J. Bateman, S. Georgiou *et al.* 2004. "An ecological economics approach to the management of a multi-purpose coastal wetland." *Regional Environmental Change* 4:86–99.

Turner, R.K., S. Georgiou, and B. Fisher. 2008. *Valuation of Ecosystem Services: The Case of Multi-functional Wetlands.* Earthscan Publications, London.

Willis, K.G., G. Garrod, R. Scarpa *et al.* 2003. *The Social and Environmental Benefits of Forests in Great Britain.* Report to Forestry Commission, UK Forestry Commission, Edinburgh, Scotland.

Woodward, R.T. and Y-S. Wui. 2001. "The economic value of wetland services: a meta-analysis." *Ecological Economics* 37:2257–2270.

World Resources Institute (WRI). 2001. *World Resources 2000–2001. People and Ecosystems: The Fraying Web of Life.* WRI, Washington, DC.

Yang, W., J. Chang, B. Xu, C. Peng, and Y. Ge. 2008. "Ecosystem service value assessment for constructed wetlands: a case study in Hangzhou, China." *Ecological Economics* 68:116–125.

Zandersen, M. and R.S.J. Tol. 2009. "A meta-analysis of forest recreation values in Europe." *Journal of Forest Economics* 15:109–130.

Zandersen, M., M. Termansen, and F. Søndergaard Jensen. 2007. "Testing benefits transfer of forest recreation values over a twenty-year time horizon." *Land Economics* 83(3):412–440.

Zedler, J.B. and S. Kercher. 2005. "Wetland resources: status, trends, ecosystem services, and restorability." *Annual Review of Environment and Resources* 20:39–74.

Zonneveld, I.S. 1989. "The land unit – a fundamental concept in landscape ecology, and its applications." *Landscape Ecology* 3:67–86.

3 | *The basic natural asset model*

Natural environments will represent irreplaceable assets of appreciating value with the passage of time.

(Krutilla 1967, p. 783)

Introduction

The purpose of the following chapter is to illustrate further the natural asset properties of ecosystems by developing a basic competing land use model as applied to ecosystems. As we saw in the previous chapter, if we are to view ecosystems as economic assets, then it is helpful to have a measure of this "ecological wealth." We suggested that by adopting ecological landscape, or land area, as the basic unit, modeling an ecosystem as a natural asset is relatively straightforward. Here, we also show how this approach facilitates applying competing land use models to the problem of whether or not to conserve or develop the remaining area of an ecosystem.

Employing the concept of an ecological landscape as the basis for analyzing development versus conservation tradeoffs is not new. The many case study examples and valuation studies cited in the previous chapter illustrate that this approach is gaining acceptance in applying integrated ecological and economic analysis to manage entire landscapes, such as floodplains, river basins, watersheds, coastal wetlands, and forests. Integrated economy–ecosystem models in economics have also started examining human transformation of an ecological landscape through land use conversion, leaving the residual land for ecological processes and habitat for species.[1] But whereas these integrated models focus on modeling the complex ecological processes and feedback effects on multiple ecosystem services that

---

[1] See, for example, Brock and Xepapadeas (2002); Eichner and Pethig (2006); Finnoff *et al.* (2008); Tschirhart (2000, 2009).

arise through land conversion, the approach in the following chapter is to adopt a much simpler model of land use change. Such models of competing land use have been employed in many contexts to analyze the allocation of land between alternative uses.[2]

In applying competing land use models to ecosystems, the starting point is the assumption that the amount of an ecological landscape that is preserved must compete with other assets in the portfolio of wealth owners in the economy. The remaining landscape area yields a flow of ecosystem services, which have value but are nonmarketed. The first version of the basic model considers a one-time irreversible development of the landscape. Land that is converted and developed has a market value, and the rate of appreciation of land awaiting development must equal the opportunity cost of the land investment, which includes an adjustment for the ratio of the value of ecosystem services to the capital value of the developed land. This basic model is extended to the case of continuous conversion of the ecological landscape over time, taking into account the costs of converting land and any capital gains from increases in the value of unconverted land. The model is solved to show the conditions under which a positive amount of ecosystem land is conserved rather than converted to commercial use. Finally, the basic model examines the case of a possible *ecological transition*, whereby it becomes technologically feasible to restore developed land as ecological landscape, leading to a new phase of land use in which ecological restoration occurs.

Although the two versions of the model developed in this chapter are necessarily technical, they will be supplemented by additional discussion of their relevance to case studies. For example, the depiction of an ecological transition is directly applicable to the growing literature on forest transitions in some countries as well as the growing literature in ecological restoration of degraded ecosystems, including coastal, estuarine, and marine systems. Other chapters in this book will develop further extensions to the natural asset model and discuss their potential applications.

[2] See, for example, Amacher *et al.* (2009); Barbier and Burgess (1997); Barbier *et al.* (2010); Benhin and Barbier (2001); Crocker (2005); Fisher *et al.* (1974); Hartwick *et al.* (2001); McConnell (1989); Parks (1995); Parks *et al.* (1998); Rowthorn and Brown (1999); and Stavins and Jaffe (1990).

One-time development of an ecological landscape

To illustrate further the natural asset properties of ecosystems, we consider the simplest problem of one-time development of an entire ecological landscape to an alternative commercial use. Such a model turns out to have properties very similar to those of early economic models of land awaiting development that might have interim use or income (Arnott and Lewis 1979; Shoup 1970) or forest land that is clear cut once for timber but also yields nontimber benefits in the meantime (Hartman 1976).

Let the initial landscape area of an ecosystem be denoted as A_0. If the landscape is completely converted and developed in its highest and best use at some future time t, then its value, expressed in terms of the optimal rent to developed land at that time, is $R(t)$. We assume that developed land is initially scarce in the economy, perhaps due to a large and growing population relative to the amount of available land, and thus the rental value of developed land increases over time, i.e., $R'(t) > 0$. But as more and more land conversion occurs through-out the economy, and because initially the best quality land for development is used first, $R''(t) < 0$. Also, until the ecological landscape is converted at time t, it yields a flow of ecosystem services, or benefits. Denote the value of these benefits in each time period i as $B(i)$, which begin during the current period 0 and end at the time of development t. It follows that the present value of the landscape at time 0 is

$$V(t) = \underset{t}{Max}\left[R(t)e^{-rt} + \int_0^t B(i)e^{-ri}di \right]. \tag{3.1}$$

The optimal date of development, t, is determined as

$$e^{-rt}\left[R'(t) - rR(t) + B(t) \right] = 0 \rightarrow R'(t) + B(t) = rR(t). \tag{3.2}$$

In (3.2) $R'(t) + B(t)$ represents the gain from delaying development one period. It includes the increase in rental value of developed land plus the additional ecosystem benefits during that period of delay. The term $rR(t)$ represents the cost of delaying development. The value of the land, if sold in period t, could be invested to earn an interest income. The average interest rate on other assets in the economy is clearly key to the opportunity cost of delaying development another period. A higher interest rate means that it is costly to delay, whereas the lower interest rate has the opposite effect. Thus, although highly basic, condition (3.2) shows how the returns to holding on to ecosystems as a natural asset can be compared to the rate of return on other assets in the economy.

Condition (3.2) can also be written in the more familiar way

$$\frac{R'(t)}{R(t)} = r - \frac{B(t)}{R(t)} \, . \tag{3.3}$$

Development should take place when the rate of change of development value of the land, $R'(t)/R(t)$, is equal to the interest rate, r, less the ratio of the ecosystem benefit flows per time period of the ecological landscape to the development value of the land. As the rate of growth in the rental value of developed land is initially high but falls over time, condition (3.3) indicates that the net or effective interest rate is key to the decision as to whether or not to postpone development an additional period. With positive ecosystem benefits, $B(t)/R(t) > 0$, the effective interest rate is lower than the market rate, implying that the ecological landscape should be developed when the rate of growth in its value is less than r, and thus development should be delayed.

Ecosystem benefits are therefore critically important to the optimal landscape development decision. When the benefits are large, development may not be optimal at all. First, as $B(t) \to \infty$, then the problem (3.1) is convex, and there is no feasible first-order condition for the optimal time for development. However, ecosystem benefits do not have to be that large for development to be delayed indefinitely. From (3.2), if $R'(t) + B(t) > rR(t)$ for all t, then the gains from delaying development always exceed the costs, and the ecological landscape should not be developed. Finally, if a solution for the optimal timing for development exists, it must also satisfy the second-order condition $R''(t) + B'(t) < rR'(t)$. If ecosystem benefits rise rapidly over time, perhaps because rapid development elsewhere in the economy has made such ecosystem services scarce, then this condition might not be satisfied and there is no solution to (3.1). Once again, development of the ecological landscape should not occur.

Valuing ecosystem services as well as changes in this value over time is therefore important to determining the optimal time to develop ecological landscape as well as whether or not development should take place at any time. As condition (3.3) indicates, the failure to value ecosystem benefits at all is tantamount to assuming that ecosystems are not natural assets. Their only value is as a potential source of developed land, and the development decision depends solely on comparing the growth in rental value to the market interest rate. Ecological landscape development will take place too soon, if it should occur at all.

Continuous conversion of an ecological landscape

Although the ecological landscape of an ecosystem might be completely converted through one-time development, a more likely scenario is that the landscape is subject to continuous but irreversible conversion to land used in economic development activities. Here, it is shown that this problem can be easily analyzed by employing a *competing land use model*, which has been used in many contexts to analyze the allocation of land between alternative uses.[3]

In the following version of the problem, it is assumed that the land conversion decision is effectively irreversible because, once the ecological landscape is converted to another land use, the cost of restoring the landscape is either technically infeasible or prohibitively expensive relative to the ecosystem benefits obtained. Later in this section, this condition is modified to allow for the possibility of future restoration of the ecological landscape.

Let $A(t)$ be the area of an ecosystem's landscape at time t and $A(0) = A_0$ is the initial landscape area. If $c(t)$ is the area of ecological landscape converted in each period to a development activity, then

$$A(t) = A_0 - \int_0^t c(s)ds \text{ and } \dot{A} = -c(t).\tag{3.4}$$

It follows that, if $D(t)$ be the area of land use in the development activity and $D(0) = D_0$ is the initial developed land area, then

---

[3] See, for example, Amacher *et al.* (2009); Barbier and Burgess (1997); Barbier *et al.* (2010); Benhin and Barbier (2001); Crocker (2005); Fisher *et al.* (1974); Hartwick *et al.* (2001); McConnell (1989); Parks (1995); Parks *et al.* (1998); Rowthorn and Brown (1999); and Stavins and Jaffe (1990).

$$D(t) = D_0 + \int_0^t c(s)\,ds \text{ and } \dot{D} = c(t) \tag{3.5}$$

The ecosystem produces a flow of goods and services, or benefits, which vary across the landscape. Let $B(A(t))$ be the periodic ecosystem service flow from the remaining landscape area. These benefits vary nonlinearly across the landscape such that $\partial B/\partial A(t) > 0$, $\partial^2 B/\partial A(t)^2 < 0$. Developed land is also heterogeneous in quality. Let R be the periodic rent associated with developed land. If the conversion decision is rational, then the highest quality land is allocated to development first, and differential rent will vary with land quality; i.e., there are decreasing marginal returns (rent) to the increase in the stock of developed land, $R(D(t))$, $\partial R/\partial D(t) > 0$, $\partial^2 R/\partial D(t)^2 < 0$. However, conditions (3.4) and (3.5) indicate that $D(t) = D_0 + A_0 - A(t)$. The latter expression implies in turn that the rents from developed land can be rewritten as $R(A(t))$, $\partial R/\partial A(t) < 0$.

If C are the costs of conversion, then more landscape conversion increases these costs, i.e., $C(c(t))$, $\partial C/\partial c\,(t) > 0$, $\partial^2 C/\partial c(t)^2 > 0$. It is also assumed that $C(0) = C'(0) = 0$.

The decision maker determining landscape use can maximize the present value of net returns from the land, V, by choosing optimal levels of land to convert, $c(t)$

$$\underset{c(t)}{Max}\, V = \int_0^\infty \left[R(D) - C(c) + B(A) \right] e^{-rt}\, dt \tag{3.6}$$

subject to (3.4) and (3.5). However, if we use the above suggested substitutions in the expression for rent from developed land, then the current value Hamiltonian of the problem is

$$H = R(A) - C(c) + B(A) - \mu c,$$

where μ is the shadow value of ecological landscape. Two of the first-order conditions of the problem are

$$\frac{\partial H}{\partial c} = 0 \rightarrow \mu = -C'(c) \tag{3.7}$$

$$-\frac{\partial H}{\partial A} = \dot{\mu} - r\mu \rightarrow \dot{\mu} = r\mu - B'(A) - R'(A). \tag{3.8}$$

Combining (3.7) and (3.8) yields

$$-B'(A) - R'(A) = \dot{\mu} + rC_c \rightarrow -R'(A) - rC'(c)$$
$$= R'(D) - rC'(c) = B'(A) + \dot{\mu},$$
(3.9)

where $-R_A = R_D$ is annual periodic rent from developed land use.

Condition (3.9) indicates that, along the optimal path of landscape conversion, the returns from the two competing land uses must be equal. The marginal profits from development less conversion costs $R'(D) - rC'(c)$ must equal the marginal benefit of holding on to the ecological landscape $B'(A) + \dot{\mu}$. Note that (3.9) can also be rewritten as $-\mu(t) = \dfrac{R'(D)}{r} - \dfrac{B'(A) + \dot{\mu}}{r} = C'(c)$. The difference between the capitalized marginal value of developed land and land retained as ecological landscape is the marginal cost of converting landscape. Denote P as the "price," or capital value, of land that is associated with each of these respective capitalized land use values, then

$$\frac{R'(D)}{r} - \frac{B'(A) + \dot{\mu}}{r} = P(D(t)) - P(A(t)) = C'(c).$$
(3.10)

The difference in land prices between developed and ecological land is the marginal cost of converting a unit of the ecological landscape into developed land.

In the long-run steady state, $\dot{A} = \dot{\mu} = 0$. It follows from (3.4) and (3.7) that both landscape conversion and the marginal value of an additional unit of ecosystem landscape approach zero asymptotically, i.e., $c = 0$ and $\lim\limits_{t \to \infty} \mu(t) = C_c(0) = 0$. The wedge between land prices will disappear, $P(D(t)) = P(A(t))$, and ecosystem landscape area will converge to a steady state level A^*.

Assume that the initial ecological landscape area is large $A(0) > A^*$. From (3.7), along the transition path to the long-run steady state, the marginal value of an additional unit of ecosystem landscape is negative $\mu < 0$. Initially, optimal landscape conversion c is very large, which reflects the fact that developed land is relatively scarce compared to ecological landscape and essentially valued as a "reserve" to be converted for developed land. But because initial landscape area is large, the marginal value of ecosystem services from that landscape $B'(A)$ is very low whereas the marginal rent earned from developed land use $R'(D)$ is extremely high. The result is that the shadow value of ecological landscape μ(*t*) is rising over time. In fact, given that A(0) > A*, along the optimal path until the steady state is reached, μ(*t*) continues rising and *c* falling.

Formally, from the necessary condition (3.7)

$$\partial\mu = -C''(c)\partial c \rightarrow \frac{\partial c}{\partial\mu} = -\frac{1}{C''(c)} < 0,$$

(3.11)

which implies that (3.4) can be written as $\dot{A} = -c(\mu)$ and confirms that, as the shadow value of the ecological landscape becomes less negative over time, optimal land conversion falls. The slope of the optimal path is

$$\frac{\partial\mu}{\partial A} = \frac{\dot{\mu}}{\dot{A}} = \frac{r\mu - B'(A) - R'(A)}{-c(\mu)} < 0,$$

(3.12)

which verifies that, although initially the ecological landscape is very large, as land conversion proceeds and *A* falls, the shadow value of the landscape becomes less negative. The optimal path for ecological landscape conversion is depicted in Figure 3.1.

However, as we have discussed previously, the problem for the decision maker determining landscape use is that markets do not take into account the value of nonmarket ecosystem services, so that typically $B'(A) = 0$ in most land use decisions. If that is the case, the only value of ecological landscape is as a "reserve" of developed land. Land will be developed until in the long run the entire landscape is converted $A^* = 0$ and $D^* = A_0$, and the capitalized value of land is zero, $R'(D^*)/r = \dot{\mu}/r = P(D^*) = 0$. This outcome is depicted in Figure 3.2.

An ecological transition

Although it might not be feasible initially to restore the ecological landscape, at some future time t_1, where $0 < t_1 < \infty$, it becomes technologically possible to restore developed land as ecological landscape. The value of restoring all developed land at time $t_1 \leq t \leq \infty$ can be denoted by the function $G(D(t))$, $G'(D(t)) > 0$.

At some finite time *T*, which occurs at the time or shortly after ecological restoration becomes feasible, i.e., $t_1 \leq T < \infty$, the future land

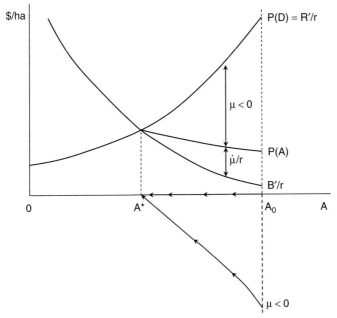

Figure 3.1 Optimal landscape conversion in the basic model

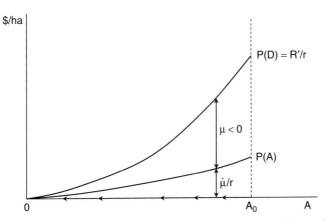

Figure 3.2 Landscape conversion when ecosystem services are ignored

rents earned from developed land are equal to the value of restoring all developed land at T

$$V\big(D(T)\big) = \int_T^\infty R\big(D(t)\big)e^{-rt}dt = G\big(D(T)\big),$$

$$G'\big(D(T)\big) \geq V'\big(D(T)\big) > 0. \tag{3.13}$$

Given that $D(t) = D_0 + A_0 - A(t)$ it follows that $V(D(T))$, which is the value of developed land from T onwards, can also be expressed as $V(A(T))$, $V'(A(T)) < 0$.

The competing land use model is now a finite time optimization problem with a designated terminal value associated with the stock of remaining ecological land at time T. The first-order conditions of the model over the interval $[0,T]$ are the same as before, but the new transversality condition is

$$\mu(T) = -C'(c) = V'(A(T)) < 0. \tag{3.14}$$

At time T the marginal (negative) value of an additional stock of ecological landscape must equal the additional cost of converting it to developed land and also equal the marginal increase in future rents from developing another unit of the landscape.

From (3.13) and using $-V'(A(T)){=}V'(D(T))$ in (3.14), the transversality condition can also be written as

$$-\mu(T) = -V'(D(T)) \leq G'(D(T)). \tag{3.15}$$

$-\mu(T)$ can be interpreted as the marginal value of an additional stock of developed land at T, which is equal to the marginal increase in the future rents from an additional unit of developed land. But this increase in the future stream of rents is equal to or less than the marginal value of restoring one unit of developed land at time T.

Two implications emerge from this transversality condition. First, conversion of ecological landscape to developed land will terminate at time T. Second, over the remaining time period $T \leq t \leq \infty$, a new phase of land use will occur involving the restoration of the stock of developed land to ecological landscape. Thus, the time period T denotes the *ecological transition* from development of ecological landscape to a period of ecological restoration.

Let $g(t)$ be the area of developed land restored in each period over $T \leq t \leq \infty$ to ecological landscape. It follows that

$A(t) = A_T + \int_T^t g(s)ds,\ A(T) = A_T$ and $\overset{*}{A} = g(t)$. If $C(g)$ is the cost

of restoration, which increases with the amount of land restored, i.e., $C'(g) > 0$, $C''(g) > 0$, $C(0) = C'(0) = 0$ then the maximization problem, from the standpoint of the beginning of the ecological transition, is now

$$\underset{g(t)}{Max}V = \int_T^\infty \left[R(A)+B(A)-C(g)\right]e^{-r(t-T)}dt \quad \text{s.t.} \quad \overset{*}{A}=g,\ A(T)=A_T.$$

The current value Hamiltonian of the problem is $H = R(A) + B(A) - C(g) + \mu g$, which yields the following two necessary conditions

$$\frac{\partial H}{\partial c} = 0 \to \mu = C'(g) \tag{3.16}$$

$$-\frac{\partial H}{\partial A} = \dot{\mu} - r\mu \to \dot{\mu} = r\mu - B' - R_A. \tag{3.17}$$

Combining (3.16) and (3.17)

$$-R'(A) = R'(D) = B'(A) - rC'(g) + \dot{\mu} \tag{3.18}$$

$$\mu = \frac{B'(A)+\dot{\mu}}{r} - \frac{R'(D)}{r} = P(A) - P(D) = C'(g). \tag{3.19}$$

After the ecological transition, the difference between the capitalized marginal value of ecological landscape can also be designated as the difference in the "price" of ecological as opposed to developed land, but now this difference must be equivalent to the marginal cost of restoring a unit of developed land as ecological landscape.

In the long-run steady state, $\dot{A} = \dot{\mu} = 0$ and $C'(0) = 0$. It follows that both landscape restoration and the marginal value of an additional unit of ecosystem landscape approach zero asymptotically, i.e., $g = 0$ and $\lim_{t\to\infty}\mu(t) = C'(0) = 0$. The wedge between land prices will disappear, $P(D(t)) = P(A(t))$, and ecosystem landscape area will converge to a steady state level A^{**}. If the initial landscape level is small, i.e. $D(T) > A(T) > A^{**}$ then from (3.16), along the ecological restoration path to the long-run steady state, the marginal value of an additional unit of ecosystem landscape is positive $\mu > 0$, and optimal landscape restoration g is very large, reflecting the fact that developed land is initially relatively abundant compared to ecological landscape. But because initial landscape area is small, the marginal value of ecosystem services from that landscape $B'(A)$ is very high whereas the marginal rent earned from developed land use $R'(D)$ is extremely low. The result is that the shadow value of ecological landscape $\mu(t)$ is falling over time. In fact, given that $A(T) < A^{**}$, along the optimal path until the steady state is reached, both $\mu(t)$ and g continue falling. The outcome is depicted in Figure 3.3.

Although the model of ecological transition developed here is relatively simple, it nonetheless captures two important aspects identified in the literature: restoration must be technologically feasible and the value of a restored ecological landscape must be sufficient to justify the costs of restoration. The notion that there may be distinct phases of ecological land use, where there is an initial phase in which irreversible landscape conversion takes place followed by a new phase where restoration is technically and economically feasible, is supported by the empirical literature on some key ecosystems.

Forest transitions

For example, there is a long-standing *forest transition* literature, which emphasizes that a country's forest cover generally declines as it develops socially and economically, but eventually as an economy develops further, the increased demand for wood products and nonmarket ecosystem services from forested land may lead to forest replenishment, and perhaps eventually a recovery in the total forest area.[4] The result is an inverted "U-shaped curve" for forest cover as a function of time (see Figure 3.4). As indicated in Figure 3.4, the forest transition occurs over the time period or periods at which forest decline halts and begins to rise.

As in the above ecological transition model, the forest transition literature recognizes that long-term forest land use consists of two distinct phases, an initial phase of forest conversion followed by a new phase where forest recovery becomes technically and economically feasible. For example, Grainger (1995) suggests that the U-shaped

---

[4] See, for example, Barbier *et al.* (2010); Grainger (1995, 2008); Kauppi *et al.* (2006); Mather (1992, 2000, and 2007); Palo and Vanhanen (2000); Rudel *et al.* (2005); and Walker (1993).

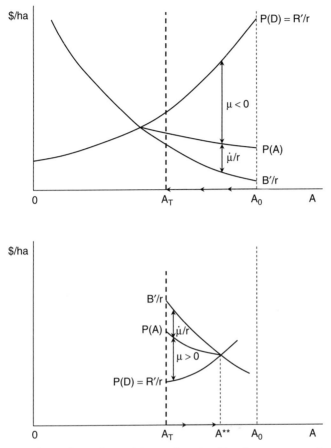

Figure 3.3 The ecological transition and optimal landscape restoration

forest cover curve is actually the aggregate of two separate land use change curves: the decline in forest area, termed the *national land use transition*, and the recovery in forest area after the transition, which he termed the *forest replenishment period* (see Figure 3.4A). These two components of the forest transition curve should be analyzed separately as each involves two fundamentally different processes of land use allocation; i.e., different factors drive forest decline as opposed to forest recovery. For most countries, the decline in forest cover that occurs during the national land use transition is mainly the result of the rapid loss of natural forest cover as agricultural area expands in

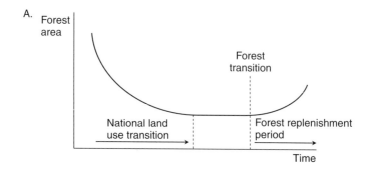

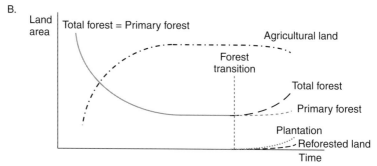

Figure 3.4 Land use change and the forest transition curve
A. The two phases of the forest transition
B. Land use changes of the forest transition
Source: Barbier *et al.* (2010, Figure 1).

response to rising demand for food and other commodities as economic development proceeds and populations grow. Agricultural land
expansion may eventually taper off as the limits of land suitability
are reached, farming modernizes and intensifies following investment
in improved technologies, and economies reach an advanced stage
of economic development such that the demand for food rises less
rapidly. In contrast, as an economy develops further, the increased
demand for wood products and nonmarket ecosystem services from
forested land may lead to forest replenishment, and perhaps eventually a recovery in the total forest area. Increased interaction in the
international trade may also play an important role in forest land use
decisions through its export demand for forest based products. In
addition, if farmland is abandoned but not necessarily converted to

other uses, e.g., to satisfy the demand for land for residential housing and urbanization, natural reforestation may also occur (Mather and Needle 1998; Rudel *et al.* 2005).

Thus, there is general agreement in the literature on the major land use changes underlying the two phases before and after the forest transition (see Figure 3.4B). Although timber harvesting and fuelwood consumption may play a role, the decline in forest cover that occurs during the national land use transition is mainly the result of conversion of primary forest to agricultural land uses. As shown in Figure 3.4B, during this phase there is an inverse relationship between the expansion of agricultural land area and total forest area decline, which is almost exclusively loss of primary forest. As agricultural land expansion slows down, so does the decrease in primary forest area. Increased environmental protection of remaining primary forest also stabilizes its size. But the two main causes of the rise in total forest area are 1) changes in land use, such as the abandonment of agricultural land which allows it to revert to forest, and 2) the establishment of timber plantations.

Historical evidence of forest cover trends suggest that most of Western Europe, North America, and the Pacific developed countries (e.g., Australia, Japan, and New Zealand) underwent some form of transition in forest land use from decline to recovery in the nineteenth or early twentieth century (Grainger 2008; Kauppi *et al.* 2006; Mather 1992, 2000; Palo and Vanhanen 2000; Rudel *et al.* 2005). As discussed in Chapter 1, for these developed countries as a group, the major land use changes underlying this transition are evident (see Figure 1.2). In the late nineteenth and early twentieth century, cropland area slowed its growth, and eventually stabilized and then declined slightly by the late twentieth century. Throughout the twentieth century, abandoned cropland increased and then rose quickly in the last decades. As a result, the decline of forest and woodland has halted in developed countries in aggregate and, since 1990, total forest area has increased (see Figure 1.2 and Table 1.2). Not only has primary forest area recovered but the growth in plantations has also been strong.

In recent years, there have been signs of forest recovery in some low- and middle-income nations, notably Bangladesh, China, Costa Rica, Cuba, Dominican Republic, India, Morocco, Peninsular Malaysia, Puerto Rico, Rwanda, and South Korea (Grainger 2008; Mather 2007;

Rudel *et al.* 2005). But on the whole, the long-run land use change for tropical developing countries is continuing a rapid decline in forest area (see Figure 1.2 and Table 1.2).[5] In the late twentieth century, cropland area in the tropics was still expanding and, consequently, forest area declining. Over the past fifty years, the contrast between changing agricultural versus forest land use in developing as opposed to developed economies could not be more dramatic. More problematic for the major developing regions of Africa, Asia, and Latin America is that the demand for new land required for future crop production growth shows little sign of abating in the near future. Almost one-fifth of new crop production in developing countries (excluding China) from 1990 to 2050 is expected to rely on expanding cultivated area, and two-thirds of this new land will come from conversion of forests and wetlands (Fischer and Helig 1997). In some regions, such as tropical Latin America, livestock grazing is also projected to cause extensive deforestation in the near future (Wassenaar *et al.* 2007).[6]

Using a competing land use framework that is similar to the natural asset model of this chapter, Barbier *et al.* (2010) explain both the continuing conversion of forest to agriculture in tropical countries and the forest transition in temperate developed countries. They show that it is the value of land under competing uses that determines ultimately whether the resulting pattern of land use leads to an increase or decrease in forest cover. Figure 3.5 illustrates the results of the analysis applied to the major global forest cover changes over time.

Figure 3.5A shows how the value of land influences agricultural land conversion during the national land transition phase depicted

---

[5] Although Grainger (2008) warns about the reliability of the data from recent tropical forest resource assessments such as FAO (2006), Table 1.2 in Chapter 1 shows that recent trends in total and primary forest area are not encouraging evidence for a forest transition across tropical developing countries. Perhaps more encouraging is the expansion of plantation tree crop and timber plantations in the tropics, which is approaching a rate of growth comparable to forest plantation increase in developed countries.

[6] In fact, Wassenaar *et al.* (2007) project that the impact of grazing on deforestation from 2010 onwards is likely to be greater than cropland expansion. Cropland expansion into forest is expected to contribute to 31 percent of deforestation in the Central American countries studied and 38 percent of deforestation in the South American countries. In comparison, pasture expansion in forest accounts for 69 percent of the deforestation in the Central American countries and 62 percent of forest loss in the South American countries.

Figure 3.5 Changing land use values and the forest transition

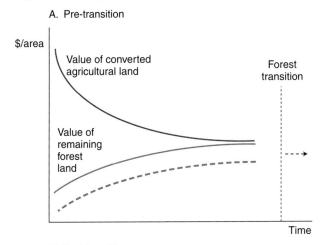

A. Pre-transition

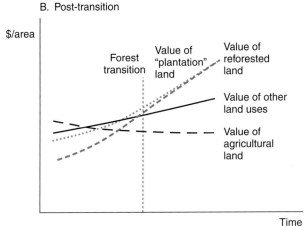

B. Post-transition

Source: Barbier *et al.* (2010, Figure 2).

in the forest transition diagrams of Figure 3.4. As the evidence on global forest cover suggests, this is the phase that applies most to tropical developing countries. Initially, there is a low level of economic development, the forest area is intact, and no forest conversion to agriculture has occurred. As economic development proceeds and populations grow, the demand for increased agricultural goods will increase the per hectare value of agricultural land. The abundance of primary forests means that the benefits, and thus the value, of retaining land as forest are much lower. Thus, considerable agricultural land conversion will take place, forest area declines quickly, and agricultural land area expands (see Figure 3.4). However, even during the national land transition phase, the continual conversion of forest to agricultural land will cause changes in relative land values. As agricultural land expansion occurs, the value of converted land from forest falls; similarly, the value of remaining primary forest will rise as it becomes relatively scarce. As shown in Figure 3.4, as these land values converge, less and less land conversion takes place. Eventually, there is no net gain from converting additional forested land to agriculture as the marginal benefits from both land uses are the same, and both the stock of remaining primary forest land and agricultural land area remain constant; i.e., the economy is on the verge of the forest transition (see Figure 3.4).

A similar analysis can be employed to show the role of changing land use values in influencing both allocations as part of the post-forest transition replenishment phase (see Figure 3.5B). As Figure 3.5B depicts, the value of land for plantations (including the management of secondary forests) or for reforested land may initially be less than the value of other uses of the land (e.g., for commercial and residential uses) and the value of agricultural land, but this will change as the economy approaches the end of the national land transition phase. In fact, as shown in Figure 3.4, the rise in total forest area that signals the forest transition is often driven by a sustained increase in both plantations and reforested land. Figure 3.5B indicates the case where the recovery occurs first due to the rising value of plantation land then followed by the rising value of reforested land. As the value of land in plantation increases, it first surpasses the value of agricultural land, suggesting that some of that land will be switched to tree crops, timber plantations, or managed secondary forest regrowth. However, soon the value of plantation land rises sufficiently to draw land from other commercial and residential uses. Similarly, as the value of agricultural land diminishes, it will eventually decline relative to naturally regenerated forest land – or *reforested land* for short. The value of the reforested land is also likely to rise, especially if it is associated with important forest ecosystem services and other scarce environmental benefits. As the value of reforested land surpasses the value of agricultural land, more and more of the latter land will be abandoned and allowed to revert to natural forest. It is possible that the value of naturally regenerated forest land may rise sufficiently to surpass other uses of land, and thus some reforested land may come from converting lower valued commercial and residential land.

Finally, Figure 3.5B shows that the values of plantation and reforested land eventually converge, suggesting that there is no competition in the post-forest transition phase between these two sources of forest replenishment. However, there is some evidence suggesting that this is an unlikely outcome. For example, Foster and Rosenzweig (2003) find that forest recovery in India was largely dominated by plantations, especially by private landowners. Rudel *et al.* (2005) confirm a similar result for Bangladesh and China, but find the rapidly developing economies of the European Union, notably Greece, Ireland, and Portugal, experienced considerable reforestation as landowners have attempted to save on agricultural labor by converting some of their fields into forests.

Tropical deforestation: the wider development and policy context

Although it is gratifying that much of the observed contemporary patterns of global forest cover decline and recovery can be explained through the type of basic natural asset model of landscape use developed in this chapter, one should also be aware that there is always a wider institutional and policy context that is behind many of these changing forest landscape trends. As argued by Barbier *et al.* (2010, p. 103), "because changes in the value of competing land uses drive the different phases of forest decline and recovery association with the forest transition, there is great scope for policy to influence these processes." This is particularly the case with tropical deforestation, where many complex institutional, political, and economic factors have interacted to affect this process over recent decades.

For example, Rudel (2005, 2007) has reviewed 270 national or subnational land use change studies conducted over 1970 to 2003 to identify the main common trends and causalities for seven tropical regions. He finds two broad trends in deforestation that are common to all regions.

First, how much abundant, accessible forest is left as "reserve land" in a country has been a critical determinant of long-run deforestation patterns. In forest-scarce regions and countries, there are signs that exploitation of the remaining forest resources and land conversion is slowing down and, in some cases, even evidence of a transition to land use stabilization and re-establishment of forest recovery through investment in large-scale reforestation and afforestation. However, in forest-rich countries and regions, deforestation has continued unchecked, with the remaining large-scale natural forests surviving only in peripheral, remote areas beyond the edge of a moving agricultural frontier and well away from central markets.

Second, Rudel found that the main "agents of deforestation" have changed over the past three decades. From the end of World War II until the 1970s, state-run road building, granting of mineral and timber concessions, and agricultural colonization programs opened up tropical regions for deforestation and settlement. However, by the 1990s, "enterprise driven deforestation" was predominant in the tropics; i.e., "the heads of farms and agribusiness enterprises assumed a more salient role in shaping agricultural expansion in rain forest regions" (Rudel 2007, p. 40). Although governments continued to contribute to forest losses, their impact was less direct and more through assisting frontier expansion by plantation owners, large-scale farmers, ranchers, and timber and mining operations. According to Rudel (2007, p. 40), "to facilitate their plans for expansion, large landowners lobbied for the construction of improved and expanded networks of roads. Local politicians and bankers joined the landowners to form 'growth coalitions' that lobbied federal and provincial governments for improved infrastructure." These governments were soon "won over by powerful interest groups of landowners whose agendas involved agricultural expansion at the expense of forests."

Other evidence confirms the latter deforestation trends in recent decades. Across the tropics, the principal activity responsible for deforestation appears to be the direct conversion of forests to permanent agriculture (Chomitz *et al.* 2007; FAO 2001, 2003a). Stratified random sampling of 10 percent of the world's tropical forests reveals that direct conversion by large-scale agriculture may be the main source of deforestation, accounting for around 32 percent of total forest cover change, followed by conversion to small-scale agriculture, which accounts for 26 percent. Intensification of agriculture in shifting cultivation areas comprises only 10 percent of tropical deforestation, and expansion of shifting cultivation into undisturbed forests only 5 percent (FAO 2001). However, there are important regional differences.

In Africa, the major process of deforestation (around 60 percent) is due to the conversion of forest for the establishment of small-scale permanent agriculture, whereas direct conversion of forest cover to large-scale agriculture, including raising livestock, predominates in Latin America and Asia (48 percent and 30 percent, respectively).

In addition, many large-scale resource-extractive activities such as timber harvesting, mining, ranching, and plantations, are often responsible for initially opening up previously inaccessible forested frontier areas to permanent agricultural conversion, especially by small-scale farmers, and for causing widespread development-related forest degradation and loss.[7] Investors in these large-scale commercial activities are attracted to frontier regions because the lack of government controls and property rights in these remote areas mean that resource rents are easily captured, and thus frontier resource-extractive activities are particularly prone to rent-seeking behavior and corruption.[8] Small-scale farmers usually follow because forest and other land is now available and more accessible for conversion. In some regions, large-scale plantation development is initiating the "opening up" of forested areas to subsequent smaller scale cropland expansion; in other regions, it may be timber, mining, or energy developments that begin this process.[9]

A study by Bulte *et al.* (2007) of nine Latin American countries over 1985 to 2000 confirms the self-reinforcing effects of rent-seeking behavior, lobbying and corruption, and low land productivity and deforestation. The analysis illustrates that, over this period, the Latin American governments tended to provide producer subsidies that in turn encouraged large-scale landowners and resource-based

---

[7] For evidence and further discussion, see Alston *et al.* (1999); Ascher (1999); Barbier (2005); Chomitz *et al.* (2007); López (2003); Matthews *et al.* (2000); and Wassenaar *et al.* (2007).

[8] For a model of this behavior and its empirical impacts on tropical agricultural land use expansion, see Barbier *et al.* (2005).

[9] For instance, Wassenaar *et al.* (2007, p. 101) note that "Amazonian cropland expansion hot spots in Brazil and Bolivia for example are adjacent to current large soybean production zones, the creation of which, largely driven by increasing animal feed needs, has caused large scale deforestation in the recent past." Ascher (1999), Barbier (2005), and Wunder (2003, 2005) provide numerous case studies of the links between mineral, energy, and timber developments across the tropics and initially opening up inaccessible frontier areas for subsequent agricultural conversion.

industries to choose more extensive modes of production thus lowering resource or land productivity and often fostering inefficient modes of production. In agriculture, the result is over-investment in land, as an instrument to attract public subsidies when governments are corrupt or extract political contributions. Large land holdings and resource claims demonstrate to government that resource-based industries can obtain greater benefits from government subsidies and, consequently, are willing and able to pay greater bribes or political contributions. As a consequence, the authors find that about 50 percent of the total rural government expenditures in Latin America are subsidies to large-scale producers instead of expenditures related to the provision of public goods for the benefit of the general population. These perverse incentives include subsidized public credit to selected producers, grants directed to particular resource extractive activities, marketing promotion targeting specific crops, free irrigation services financed with public monies directed mainly to a small number of often wealthy producers, fertilizer subsidies, and other producer subsidies. Such subsidy schemes have been generally counterproductive in terms of economy-wide development and agricultural benefits, leading to low land and resource productivity, while promoting and triggering excessive agricultural land expansion, forest conversion, and depletion of other natural resources.

The effect of these wide-ranging market, policy, and institutional failures is to prolong and exacerbate the process of forest land conversion in tropical developing economies. This can occur in several ways.

First, similar to the natural asset model depicted in Figure 3.2, many policy decisions determining the allocation of remaining forest land in tropical countries routinely ignore the nonmarket ecosystem services of primary forest landscapes. Such diverse environmental values may include harvested wood and other products collected by local populations, which may be consumed by them or sold for cash income; ecosystem services arising from ecological regulatory and habitat functions such as watershed protection, habitat for forest-dwelling species, and so forth; and tourism, recreational, and amenity benefits associated with relatively undisturbed, primary forests. Ignoring these values is tantamount to undervaluing the total benefits of the remaining forest area. As shown in Figure 3.5A, the value curve for the remaining forest benefits is now the lower dotted curve.

A second implication of the policy, institutional, and market failures encouraging excessive tropical deforestation is that not only does too much agricultural conversion occur in each time period, but also the cumulative deforestation over time will be excessive. What is more, the undervaluing of the remaining forest area means that the forest transition will be postponed; i.e., as Figure 3.5A indicates, the timing of the forest transition is now shifted to a much later period. The excessive levels of forest conversion and the failure to capture the full value of forest land use will in turn undermine both economic development and forest landscape management in the long run.

Wetland restoration

Wetlands are another ecosystem that has been the subject of considerable restoration efforts in recent decades. According to the EPA (2001), wetland restoration is "the return of a degraded wetland or former wetland to its preexisting naturally functioning condition, or a condition as close to that as possible." Interest in wetland restoration has grown because of concerns over the impact of climate change on a wide variety of global wetland systems, including floodplains, mangroves, salt marshes, arctic wetlands, peatlands, freshwater swamps, marshes, and riparian forests (Erwin 2009; Twilley 2007). The 2004 Indian Ocean tsunami and the 2005 Hurricanes Katrina and Rita have also spurred efforts on restoring mangroves, marshes, and other coastal and estuarine wetlands as natural storm barriers (Barbier 2006; Biswas *et al.* 2009; Bosire *et al.* 2008; Day *et al.* 2007; Simenstad *et al.* 2006).

However, to date, much of the global efforts at wetland restoration have occurred in the United States, Europe, and other developed economies, and have focused largely on the restoration of temperate inland wetlands, such as freshwater marshes, swamps, and riparian forests and peatlands. Reviews of these wetland restoration efforts have identified three important lessons. First, to be successful, wetland restoration strategies need to be conducted at watershed or landscape scales. Second, as hydrological conditions provide the basic control of wetland structure and function, the re-establishment of the ecological production of key wetland ecosystem services is critically dependent on determining the appropriate hydrological regime and water management for the restored wetlands. Third, in terms of providing key ecosystem services, restored wetlands tend to perform better than *created wetlands*, i.e., establishing wetlands where they previously did not exist (Acreman *et al.* 2007; Bedford 1996, 1999; Gwin *et al.* 1999; NRC 2001; Simenstad *et al.* 2006; Zedler 2000; Zedler and Kercher 2005).

In comparison, ecological restoration of coastal and estuarine wetland systems has only received attention very recently (for reviews, see Bosire *et al.* 2008; Elliott *et al.* 2007; Simenstad *et al.* 2006). As discussed in Chapter 2, for example, restoring mangroves on abandoned shrimp farm sites is very costly, as it requires re-establishing tidal flows, treating and detoxifying the soil, replanting vegetation, and maintaining and protecting mangrove seedlings for several years. Nevertheless, improvements in the technical feasibility of restoring estuarine hydrology and vegetation replanting methods have led to noticeable transitions to restoration of degraded and converted landscapes in locations where the services of these coastal ecosystems are especially valuable (Bosire *et al.* 2008; Elliott *et al.* 2007; Lewis 2000, 2005; Lewis and Gilmore 2007; Reed and Wilson 2004; Simenstad *et al.* 2006).

Thus, as the above natural asset model suggests, in the case of many global wetlands we are reaching the phase where the long period of irreversible landscape conversion may be on the verge of an ecological transition where widespread wetland restoration becomes both technically and economically feasible. The natural asset model also indicates that assessing and valuing the ecosystem services provided by the restored landscape is critical to this ecological transition. As we saw in Chapter 2, both ecology and economics have an important role in assessing the ecological production of key ecological services and their economic valuation. Ecological and economic studies of wetland restoration also highlight the importance of this role.

For example, since the Clean Water Act of the 1970s, the US government has instigated a variety of policies to encourage wetland creation or restoration as compensation for wetlands damaged or lost through development. This policy of "compensatory wetland mitigation" to achieve "no net loss" of wetlands in the United States has assumed that both the structure and functions of destroyed wetlands can be adequately re-established elsewhere by the new wetlands. However, this critical assumption has been challenged by a number of studies, which have found that too much emphasis has been placed on recreating the acreage of wetland area lost rather than ensuring that the restored or created wetlands provide an equivalent ecological structure and functions.[10] As summarized by Kihslinger (2008, p. 16): "Currently, many permits simply require a certain percentage of herbaceous cover as a criterion for accessing the success of a mitigation site because it is easily measured and may quickly reach required thresholds. However, percent herbaceous cover may not be a sufficient surrogate for most wetland functions." In addition, delays in initiating and completing restoration activities frequently occur, which means that the waiting lag between wetlands lost and new ones restored can lead to a consistent and considerable net functional loss over time (Bendor 2009).

A series of ecological studies of wetland restoration in Illinois confirm that compliance with wetland mitigation permit conditions is often a poor indication of a new wetland's success at replacing the structure and functions of a destroyed natural wetland (Matthews and Endress 2008; Matthews *et al.* 2009). Reviewing compliance performance for seventy-six restored wetland sites, Matthews and Endress (2008) found that the monitored indicators of success were based exclusively on the quantity and quality of the plant communities established in restored wetlands, and that the performance standards were often unclear, do not set measurable targets, vary considerably from site to site, are poor indicators of site performance and wetland functions, and are set arbitrarily without reference to similar natural or restored wetlands. Moreover, these problems appear not to be exclusive to Illinois but are consistently found by other studies of wetland mitigation at the regional or national level. In addition, the overall criterion of restoring particular wetland plant community types is not an appropriate goal if the objective is to restore wetlands with a high conservation value or provision of ecosystem services; instead, consideration of hydrological and landscape processes and the appropriate species assemblage in the restored wetlands is essential (Matthews *et al.* 2009). Similar findings have been noted for restoring coastal and estuarine wetlands in the United States, where poor site location with respect to the surrounding landscape and lack of consideration of the appropriate hydrological regime have been common

---

[10] For reviews, see Bendor (2009); Burgin (2010); Dale and Gerlak (2007); Kihslinger (2008); NRC (2001); and Zedler and Kercher (2005).

ecological factors in restoration failure (Lewis 2000, 2005; Lewis and Gilmore 2007; Reed and Wilson 2004; Simenstad *et al.* 2006)

The increasing focus on landscape level considerations in the restoration of wetlands has meant that economic valuation of alternative land use scenarios and their impacts on conservation versus development tradeoffs is becoming a priority. For example, Posthumus *et al.* (2010) examine six alternative floodplain management scenarios to reflect different priorities for land use in lowland floodplain areas of England. Although obvious conflicts emerge, such as between agricultural production and water quality, carbon sequestration and habitat and species conservation, some development and environmental benefits are complementary, such as agricultural production and flood storage and control. Because the financial returns to different land uses are sensitive to farm input and output prices, there is scope to develop combined floodplain restoration and agricultural regimes that provide a balance of land and water management benefits that appeal to a wide range of stakeholders, including farmers and local communities, conservationists, and flood managers.

Jenkins *et al.* (2010) conduct a more conventional cost–benefit analysis of restoring over 200,000 hectares (ha) of forested wetlands in the Mississippi Alluvial Valley, a floodplain area below the confluence of the Mississippi and Ohio Rivers in the United States. The authors were able to provide lower bound estimates on the total ecosystem value of the wetland restoration by quantifying the benefits from three ecosystem services: carbon sequestration, nitrogen runoff abatement, and waterfowl recreation. The total social value of these services amounts to between $1,435 and $1,486 per ha annually, which exceeds the full costs of wetland restoration after only one year and indicates a high social return on the public investment. In comparison, given existing markets that generate actual payments for these ecosystem services, their market value is only $70 per ha. But when fully accounting for potential markets, this value rises to $1,035 per ha annually. This potential market value suggests that payments to private landowners to restore wetlands could also be profitable for individual landowners.

Large-scale wetland restoration projects need also to be assessed for their appeal to different stakeholder groups, especially when there are several alternative restoration options. Milon and Scrogin (2006) analyze three distinct groups, who vary significantly in socio-economic characteristics and in their preferences for ecosystem restoration of the Greater Everglades in Florida, to assess their willingness to pay (WTP) for different restoration options. The Greater Everglades wetlands ecosystem extends over 69,000 sq. km, but by 1990, it had declined to less than 50 percent of its original area due to extensive land use conversion and hydrological changes. Two overall restoration options for the Everglades were offered as comparison to the stakeholder groups surveyed: a *functional* restoration option that focused on the hydrological regime and its management as the primary restoration strategy and a *structural* restoration option that focused on conserving key populations of native fauna (e.g., birds, alligators, deer, hawks, and fish). In addition, a comparison was made of partial and full restoration scenarios under each of these options. The analysis reveals that the structural restoration option was generally preferred to the functional option. For both options, the groups that expressed a strong preference for Everglades restoration had a higher WTP for restoration than other groups. Thus, the results suggest that public support and WTP for Everglades restoration is more likely to favor plans that emphasize conserving key populations of native fauna rather than hydrological regime restoration and management, which is currently stressed by wetland scientists and the US Army Corps of Engineers as the proposed restoration plan.

In concluding their analysis of stakeholder preferences for Everglades restoration options, Milon and Scrogin (2006, p. 172) make an important observation: "Policy analysis for wetland ecosystems is especially difficult because these systems provide multiple, interdependent services that vary by type of wetland, location, ecohydrological management, and other factors." Too often, policies for ecological restoration focus exclusively on the rehabilitation of natural systems for one primary service at the exclusion of others, and ignore the wider political and developmental context that led to the destruction of the natural systems in the first place. As we shall see in the following case study of mangrove replanting in Asia in response to the 2004 Indian Ocean tsunami, the result could prove counterproductive to overall ecological restoration efforts.

Replanting mangroves: the wider development and policy context

There is little doubt that the December 2004 Indian Ocean tsunami led to a "sea change" in the attitude of policymakers and the public towards mangroves in the region. As a result of the tsunami, governments of Indian Ocean countries and the wider international community are now convinced of the need to replant mangroves as "natural barriers," and plans for large-scale rehabilitation programs have been funded throughout Asia. For example, the United Nations, the World Conservation Union (IUCN), and the UN Development Programme in October 2006 launched a six-year, $62 million initiative called Mangroves for the Future that involves replanting mangroves and rehabilitating other coastal systems as "natural barriers" in the twelve tsunami-hit Indian Ocean countries (Stone 2006). Behind this view is the belief that widespread mangrove deforestation has left Asian coastlines and communities vulnerable to the devastating damages caused by large-scale storm events, such as tsunamis and cyclones. Three days after the May 3, 2008 cyclone that devastated Burma, Surin Pitsuwan, the Association of South-East Asian Nations' Secretary-General, announced that the combination of more people living in coastal areas and the loss of mangroves had exacerbated the tragedy (Kivener 2008).

While Asian policymakers and international donors have become increasingly convinced of the need to replant mangroves as "natural barriers" against tsunami, cyclones, and other large storms, scientists express concerns about whether mangroves can always effectively reduce coastal damages caused by such extreme storm events. Although initial assessments suggested that healthy mangroves may have mitigated damages caused by the Asian tsunami (Danielson *et al.* 2005; Dahdouh-Guebas *et al.* 2005; Kathiresan and Rajendran 2005), other scientists have concluded that there is little evidence that mangroves reduced the damage caused by the tsunami (Kerr *et al.* 2006; Kerr and Baird 2007). Ecohydrology studies have also shown that mangroves are unlikely to stop waves created by a tsunami, cyclone, or other storms that are larger than 6 meters (Alongi 2008; Cochard *et al.* 2008; Forbes and Broadhead 2007; Wolanski 2007a and Wolanski 2007b). In fact, large wave surges from extreme storm events can uproot mangroves, thus increasing damages and loss of life (Forbes and Broadhead 2007). Wave attenuation by mangroves is "qualitatively different" for "large, infrequent disturbances," such as tsunamis, hurricanes (typhoons), and tidal bores, compared to "small, frequent disturbances," such as tropical storms, coastal floods, and tidal waves (Alongi 2008). In short, the evidence that mangroves can act as natural barriers against big storms such as the Asian tsunami is at best mixed: "in several locations (particularly farther away from the tsunami source), mangroves and other vegetation probably provided some protection against the 2004 tsunami" (Cochard *et al.* 2008).

However, lost in this debate over whether or not to replant mangroves as natural storm barriers are three fundamental questions:

- Why has widespread mangrove deforestation been occurring in Asia, and indeed globally, in recent decades?
- Has this widespread loss of mangroves increased the vulnerability of coastal populations to economically damaging storm events, not just the occasional "big" tsunami but the more frequent storm surges, typhoon and other tropical wind storms, and coastal floods that occur?
- Are current institutions and incentives adequate for, first, encouraging local coastal communities to participate in mangrove replanting schemes, and second, to allow these communities a stake in the long-term management of the rehabilitated forests?

With regard to the first question, mangrove forests are among the most threatened global ecosystems, especially in Asia. At least 35 percent of global mangrove area has been lost since the 1970s, and in Asia, 36 percent of mangrove area has been deforested, at the rate of 1.52 percent per year (Valiela *et al.* 2001). Although many factors are behind global mangrove deforestation, a major cause is aquaculture expansion in coastal areas, especially the establishment of shrimp farms, although other activities, such as logging, freshwater diversion, land reclamation, and agriculture, also contribute (Barbier and Cox 2003; Valiela *et al.* 2001).

However, many of these coastal developments causing mangrove loss rarely benefit local coastal communities. Traditional uses of the mangroves by these communities involve harvesting fish, wood products, honey and even medicines from the mangrove forests and swamps, and fishing in the nearby coastal waters stocked by fish that depend on the mangroves for breeding grounds and nurseries (Walters *et al.* 2008). In contrast, commercial shrimp farming and aquaculture, logging operations, salt ponds, large-scale agricultural developments, and resort hotels are usually owned and financed by outside investors who profit handsomely from these developments. Not only are local coastal people largely excluded from sharing these lucrative financial rewards, they hardly benefit at all, except perhaps for the lucky few who find employment as low-skill labor in these coastal development activities. Meanwhile, the traditional livelihoods of whole communities are often laid to waste along with the mangroves that support these livelihoods.

With regard to the second question, simply because the evidence is mixed that mangroves can mitigate coastal damages from extreme events, such as tsunamis, does not mean that mangroves offer little or no coastal storm protection at all. First, field studies do show that healthy mangrove forces can attenuate storm waves under 6 meters and buffer wind storms.[11] Second, tropical coasts are battered frequently by other storm events, not just massive tsunamis (see Figure 3.6).

As Figure 3.6 shows, a variety of damaging coastal storm events occur frequently in Thailand, and the incidence events (the number annually) has increased in recent years (Barbier 2007). Of these events, only four could be considered extreme storm events: three typhoons and of course the 2004 Indian Ocean tsunami. Moreover, the frequency of the smaller storm events appears to be increasing; over 1975–1987, Thailand experienced on average 0.54 coastal natural disasters per year, whereas over 1987–2004, the incidence increased to 1.83 disasters per year. It is against these small, frequent but economically damaging events that we are likely to see mangroves offer the greatest value in terms of storm protection.

Over the same time period, 1975–2004, extensive mangrove deforestation occurred in Thailand (see Figure 3.7). Thus, over the past two decades, Thailand experienced both a rise in the number and frequency of coastal natural disasters and the simultaneous rapid decline in coastal mangrove systems. This suggests an important hypothesis: did the widespread loss of mangroves in coastal areas of Thailand

[11] See, for example, Alongi (2008); Cochard *et al.* (2008); Forbes and Broadhead (2007); Kathiresan and Rajendran (2005); Massel *et al.* (1999); Mazda *et al.* (1997, 2006); Wolanski (2007a and 2007b).

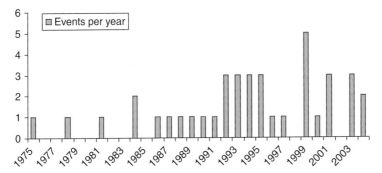

Figure 3.6 Number of coastal natural disaster events per year in Thailand, 1975–2004

Notes: Coastal natural disasters included wave/surge (tsunami and tidal wave), wind storm (cyclone/typhoon and tropical storm), and flood (significant rise of water level in coastal region. In order for EM-DAT (2005) to record an event as a disaster, at least one or more of the following criteria must be fulfilled: ten or more people reported killed; 100 people reported affected; declaration of a state of emergency; call for international assistance.

Source: Barbier (2007) based on data from EM-DAT (2005).

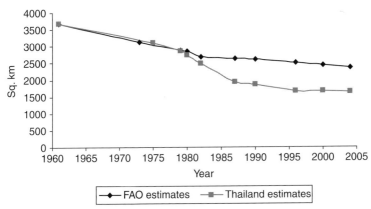

Figure 3.7 Mangrove area (km²) in Thailand, 1961–2004

Source: FAO estimates from FAO (2003b). 2000 and 2004 data are estimated from 1990–2000 annual average mangrove loss of 18.0 km². Thailand estimates from various Royal Thailand Forestry Department sources reported in Aksornkoae and Tokrinsa (2004). 2000 and 2004 data are estimated from 1993–1996 annual average mangrove loss of 3.44 km².

increase the vulnerability of these areas to more incidences of economically damaging natural disasters? This hypothesis was tested
statistically using a count data model (Barbier 2007). The analysis for
Thailand over 1979–1996 and across twenty-one coastal provinces
shows that a 1 sq. km decline in mangrove area increases the expected
number of disasters by 0.36 percent. This relationship was statistically significant, and suggests that one cannot reject the hypothesis
of correlation between mangrove deforestation and the incidence of
damages from coastal storms in Thailand over 1979–1996. In sum,
consistent with most of the prevailing ecological literature on the
coastal protection service of mangrove forests, the Thailand study
shows that widespread deforestation over a significant period of time
will increase the vulnerability of coastal areas to a variety of economically damaging storm events.

The final question above raises concerns about the institutions and
incentives in many coastal areas. In other words, even if we think that
current calls to expand mangrove replanting and rehabilitation in Asia
for coastal protection are worthwhile, will such schemes succeed?
Although the post-tsunami change in attitude towards mangroves in
the region is welcomed, focusing solely on replanting projects is not
sufficient to reverse the decades-long decline in mangrove forests in
the region (Barbier 2006). Unless local coastal communities have more
of a say in the control, use, and protection of mangroves, current and
future restoration projects will fail to have any lasting results. Instead,
a new institutional and policy framework that involves local communities more directly in coastal mangrove management could make a
difference to the sustainability of mangrove rehabilitation projects in
the Indian Ocean region, and may improve community participation
in these projects.

Several studies of replanting mangroves in Thailand illustrate
this connection. An analysis of four coastal communities reveals
that awareness of community conservation efforts, community-
imposed utilization rules, and the environmental damages imposed
by shrimp farms are key motivating factors in the decision by male
and female members of mangrove-dependent households to participate in replanting activities (Barbier 2008). As a consequence, there
may be more willingness to participate in mangrove rehabilitation as
a means to combat mangrove loss due to shrimp farm expansion and
other developments, but equally important is the degree of control

Tl
the l
impc
benc
all. ,
cum
mad
land
we (
syst(
inflt
dete
A
vert
the
lanc
the
Onc
the
ing
valt
thai
ing
ope
unt
a fe
sca
if e
bec
pro
trai
dis:
eco
tim
as (
ecc
to (
a r
of :

the community has over managing the mangroves and their utilization. Similarly, in a mangrove forest rehabilitation project in Pattani Bay, local ownership of the project and effective community participation by three surrounding villages were crucial to the successful restoration of degraded mangroves (Erftemeijer and Bualuang 2002). Approximately ten years after the mangrove replanting project was initiated, the forest is still thriving (Erftemeijer 2008). Community surveys throughout Thailand have confirmed that, where local villages have been allowed to design and maintain well-defined governance structures over mangroves, stand structure was superior in these community-managed forests than in open-access state forests (Sudtongkong and Webb 2008). The lessons learned from these and similar studies of the motivation of local communities to participate in local mangrove replanting projects should be applied to designing the correct institutions and incentives for the larger mangrove rehabilitation schemes planned for many coastal areas across Asia.

For example, a new institutional framework for coastal mangrove management in Thailand and other Indian Ocean countries that could make a difference to coastal communities, including their willingness to restore and protect local mangroves, might contain the following features (Barbier 2006; Barbier and Sathirathai 2004; Sudtongkong and Webb 2008).

First, remaining mangrove areas should be designated into conservation (i.e., preservation) and economic zones. Shrimp farming and other extractive commercial uses (e.g., wood concessions) should be restricted to the economic zones only. However, local communities who depend on the collection of forest and fishery products from mangrove forests should be allowed access to both zones, as long as such harvesting activities are conducted on a sustainable basis.

Second, the establishment of community mangrove forests should also occur in both the economic and conservation zones. However, the decision to allow such local management efforts should be based on the capability of communities to effectively enforce their local rules and manage the forest to prevent over-utilization, degradation, and conversion to other land uses. Moreover, such community rights should not involve full ownership of the forest but be in the form of user rights.

Third, the community mangrove forests should be co-managed by the government and local communities. Such effective co-management

spatial pattern of the ecological production of these services might vary across the landscape.

Yet, evidence from ecology suggests that scale matters to the structure and functions of ecosystems. In particular, there are two main reasons why the structure and functions underlying the ecological production of key ecosystem goods and services are likely to be spatially variant across landscapes.

First, as pointed out by Schneider (2001, p. 545), "patterns measured at small scales do not necessarily hold at larger scales; nor do processes prevailing at small scales necessarily prevail at large scales." This implies, for example, that ecological functions for an entire forested watershed, such as water flow regulation and control, soil retention, and sediment stabilization, cannot always be inferred from field observations of these functions at smaller plots and sites within the watershed. Thus, one cannot simply "scale up" the pattern of functions observed at specific field sites within a landscape to determine how the entire landscape functions.

Second, as argued by Turner (1989, p. 173), "Because landscapes are spatially heterogeneous areas (i.e. environmental mosaics), the structure, function, and change of landscapes are themselves scale-dependent." In other words, as a landscape is not spatially uniform, including the ecological landscape of a single ecosystem, its structure and functions are likely to vary at different locations within the landscape. For a forested watershed, for example, water flow regulation and control, soil retention, and sediment stabilization may vary considerably from the upper most part of the watershed compared to further downstream.

The purpose of the following chapter is to examine how spatial variation in the structure and functions of an ecological landscape influences the provision of ecosystem goods and services. If these benefits are not uniformly distributed across an ecological landscape, then there are also implications for the decision as to whether or not to develop the landscape as well as the extent of development. Scale not only matters to ecosystem properties but also to the management of ecosystems as natural assets.

To help focus the analysis of the chapter, we will use the example of coastal landscapes to illustrate the ecological and economic importance of spatial variation in ecosystems. First, we review ecological evidence of the spatial heterogeneity of key coastal landscapes, and the implications for the provision of two key ecosystem services: estuarine habitat-fishery linkages and protection against damaging storm events. Evidence of spatial heterogeneity of landscapes is explored further, with the example of nonlinear wave attenuation across a mangrove landscape that affects the value of the coastal protection service and how it affects the mangrove–shrimp farm competing use problem in Thailand. The chapter then develops a simple spatial model of allocating an ecological landscape that takes into account variation in ecological functions across the landscape, thus affecting the location and extent of landscape conversion. The model is illustrated through simulation with data from the mangrove–shrimp farm competing use problem in Thailand. Finally, we look beyond the provision of ecological goods and services at the coastal landscape and examine entire seascapes of interconnected land, coastal, and marine systems.

Coastal landscapes

Because the functional relationships inherent in many ecological processes are understudied, and there is so little corresponding economic information on the value of important services, estimations of how the value of an ecosystem service varies across an ecological landscape are rare. However, studies of coastal systems suggest that, for a handful of key ecosystem services, it is possible to track how the ecological functions vary spatially and thus influence the economic benefits that they provide.[3] What is more, much of the evidence suggests that benefits tend to decline with the distance inshore from the seaward edge of most coastal wetland habitats, such as mangroves and salt marshes.

For example, various coastal ecosystems, including mangroves, salt marshes, seagrass beds, nearshore coral reefs, and sand dunes, can provide protection against wave damage caused by storms, hurricanes, tidal waves, and other storm events, provided that such storm events are not too extreme in their magnitude (Barbier *et al.* 2008; Koch *et al.* 2009). However, for all these coastal habitats, nonlinear

---

[3] See, for example, Aburto-Oropeza *et al.* (2008); Aguilar-Perera and Appeldorn (2008); Barbier *et al.* (2008); Koch *et al.* (2009); Meynecke *et al.* (2008); Petersen *et al.* (2003); Peterson and Turner (1994); and Rountree and Able (2007).

landscape relationships exist between habitat area and measurements of the ecosystem function of wave attenuation (i.e., reduction of wave height). For mangroves and salt marshes, wave attenuation diminishes with increasing habitat distance inland from the shoreline. In the case of seagrasses and near-shore coral reefs, wave attenuation is a function of the water depth above the grass bed or reef, and these relationships are also nonlinear. There is also a spatial relationship between the percent cover of dune grasses and the size of oceanic waves blocked by the sand dunes produced by the grasses.

Coastal systems also strongly influence the abundance, growth, and structure of neighboring marine fisheries by providing nursery, breeding, and other habitat functions for commercially important fish and invertebrate species that spend at least part of their life cycles in coastal and estuarine environments. Evidence of this coastal habitat-fishery linkage is increasingly indicating that the value of this service is higher at the seaward edge or "fringe" of the coastal habitat than further inland.[4] For example, Peterson and Turner (1994) find that densities of most fish and crustaceans were highest in salt marshes in Louisiana within 3 meters of the water's edge compared to the interior marshes. In the Gulf of California, Mexico, the mangrove fringe with a width of 5–10 m has the most influence on the productivity of near-shore fisheries, with a median value of $37,500 per hectare. Fishery landings also increased positively with the length of the mangrove fringe in a given location (Aburto-Oropeza *et al.* 2008).

Ecological field studies illustrate how the key ecological functions and indicators underlying storm protection and habitat-fishery linkages vary nonlinearly across a typical mangrove landscape that extends inshore from a seaward edge or boundary.

As discussed above, the protection against storms provided by mangroves depends on their critical ecological function in terms of "attenuating," or reducing the height, of storm waves. That is, the ecological damages arising from tropical storms come mostly from the large wave surges accompanying these storms. Ecological and hydrological field studies suggest that mangroves are unlikely to stop storm waves that are greater than 6 meters (Alongi 2008; Cochard *et al.* 2008; Forbes and Broadhead 2007; Wolanski 2007). On the other

---

[4] See, for example, Aburto-Oropeza *et al.* (2008); Aguilar-Perera and Appeldorn (2008); Manson *et al.* (2005); and Peterson and Turner (1994).

hand, where mangroves are effective as "natural barriers" against storms that generate waves less than 6 m in height, the wave height of a storm decreases nonlinearly for each 100 m that a mangrove forest extends out to sea (Barbier *et al.* 2008; Mazda *et al.* 1997). In other words, wave attenuation is greatest for the first 100 m of mangroves but declines as more mangroves are added to the seaward edge.

Figure 4.1 illustrates the nonlinear wave attenuation function of mangroves based on field study data by Mazda *et al.* (1997) from a coastal site in Vietnam where *Kandelia candel* and *Sonneratia caseolaris* mangrove plantations have been created over a wide intertidal shoal as a coastal defense against typhoon waves. Wave data was measured *in situ* at the seaward edge of the forest up to a distance inland of approximately 1000 m. Koch *et al.* (2009) employ these data to construct a wave attenuation relationship as a function of 100 m inshore mangrove distance, assuming a mangrove forest extending 1,000 m seaward along a 10 km coastline (i.e., a 10 sq. km mangrove landscape). Figure 4.1 plots the wave attenuation relationship for *Sonneratia* spp. at mid-level tide, showing the change in wave height corresponding to every 100 m that the 10 sq. km mangrove landscape extends inshore from its seaward boundary. With no mangroves (distance 0 m) waves have a maximum height of 1.1 m, which would remain virtually unchecked across the 1,000 m landscape if it was not vegetated. But the presence of mangroves over the first 100 m from the seaward boundary reduces wave height significantly (0.38 m). However, as shown in the figure, this wave attenuation effect is nonlinear across the 1,000 m mangrove landscape. The change in wave height due to the presence of subsequent mangroves declines exponentially, until the fall in wave height is negligible for the last 100 m of mangroves (e.g., only 0.004 m). Koch *et al.* find similar nonlinear wave attenuation across other mangrove landscapes, regardless of the species (*Kandelia* or *Sonneratia*) or the tide level (mid or high tide).

Figure 4.2 shows that the habitat function of a mangrove ecosystem, which underlies its role as a nursery and breeding habitat for fish species, also declines nonlinearly across a mangrove landscape. The data for the figure are drawn from Aguilar-Perera and Appledoorn (2008), who sample fish density (numbers per square meter, N/m^2) as a measure of the habitat function along an inshore–offshore gradient, including a mangrove–seagrass–coral reef continuum, that reached a length of about 5 km from shore at Montalva Bay, southwestern

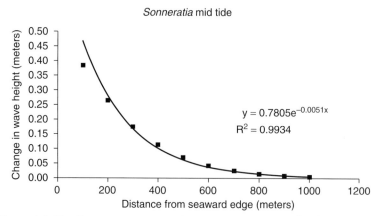

Sonneratia mid tide

Figure 4.1 Nonlinear wave attenuation across a mangrove landscape
Source: Koch *et al.* (2009) based on data in Mazda *et al.* (1997).

Puerto Rico. The data in Figure 4.2 correspond to the two mangrove strata (all *Rhizophora mangle*) that were sampled along this gradient according to orientation from shore: mangroves on the seaward edge and mangroves further inshore. The figure displays average fish density for ten families that inhabit the mangroves, and it shows that fish density is significantly lower for mangroves located 30–50 m or more inshore than compared to the mangroves on the seaward edge. No fish were found more than 50 m inshore from the sea.

Storm protection by mangroves, Thailand

To illustrate the influence of spatial variability on an ecosystem service and thus on the conversion of a coastal landscape for development, we return to the Thailand mangrove case study of Chapter 2. Recall that this study compared per hectare land use values between various mangrove ecosystem benefits and conversion of the mangrove to shrimp ponds in Thailand (see Table 2.5). But what if these per hectare values for mangroves were used to inform a land use decision weighing conversion of an entire mangrove ecosystem to shrimp aquaculture? For example, deciding how much of a mangrove forest extending 1,000 m seaward along a 10 km coastline to convert to shrimp aquaculture may depend critically on whether or not all the mangroves in the 10 sq. km ecosystem are equally beneficial in terms of coastal storm protection (Barbier *et al.* 2008).

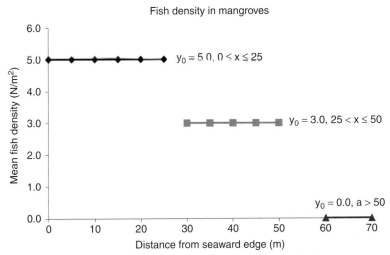

Figure 4.2 Nonlinear habitat function across a mangrove landscape
Source: Based on data in Aguilar-Perera and Appledorn (2008).

Suppose that it is assumed initially that the annual per hectare (ha) values for the various ecosystem benefits are spatially uniform, and thus vary linearly, across the entire 10 sq. km mangrove landscape. Following this assumption, a mangrove area of 10 sq. km would have an annual storm protection value of 1,000 times the $1,879 per ha "point estimate," which yields an annual total benefit estimate of nearly $1.9 million. Barbier *et al.* (2008) indicate how this assumption translates into a comparison of the net present value (10 percent discount rate and twenty-year horizon) of shrimp farming to the three mangrove services – coastal protection, wood product collection, and habitat support for off-shore fisheries – as a function of mangrove area (sq. km) for the example of a 10 sq. km coastal landscape. Figure 4.3 shows a comparison of these benefits.

Figure 4.3 aggregates all four values to test whether an integrated land use option involving some conversion and some preservation yields the highest total value. When all values are linear, as shown in the figure, the outcome is a typical "all or none" scenario; either the aggregate values will favor complete conversion or they will favor preserving the entire habitat. Because the ecosystem service values are large and increase linearly with mangrove area the preservation option is preferred. The aggregate value of the mangrove system is at

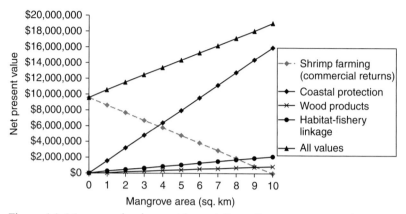

Figure 4.3 Mangrove land use with spatially uniform ecosystem values
Source: Barbier *et al.* (2008).

its highest ($18.98 million) when it is completely preserved, and any conversion to shrimp farming would lead to less aggregate value compared to full preservation, thus any land use strategy that considers all the values of the ecosystem would favor mangrove preservation and no shrimp farm conversion.

However, as discussed above, not all mangroves along a coastline are equally effective in storm protection. It follows that the storm protection value is unlikely to be uniform across all mangroves. The reason is that the storm protection "service" provided by mangroves depends on their critical ecological function in terms of "attenuation" of storm waves. That is, the ecological damages arising from tropical storms come mostly from the large wave surges associated with these storms. Ecological and hydrological field studies suggest that mangroves are unlikely to stop storm waves that are greater than 6 m (Alongi 2008; Cochard *et al.* 2008; Forbes and Broadhead 2007; Wolanski 2007). On the other hand, where mangroves are effective as "natural barriers" against storms that generate waves less than 6 m in height, the wave height of a storm decreases quadratically for each 100 m that a mangrove forest extends out to sea (Barbier *et al.* 2008; Mazda *et al.* 1997). In other words, wave attenuation is greatest for the first 100 m of mangroves but declines as more mangroves are added to the seaward edge.

Barbier *et al.* (2008) employ the nonlinear wave attenuation function for mangroves based on the field data collected by Mazda *et al.*

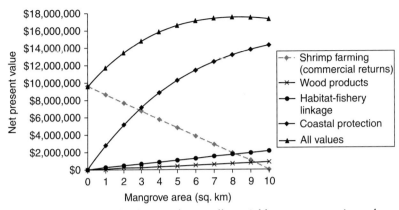

Figure 4.4 Mangrove land use with spatially variable storm protection values
Source: Barbier *et al.* (2008).

(1997) to revise the estimate of storm protection service value for the Thailand case study.[5] The result is depicted in Figure 4.4.

The storm protection service of mangroves still dominates all values, but small losses in mangroves will not cause the economic benefits of storm buffering by mangroves to fall precipitously. The consequence is that the aggregate value across all uses of the mangroves, shrimp farming, and ecosystem values, is at its highest ($17.5 million) when up to 2 sq. km of mangroves are allowed to be converted to shrimp aquaculture and the remainder of the ecosystem is preserved.

Thus, taking into account how an ecological function varies spatially and influences the value of the ecosystem service it provides can have a significant impact on a land use decision at the landscape scale.

A model with spatial production of ecosystem services

Assume that 0 denotes one ecologically defined boundary (e.g., the seaward edge of a coastal ecosystem) and *A* denotes the distance

---

[5] In addition to measuring the wave attenuation by *Sonneratia caseolaris* mangroves, which is depicted in Figure 4.1, Mazda *et al.* (1997) also analyze the wave attenuation for *Kandelia candel.* It is the latter data that were used as the basis for the simulations conducted by Barbier *et al.* (2008). A very similar pattern of wave attenuation was obtained for *K. candel* as for the *S. caseolaris* mangroves shown in Figure 4.1. See Barbier *et al.* (2008) for further details.

across to the furthest boundary of the ecological landscape (e.g., the furthest landward edge of the coastal ecosystem). A is predetermined by the biophysical characteristics of the landscape. Let a denote any specific location along the width $[0,A]$ of the coastal landscape. Based on the above ecological evidence on declining wave attenuation and fish density, it is assumed that ecological production of ecosystem services $s(a)$ at any location a varies spatially according to

$$s = s(a), \, s' < 0. \tag{4.1}$$

That is, spatial production of ecosystem services is highest at the seaward boundary ($a = 0$) and declines for locations further inshore.

If v is the value of a unit of ecosystem services and m is the cost of maintaining that service, then the net benefit of these services is simply $(v - m)s(a)$. However, the coastal landscape could also have an alternative land use in some development activity, such as agriculture, aquaculture, property development, etc. As the social planner is aware that ecosystem services are highest at the seaward edge, the decision to develop begins first at the landward boundary. Thus, for example, if the planner chooses to preserve a landscape area of width $[0,a]$, then the total rents earned from use of the remaining landscape for development can be denoted as $R(A - a)$, $R' > 0$ The social planner's decision is therefore to choose the optimal width of the coastal landscape, a^*, that maximizes

$$\underset{a}{Max} \, W(a) = \int_0^a (v - m)s(i)\,di + R(A - a) \tag{4.2}$$

from the first-order condition

$$(v - m)s(a^*) = R'(A - a^*). \tag{4.3}$$

The optimal width of coastal landscape to preserve is where the marginal ecosystem service benefits of an additional distance inward from the seaward boundary just equals the opportunity cost of foregone development rents at that location.

The implications of (4.3), and of the spatial production function, for optimal landscape conversion are portrayed in Figure 4.5. Assume that the foregone marginal rents across the landscape are constant, i.e., $R'(A - a^*) = R$. As shown in the figure, if the ecological production

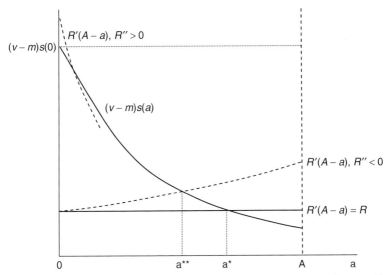

Figure 4.5 Optimal conversion of a coastal landscape with spatially variable benefits

of ecosystem services inland is the same inland as it is at the seaward edge, and assuming $(v - m)s(0) > R$, then it would be optimal to conserve the entire coastal landscape. Alternatively, although not depicted in Figure 4.5, if $R > (v - m)s(0)$, then all the landscape should be developed. However, if the spatial production of ecosystem services declines across the coastal ecosystem, $(v - m)s(a)$, then with constant marginal development rents, R, it is optimal to convert only $A - a^*$ of the coastal landscape. Of course marginal development rents may not be constant across the landscape either. As shown in Figure 4.5, if these rents are highest at the inland boundary of the coastal landscape, A, but then decline to R at the seaward edge, a greater amount of the coastal landscape will be converted, $A - a^{**}$.

Simulation of a mangrove ecosystem

The above spatial model can be simulated using empirical estimates applied to a mangrove ecosystem. Each location, a, in the landscape represents a hectare along the 1,000 m distance from the seaward edge inland, where $a = 0$ is the seaward edge and $A = 1000$ is the maximum distance inward of the mangrove landscape from the seaward edge. Since the entire ecosystem contains an area of 10 sq. km, which is equivalent to 1,000 ha, each 1,000 m location *a* across the landscape from the seaward edge to its inshore boundary comprises a 1 ha unit of land.

In the simulation, the services of the mangrove ecosystem consist of three benefits. These are the role of mangroves as natural "barriers" to periodic damaging coastal storm events, their role as nursery and breeding habitats for offshore fisheries, and the exploitation of mangrove forests by coastal communities for a variety of wood and non-wood products. These assumptions allow the simulations to draw on valuation studies from Thailand for the constant value per ha, *v*, for each of the three mangrove ecosystem services. The value of coastal protection from storms is based on a marginal value per ha of damages avoided (in 1996 $) of $1,879; over a twenty-year time horizon and a 10 percent discount rate this yields a net present value (NPV) of $15,997 per ha (Barbier 2007). The value of habitat-fishery linkages is based on a net value per ha (in 1996 $, assuming a price elasticity for fish of -0.5) of mangrove habitat of $249; over a twenty-year time horizon and a 10 percent discount rate this yields an NPV of $2,117 per ha (Barbier 2003). The value of wood and nonwood products is based on net income per ha from mangrove forests to local community (updated to 1996 $) of $101; over a twenty-year time horizon and a 10 percent discount rate this yields an NPV of $864 per ha (Sathirathai and Barbier 2001). Thus, the total value for all three mangrove services at the seaward edge, *vs*(0), amounts to a total NPV of $18,978 per ha.

Whereas it is difficult to determine whether the various resource products collected by local communities vary significantly across the mangrove landscape, the ecological evidence reviewed in this paper suggests strongly that the seaward fringe of the mangroves offer greater protection against storms and contain higher density of fish species that eventually populate near-shore fisheries. Thus, the spatial production function (4.1) is assumed to apply to storm protection and habitat-fishery linkages. In the case of storm protection, ecological production is assumed to decline exponentially, $s(a) = vs(0)e^{-\delta a}$, at the rate indicated in Figure 4.1. Mangroves on the first meter of the seaward edge are assumed to have the full value of $15,997 per ha, but this value declines for locations further inland at the exponential rate of $\delta = -0.014$. For habitat-fishery linkages, spatial production is simulated by the fish density estimates shown in Figure 4.2. The first 25 meters of mangroves on the seaward edge have the highest habitat-fishery linkage value of $2,117 per ha, but this declines to three-fifths of this value for mangroves located 30–50 m inshore, and to zero for the remaining mangroves located inland.

Unfortunately, there is no corresponding estimate of the maintenance costs m of mangrove ecosystems and their services. In many tropical developing countries, such as Thailand, the local coastal communities that benefit from mangrove goods and services do not have formal property rights over the mangroves, which instead come under the legal jurisdiction of the central government. This has had two implications for management of mangrove ecosystems (Barbier and Sathirathai 2004). First, while local communities have exercised de facto use rights over exploitation of various products extracted from forests, neither these communities nor the government have had much incentive to invest in maintaining or protecting existing mangrove ecosystems or in restoring degraded landscapes. Second, the virtual open access conditions have contributed to the widespread loss of mangroves from shrimp aquaculture. For example, over 1975 to 1996, 50–65 percent of Thailand's mangroves were lost to shrimp farm conversion (Aksornkoae and Tokrisna 2004).

Thus, in the model simulation, the foregone marginal rents that could be earned from developing the entire mangrove landscape, $R'(A - a)$, are represented by the returns to shrimp farming. Two estimates are used for this per hectare value, a commercial and an economic net return. The net present value (NPV) per ha for the commercial net returns to shrimp farming over a twenty-year time horizon and 10 percent discount rate is based on Sathirathai and Barbier (2001) updated to 1996 $; this amounts to a value of $9,632 per ha. However, many of the inputs used in shrimp pond operations are subsidized, below border-equivalent prices, thus increasing artificially the private returns to shrimp farming. Without these subsidies, the resulting economic net returns to shrimp farming result in an NPV of $1,220 per ha. As shrimp ponds can be located in any part of the mangroves with little loss of productivity, it is assumed that $R'(A - a)$ is constant across the landscape.

Figure 4.6 displays the results of the simulation for the basic spatial model. In the absence of any spatially declining production of

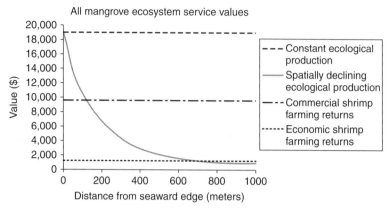

Figure 4.6 Simulation of the spatial model

storm protection and habitat-linkage benefits, the total value of all mangrove ecosystem services ($18,978/ha) easily exceeds either the commercial net returns to shrimp farming ($9,632/ha) or the economic net returns ($1,220/ha). If the benefits of mangrove ecosystem services are constant across the landscape, then the entire ecosystem should be preserved.

However, Figure 4.6 also shows that the spatial variation in the production of storm protection and habitat-fishery linkages changes the land use outcome significantly. As shown in the figure, when these two mangrove services decline spatially across the landscape, it causes the total net benefit of all ecosystem services to diminish significantly from the seaward edge to the landward boundary. When the value of preserving the mangroves is compared to the commercial net returns to shrimp farming, it is optimal to conserve only the first 118 m of mangroves from the seaward edge, and to convert the rest to aquaculture. When compared to the net economic returns to shrimp farming, mangroves up to 746 m from the seaward edge should be preserved, and the remaining mangroves inland converted.

Synergies across seascapes

One unique feature of coastal ecosystems is that they occur at the interface between watersheds, the coast, and the oceans. The location of coastal landscapes in the land–sea interface, or *seascape*, leads to a high degree of interconnectedness or connectivity across these systems and their services. The presence of these interlinked ecosystems in a seascape may considerably enhance the ecosystem service provided by one single ecosystem. For example, many fish and shellfish species utilize mangroves and seagrass beds as nursery grounds, and eventually migrate to coral reefs as adults, only to return to the mangroves and seagrasses to spawn (Moberg and Rönnbäck 2003; Mumby 2006; Mumby *et al.* 2004). Similar synergies exist for salt marshes, seagrass beds, and near-shore marine systems in estuaries (Rountree and Able 2007; Shackeroff *et al.* 2009).

There are two ways in which current studies of seascape services are incorporating such synergies. One approach is to assess the multiple benefits arising from entire interconnected ecosystems, such as estuaries. A second method is to allow for the biological connectivity of habitats, food webs, and migration and life-cycle patterns across specific seascapes, such as mangrove–seagrass–reef systems and large marine systems.

For example, Johnston *et al.* (2002) estimate the benefits arising from a wide range of ecosystem services provided by the Peconic Estuary in Long Island, New York. The tidal mudflats, salt marshes, and seagrass (eelgrass) beds of the estuary support the shellfish and demersal fisheries. In addition, birdwatching and waterfowl hunting are popular activities. Incorporating production function methods, the authors simulate the biological and food web interactions of the ecosystems to assess the marginal value per acre in terms of gains in commercial value for fish and shellfish, birdwatching, and waterfowl hunting. The aggregate annual benefits are estimated to be $67 per acre for intertidal mud flats, $338 for salt marsh, and $1,065 for seagrass across the estuary system. Using these estimates, the authors calculate the asset value per acre of protecting existing habits to be $12,412 per acre for seagrass, $4,291 for salt marsh, and $786 for mud flats; in comparison, the asset value of restored habitats is $9,996 per acre for seagrass, $3,454 for marsh, and $626 for mudflats.

Sanchirico and Mumby (2009) develop an integrated seascape model to illustrate how the presence of mangroves and seagrasses enhance considerably the biomass of coral reef fish communities. A key finding is that mangroves become more important as nursery habitat when excessive fishing effort levels are applied to the reef, because the mangroves can directly offset the negative impacts of fishing effort. Such results support the development of "ecosystem-based" fishery management and the design of integrated coastal–marine reserves that emphasize four key priorities: 1) the relative importance of mangrove nursery sites; 2) the connectivity of individual reefs to mangrove nurseries; 3) areas of nursery habitat that have an unusually large importance to specific reefs; and 4) priority sites for mangrove restoration projects (Mumby 2006).

Economic studies of large marine ecosystems have extended simple single-species or predator–prey harvesting models to consider multi-species relationships and their impacts on harvesting the commercially valuable species from the ecosystem (Finnoff and Tschirhart 2003a, 2003b; Flaaten and Stollery 1996; Sanchirico *et al.* 2008; Wacker 1999). These studies find that the inter-specific links between noncommercial species in marine ecosystems and the harvesting of commercial fish species are highly important. For example, results for a marine ecosystem in the East Bering Sea off Alaska show that predator–prey relations between Orca whales and Stellar sea lions are intricately linked to the stock density of the sea lions' commercially harvested prey, pollack (Finnoff and Tschirhart 2003a, 2003b). Killer whales also feed on otter, which in turn prey on sea urchins. This complex food web implies that changes in any one population will impact all other species. Such a result suggests that the noncommercial species have value because they support the fisheries indirectly via the effect of total diversity on the productivity of commercial fisheries and overall ecosystem stability. Similarly, Sanchirico *et al.* (2008) demonstrate that, if total allowable catch levels for Chesapeake Bay fisheries accounted for species interdependencies and other environmental factors, fishing revenues would increase and their variability could be reduced.

Larval dispersal and fish migration between reserve and fishery areas may be important factors determining whether marine reserves enhance the productivity of neighboring fishery areas (Grafton *et al.* 2005, 2009; Rodwell *et al.* 2002; Sanchirico 2005; Sanchirico and Wilen 2002; Smith *et al.* 2008). In tropical systems, the quality of critical habitat, such as coral reefs, is also relevant. Evidence from Kenya indicates that coral reefs may also be critical to larval dispersal to fishing areas, which could influence the effectiveness of marine reserves and closed fishing grounds in inducing stock recovery and thus eventual re-opening to fishing (Rodwell *et al.* 2003).

Final remarks

This chapter has argued that the ecological functions underlying some key goods and services provided by ecosystems show considerably spatial variation across landscapes. For example, in the case of many coastal ecosystems, both attenuation of storm waves and fish density tend to decline with the distance inshore from the seaward edge of the landscape. The resulting storm protection and support for near-shore fisheries provided by coastal ecosystems, such as mangroves and salt marshes, will also be greater for the seaward fringe compared to further inland. By developing a model to depict the spatial flow of ecosystem benefits across an ecological landscape, it is possible to illustrate that accounting for the spatial variability of key economic benefits across an ecological landscape may have significant implications for decisions to convert or conserve ecosystems. Several observations emerge from this analysis.

One interesting outcome, which especially results from the application of the model to the example of coastal ecosystems, is that when conversion of the landscape is optimal, it always occurs in certain locations only. For example, because the seaward fringe of coastal ecosystems appears to be more valuable in terms of generating key ecosystem services, any conversion of the landscape should take place further inland. Spatial variation in ecosystem benefits may therefore determine not only how much of a landscape to convert, but where the conversion should be located.

Although the spatial problem examined here is highly simplistic, assuming that the ecological function underlying an ecosystem service declines unidirectionally across a landscape, this example does show the importance of spatial variation in determining conservation decisions. Increasingly, economists are taking into account such considerations, and showing in particular how the spatial variability of costs and the need for agglomeration bonuses across heterogeneous landscapes will have an important bearing on the decision as to how much land area to protect, which landscapes to include cost-effectively for achieving overall conservation targets, and the selection of alternative possible sites for protected areas.[6] For example,

---

[6] See, for example, Ando *et al.* (1998); Balmford *et al.* (2003); Carwardine *et al.* (2008); Ferraro (2003, 2004); Naidoo *et al.* (2006); Parkhurst and Shogren (2008); Polasky *et al.* (2001).

Ferraro (2004, p. 907) argues that, in a given landscape, "each land parcel is a production unit, a 'manufacturing plant that produces biophysical attributes,' and these attributes can only be secured for conservation purposes through investment into a contract." As a result, "the degree to which a contracting agent can identify the 'true' cost-efficient land portfolio ... depends on the degree to which environmental benefits ... can be measured accurately." Ferraro shows, with the example of managing a riparian buffer zone to provide water for urban residents in Syracuse, New York, that conservation investment opportunities can still be ranked without a parametric specification of the amenity function or the cost function, provided that the decision maker is at least able to identify the important biophysical and economic attributes of each landscape parcel in each location.

Perhaps the most important contribution of this chapter is to provide further illustration of how the spatial variability of ecosystem benefits across a landscape can have a considerable influence on conservation and land use decisions.

Finally, as this chapter has shown, maintaining coastal and marine ecosystems for their multiple and synergistic ecosystem services invariably involves managing seascapes across different spatial scales. For a number of key ecosystem services, such as coastal protection, productivity of marine systems, and habitat-fishery linkages, there is now sufficient evidence to suggest that these services are not uniform across a seascape. Incorporating spatial and synergistic characteristics of these seascapes into management scenarios is likely to result in the most ecologically and economically sustainable management plan possible (Granek *et al.* 2010; McLeod and Leslie 2009). Because the connectivity of ecological structure and functions across land–sea gradients has implications for the provision of certain ecosystem services, management of the entire seascape may be necessary to preserve such synergistic effects.

References

Aburto-Oropeza, O., E. Ezcurra, G. Danemann *et al.* 2008. "Mangroves in the Gulf of California increase fishery yields." *Proceedings of the National Academy of Sciences* 105:10456–10459.

Aguilar-Perera, A. and R.S. Appeldoorn. 2008. "Spatial distribution of marine fishes along a cross-shelf gradient containing a continuum of mangrove-seagrass-coral reefs off southwestern Puerto Rico." *Estuarine, Coastal and Shelf Science* 76:378–394.

Aksornkoae, S. and R. Tokrisna. 2004. "Overview of shrimp farming and mangrove loss in Thailand." In Barbier and Sathirathai, eds.

Albers, H.J. 1996. "Modeling ecological constraints on tropical forest management: spatial interdependence, irreversibility and uncertainty." *Journal of Environmental Economics and Management* 30:73–94.

Alix-Garcia, J. 2007. "A spatial analysis of common property deforestation." *Journal of Environmental Economics and Management* 53:141–157.

Alongi, D.M. 2008. "Mangrove forests: resilience, protection from tsunamis, and responses to global climate change." *Estuarine, Coastal and Shelf Science* 76:1–13.

Ando, A.W., J. Camm, S. Polasky, and A. Solow. 1998. "Species distributions, land values, and efficient conservation." *Science* 279:2126–2128.

Balmford, A., K.J. Gaston, S. Blyth, A. James, and V. Kapos. 2003. "Global variation in terrestrial conservation costs, conservation benefits, and unmet conservation needs." *Proceedings of the National Academy of Sciences* 100:1046–1050.

Barbier, E.B. 2003. "Habitat-fishery linkages and mangrove loss in Thailand." *Contemporary Economic Policy* 21:59–77.

2007. "Valuing ecosystems as productive inputs." *Economic Policy* 22:177–229.

2008. "Ecosystems as natural assets." *Foundations and Trends in Microeconomics* 4:611–681.

Barbier, E.B. and S. Sathirathai, eds. 2004. *Shrimp Farming and Mangrove Loss in Thailand*. Edward Elgar, London.

Barbier, E.B., E.W. Koch, B.R. Silliman *et al.* 2008. "Coastal ecosystem-based management with nonlinear ecological functions and values." *Science* 319:321–323.

Bockstael, N.E. 1996. "Modeling economics and ecology: the importance of a spatial perspective." *American Journal of Agricultural Economics* 78:1168–1180.

Brown, G. and J. Roughgarden. 1997. "A metapopulation model with a common pool." *Ecological Economics* 22:65–71.

Carwardine, J., K.A. Wilson, G. Ceballos *et al.* 2008. "Cost-effective priorities for global mammal conservation." *Proceedings of the National Academy of Sciences* 105:11446–11450.

Clark, C.W. 1976. *Mathematical Bioeconomics*. Wiley Interscience, New York.

Cochard, R., S.L. Ranamukhaarachchi, G.P. Shivakoti *et al.* 2008. "The 2004 tsunami in Aceh and Southern Thailand: a review on coastal ecosystems, wave hazards and vulnerability." *Perspectives in Plant Ecology, Evolution and Systematics* 10:3–40.

Costello, C. and S. Polasky. 2008. "Optimal harvesting of stochastic spatial resources." *Journal of Environmental Economics and Management* 56:1–18.

Ferraro, P.J. 2003. "Assigning priority to environmental policy interventions in a heterogeneous world." *Journal of Policy Analysis and Management* 22:27–43.

2004. "Targeting conservation investments in heterogeneous landscapes: a distance-function approach and application to watershed management." *American Journal of Agricultural Economics* 86:905–918.

Finnoff, D. and J.T. Tschirhart. 2003a. "Protecting an endangered species while harvesting its prey in a general equilibrium ecosystem model." *Land Economics* 70:160–180.

2003b. "Harvesting in an eight-species ecosystem." *Journal of Environmental Economics and Management* 45:589–611.

Flaaten, O. and K. Stollery. 1996. "The economic costs of biological predation: theory and application to the case of the North Atlantic minke whale's (*Balaenoptera Acutorostrata*) consumption of fish." *Environmental and Resource Economics* 8:75–95.

Forbes, K. and J. Broadhead. 2007. "The role of coastal forests in the mitigation of tsunami impacts." FAO, Bangkok.

Gaudet, G., M. Moreaux, and S. Salant. 2001. "Intertemporal depletion of resource sites by spatially distributed users." *American Economic Review* 91:1149–1159.

Grafton, R.Q., T. Kompas, and V. Schneider. 2005. "The bioeconomics of marine reserves: a selected review with policy implications." *Journal of Bioeconomics* 7:161–178.

Grafton, R.Q., T. Kompas, and P.V. Ha. 2009. "Cod today and none tomorrow: the economic value of a marine reserve." *Land Economics* 85:454–469.

Granek, E.F., S. Polasky, C.V. Kappel *et al.* 2010. "Ecosystem services as a common language for coastal ecosystem-based management." *Conservation Biology* 24:207–216.

Johnston, R.J., T.A. Grigalunas, J.J. Opaluch, M. Mazzotta, and J. Diamantedes. 2002. "Valuing estuarine resource services using economic and ecological models: the Peconic Estuary system." *Coastal Management* 30(1):47–65.

Koch, E.W., E.B. Barbier, B.R. Silliman *et al.* 2009. "Non-linearity in ecosystem services: temporal and spatial variability in coastal protection." *Frontiers in Ecology and the Environment* 7:29–37.

Kolstad, C. 1994. "Hotelling rents in hotelling space: product differentiation in exhaustible resource markets." *Journal of Environmental Economics and Management* 26:163–180.

Levin, S.A. 1992. "The problem of pattern and scale in ecology: the Robert H. MacArthur Lecture." *Ecology* 73(6):1943–1967.

Manson, F.J., N.R. Loneragan, G.A. Skilleter, and S.R. Phinn. 2005. "An evaluation of the evidence for linkages between mangroves and fisheries: a synthesis of the literature and identification of research directions." *Oceanography and Marine Biology: An Annual Review* 43:483–513.

Mazda, Y., M. Magi, M. Kogo, and P.N. Hong. 1997. "Mangroves as a coastal protection from waves in the Tong King Delta, Vietnam." *Mangroves and Salt Marshes* 1:127–135.

McLeod, K. and H. Leslie, eds. 2009. *Ecosystem-based Management for the Oceans.* Island Press, Washington, DC.

Meynecke, J.-O., S.Y. Lee, and N.C. Duke. 2008. "Linking spatial metrics and fish catch reveals the importance of coastal wetland connectivity to inshore fisheries in Queensland, Australia." *Biological Conservation* 141:981–996.

Moberg, F. and P. Rönnbäck. 2003. "Ecosystem services of the tropical seascape: interactions, substitutions and restoration." *Ocean and Coastal Management* 46:27–46.

Mumby, P.J. 2006. "Connectivity of reef fish between mangroves and coral reefs: algorithms for the design of marine reserves at seascape scales." *Biological Conservation* 128:215–222.

Mumby, P.J., A.J. Edwards, J.E. Arias-Gonzalez *et al.* 2004. "Mangroves enhance the biomass of reef fisheries in the Caribbean." *Nature* 427:533–536.

Naidoo, R., A. Balmford, P.J. Ferraro *et al.* 2006. "Integrating economic costs into conservation planning." *TRENDS in Ecology and Evolution* 21:681–687.

Parkhurst, G.M. and J.F. Shogren. 2008. "Smart subsidies for conservation." *American Journal of Agricultural Economics* 90:1192–1200.

Petersen, J.E., W.M. Kemp, R. Bartleson *et al.* 2003. "Multiscale experiments in coastal ecology: improving realism and advancing theory." *BioScience* 53:1181–1197.

Peterson, G.W. and R.E. Turner. 1994. "The value of salt marsh edge versus interior as habitat for fish and decapods crustaceans in a Louisiana tidal marsh." *Estuaries* 17:235–262.

Polasky, S., J.D. Camm, and B. Garber-Yonts. 2001. "Selecting biological reserves cost-effectively: an application to terrestrial vertebrate conservation in Oregon." *Land Economics* 77:68–78.

5 | *The open economy*

There is no pleasure in reporting the *suspicion* that despite all the rhetoric, the world does not care too much about biodiversity conservation. Maybe the efforts of economists and ecologists will force a change of policy in the future. But the proper place to begin is with an honest appraisal of just how little we do.

(Pearce 2007, p. 331)

Introduction

Many of the world's most important ecosystems are found in developing countries that are undergoing rapid land use change and resource extraction as part of the process of development (see Chapter 1). The majority of these economies are highly *resource dependent*, in that primary product exports comprise at least half of their total merchandise exports (Barbier 2005). The result is that there is a trade-off between increased development activities, the products of which are often sold on world markets, and the conservation of ecological landscapes.

As many developing countries participate as small open economies in world markets for their products, the implications for changes in the terms of trade are relevant. At the same time, there is increased policy interest in international payments for ecosystem services as a way of increasing conservation in developing economies. One possibility is to compensate these economies for foregoing the export earnings that could otherwise be earned from development activities that require converting ecological landscapes. Such compensatory transfers serve indirectly as *payment for ecosystem services*, because they essentially subsidize developing economies to conserve rather than convert ecological landscapes, thus generating a greater flow of ecosystem services. Payments for the conservation of standing forests or wildlife habitat are the most frequent type of compensation programs used in developing countries, and they have been mainly aimed at reimbursing landowners for the opportunity costs of carbon sequestration, watershed protection, and biodiversity and landscape conservation.

To explore these issues further, the following chapter extends the natural asset model to include the effects of trade and the international payment of ecosystem services on ecological landscape management. These modeling extensions have important policy implications, which will be discussed in detail. In particular, the chapter will explore the scope for negotiating and developing international payment schemes for ecosystem services that involve transfers from rich to poor countries as well as the success and limitations of existing and planned payment for ecosystem services schemes.

To provide some background to this analysis, we begin with an overview of resource dependency in low- and middle-income economies and its implications for economic development and global ecological scarcity.

Resource dependency, rural poverty, and ecosystem loss

As we saw in Chapter 1, over the past fifty years, ecosystems have been modified more rapidly and extensively than in any comparable period in human history, largely to meet rapidly growing demands for food, fresh water, timber, fiber, and fuel. Around 50 percent of the world's surface area has been converted to grazing or agricultural land, and more than half of the world's forests have been lost due to this land conversion (MEA 2005). About 50 percent of global wetlands have disappeared as a result of human activities (Zedler and Kercher 2005). Estuarine, coastal, and marine ecosystems are some of the most heavily used and threatened systems globally, due to overfishing, coastal development, pollution, and climate change (Beddington *et al.* 2007; FAO 2009; Halpern *et al.* 2008; Jackson *et al.* 2001; Lotze *et al.* 2006; Worm *et al.* 2006, 2009). Freshwater ecosystems have deteriorated as the demand for water to satisfy economic development and human population growth continues to rise (Rosegrant *et al.* 2002). At best, only 17 percent of the Earth's land area has escaped direct influence by humans (Kareiva *et al.* 2007).

Much of the remaining areas of relatively undisturbed ecosystems and species richness is found in tropical developing regions. For example, approximately two-thirds of all species occur in the tropics, largely in tropical forests (Dirzo and Raven 2003). Other important tropical ecosystems include coral reefs, mangroves, marshes, seagrass systems, marine ecosystems, freshwater wetlands, watersheds, and floodplains.

Yet, as we saw in Chapter 1, human development activities and land conversion are occurring most rapidly in tropical developing economies. The demise of key ecosystems of the developing world include mangroves (35 percent either lost or degraded), coral reefs (30 percent), and tropical forests (30 percent) (FAO 2006, 2007; MEA 2005; UNEP 2006; Valiela *et al.* 2001). As a result of these changes, over the next fifty years, the rate of global biodiversity loss is also expected to accelerate, leading to the extinction of at least 500 of the 1,192 currently threatened bird species and 565 of the 1,137 mammal species (Dirzo and Raven 2003). Low- and middle-income countries already account for 71 percent of global water withdrawal, and their demand is expected to grow by 27 percent by 2025 (Rosegrant *et al.* 2002). In addition, tropical and subtropical developing regions are experiencing greater conversion of wetlands to alternative land uses (Zedler and Kercher 2005).

The rapid loss of many ecosystems and biodiversity in low- and middle-income economies is mainly related to how these economies develop, maintain their growing populations, and combat widespread poverty. As we shall see, this process is complex. Yet one aspect of the pattern of economic development is clear: most developing economies, and certainly the majority of the populations living within them, depend directly on natural resources. For many of these economies, primary product exports account for the vast majority of their export earnings, and one or two primary commodities make up the bulk of exports (Barbier 2005). Agricultural value added accounts for an average of 40 percent of Gross Domestic Product (GDP), and nearly 80 percent of the labor force is engaged in agricultural or resource-based activities (World Bank 2008). Further adding to these disparities, by 2025, the rural population of the developing world will have increased to almost 3.2 billion, placing increasing pressure on a declining resource base (Population Division of the United Nations Secretariat 2008).

Moreover, much of the rural poor continue to be concentrated in the less favored areas of developing regions, a long-run trend of the post-war era of global economic development (Barbier 2011). Since

1950, the estimated population in developing economies on "fragile lands" has doubled (World Bank 2003). These less-favored environments are prone to land degradation, and consist of upland areas, forest systems, and drylands that suffer from low agricultural productivity, and which, according to the World Bank (2003, p. 59) are "areas that present significant constraints for intensive agriculture." Today, nearly 1.3 billion people – almost a fifth of the world's population – live in such areas in developing regions (see Table 5.1a). Almost half of the people living in these marginal environments (631 million) consist of the rural poor, who throughout the developing world outnumber the poor living on favored lands by two to one (see Table 5.1b). The populations living in less-favored areas in developing countries include 518 million inhabiting arid regions with no access to irrigation systems, 430 million on soils unsuitable for agriculture, 216 million on land with steep slopes, and more than 130 million in fragile forest systems (World Bank 2003).

Figure 5.1 further illustrates that rural poverty is correlated with the fraction of the population in developing countries found on fragile lands. As the figure indicates, for a sample of seventy-six developing economies from Africa, Asia, and Latin America, the incidence of rural poverty rises as developing countries have more of their populations concentrated on fragile lands. Although the average poverty rate across all economies is 45.8%, the rate falls to 36.8% for those countries with less than 20% of their population in fragile environments. For those with more than 50% of their populations in marginal areas, however, the incidence of rural poverty rises to 53% or more.

The tendency for the most marginal environments to contain large numbers of the rural poor is also supported by studies at the regional and country level, although there can be important differences within and between countries. For example, researchers from the World Bank have examined the "poverty–environment nexus" in three of the poorest countries in Southeast Asia – Cambodia, Laos, and Vietnam (Dasgupta *et al.* 2005; Minot and Baulch 2005). In Cambodia, the core poor in rural areas appear to be located in areas that are already heavily deforested; on the other hand, poor populations tend to be more concentrated in the lowlands rather than steeply sloped lands. In Laos, the poorest provinces in the north and north-east also have the highest incidence of poor rural populations, who appear to be located mainly in forested areas and the highlands. In Vietnam, the

Table 5.1 *Distribution of world's population and rural poor on fragile land*

(a) Distribution of world's population

	Population in 2000 (millions)	Population in fragile lands	
Region		Number (millions)	Share of total (%)
Latin America and the Caribbean	515.3	68	13.1
Middle East and North Africa	293.0	110	37.6
Sub-Saharan Africa	658.4	258	39.3
South Asia	1,354.5	330	24.4
East Asia and Pacific	1,856.5	469	25.3
Eastern Europe and Central Asia	474.7	58	12.1
OECD Group[1]	850.4	94	11.1
Other	27.3	2	6.9
Total	6,030.1	1,389	23.0
Total developing economies[2]	5,179.7	1,295	25.0
Total Latin America, Africa, and Asian developing economies[3]	4,677.7	1,235	26.4

(b) Distribution of rural poor in developing regions

	Rural poor on favored lands (millions)	Rural poor on fragile lands	
Region		Number (millions)	Share of total (%)
Central and South America	24	47	66
West Asia and North Africa	11	35	76
Sub-Saharan Africa	65	175	73
Asia	219	374	63
Total	319	631	66

Notes: In Table 5.1(a), fragile lands are defined as areas that present significant constraints for intensive agriculture and where the people's links to the land are critical for the sustainability of communities, pastures, forests, and other natural

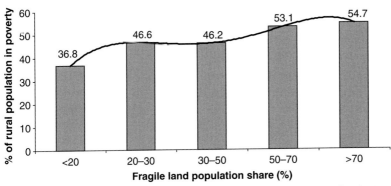

Figure 5.1 The rural poor and population on fragile lands in developing economies

Notes: Developing economies are all economies from East Asia and the Pacific, Latin America and the Caribbean, Middle East and North Africa, South Asia, and Sub-Saharan Africa with 2006 per capita income of $11,115 or less, following World Bank (2008).

Percentage of rural population in poverty is from World Bank (2008).

Percentage of population on fragile land is from World Bank (2003).

Number of observations = 76 countries, of which 12 (<20% of population on fragile land), 26 (20–30%), 28 (30–50%), 7 (50–70%), and 3 (> 70%). The average rural poverty rate across all countries is 45.8%, and the median is 42.6%.

Notes to Table 5.1 *(cont.)*

resources; they include arid regions with no access to irrigation, areas with soils unsuitable for agriculture, land with steep slopes, and fragile forest systems (see World Bank 2003). In Table 5.1(b), fragile lands are equated with marginal lands, which are defined as areas with the greatest potential for land and water degradation; i.e., land with highly weathered soils, steep slopes, inadequate or excess rainfall, and high temperatures (see Comprehensive Assessment of Water Management in Agriculture 2007).

[1] OECD Group: Australia, Austria, Belgium, Canada, Denmark, Finland, France, Germany, Greece, Iceland, Ireland, Italy, Japan, Luxembourg, Netherlands, New Zealand, Norway, Portugal, Spain, Sweden, Switzerland, United Kingdom, and United States.

[2] World Total less OECD Group.

[3] World Total less OECD Group, East Europe and Central Asia, and Other.

Sources: Barbier (2008). Table 5.1(a) is adapted from World Bank (2003, Table 4.2). Table 5.1(b) is adapted from Comprehensive Assessment of Water Management in Agriculture (2007, Table 15.1) and Scherr (1999).

incidence of poverty is highest in the upland provinces comprising the Northern and Central Highlands. In some districts, especially in the more remote upland areas, over 90 percent of the population lives below the poverty line.

Despite its robust growth and reduction of poverty overall, China has seen rural poverty persist and concentrate geographically in the relatively poor agricultural areas of the west and south-west (Gustafsson and Zhong 2000; Jalan and Ravallion 2002; Ravallion and Chen 2007). In general, households living in the lowlands and plains are less poverty prone than those living in hilly and mountainous regions. As poverty declines in coastal and lowland areas, the rural poor are increasingly found in upland areas. For example, the proportion of China's rural poor living in the mountains increased from less than one-third in 1988 to a majority in 1995 (Gustafsson and Zhong 2000).

A study of the spatial pattern of rural poverty in Bangladesh concludes that "the pocket of high poverty incidence generally coincides with the ecologically poor areas" (Kam *et al.* 2005, p. 564). Overall, four such areas could be considered poverty "hot spots" in Bangladesh: the low-lying depression area in the north-east; the drought-prone upland area in the north-west; several flood-prone subdistricts fringing major rivers; and several of the subdistricts in the south-eastern hilly regions. A similar poverty-mapping exercise in Mexico also finds that the rural poor are concentrated in particular regions, especially those with marginal lands (Bellon *et al.* 2005). Poverty is especially concentrated in mountainous regions in central, southern, and north-west Mexico. As the authors note, "these 'islands' of poverty exhibit specific circumstances such as the presence of indigenous populations, higher rainfall, steep slopes, erodable soils and lack of access to services," reflecting that these areas are both ecologically fragile and remote (Bellon *et al.* 2005, p. 489).

Much of Africa's population, and its rural poor, is located in ecologically fragile regions of landlocked, resource-scarce countries (Collier 2007). But even in coastal African economies, the rural poor continue to be clustered in marginal environments. For example, in Kenya locations with poor quality soil, a high percentage of steep land, and variable rainfall have much higher poverty levels among populations compared to areas with more favorable land and environmental conditions (Okwi *et al.* 2007). According to Dercon (2006,

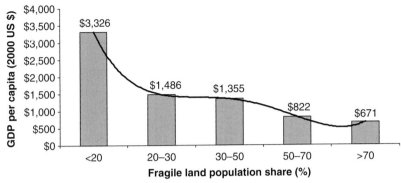

Figure 5.2 Fragile land population and GDP per capita in developing economies
Notes: Developing economies are all economies from East Asia and the Pacific, Latin America and the Caribbean, Middle East and North Africa, South Asia, and Sub-Saharan Africa with 2006 per capita income of $11,115 or less, following World Bank (2008).
GDP per capita ($ 2000), latest year, is from World Bank (2008).
Percentage of population on fragile land is from World Bank (2003).
Number of observations = 90 countries, of which 12 (<20% of population on fragile land), 27 (20–30%), 37 (30–50%), 9 (50–70%), and 5 (> 70%). The average GDP per capita ($ 2000) across all countries is $1,566 and the median is $661.

p. 23), in Ethiopia, "the poor contain mainly households with poor endowments in terms of poor land, far from towns or with poor road infrastructure."

Developing economies with high concentrations of their populations on fragile lands not only display high rates of rural poverty but also are some of the poorest countries in the world today. As indicated in Figure 5.2, for a sample of ninety low- and middle-income economies from Africa, Asia, and Latin America, real GDP per capita declines sharply with the share of the population in fragile environments. For all economies, the average GDP per capita is $1,566, but for those economies with less than 20 percent of their populations on fragile lands, real GDP per capita more than doubles to $3,326. In contrast, for those economies with 50 percent or more of the population in fragile lands, GDP per capita is only $822 and for those economies with 70 percent or more of the population in marginal rural environments, real GDP per capita is $671. According to the World

Bank (2008), the low-income, or poorest, economies of the world are those in which per capita income was $905 or less.

The clustering of rural populations in less-favored areas and fragile environments is likely to continue into the foreseeable future, given current global rural population and poverty trends. First, despite rapid global urbanization, the rural population of developing regions continues to grow, albeit at a slower rate in recent years. From 1950 to 1975, annual rural population growth in these regions was 1.8 percent, and from 1975 to 2007 it was just over 1.0 percent (Population Division of the United Nations Secretariat 2008). Second, around three-quarters of the developing world's poor still live in rural areas, even allowing for the higher cost of living facing the poor in urban areas. In general, about twice as many poor people live in rural than in urban areas in developing countries (Chen and Ravallion 2007).[1]

As developing regions continue to be the main source of the world's supply of mineral, energy, and raw material commodities, their economic development remains largely *resource dependent* – as measured by the ratio of primary products to total merchandise exports (see Figure 5.3). Although all types of economies have on average experienced a decline in primary product export share, resource dependency remains relatively high in low- and middle-income economies compared to wealthy economies (see Figure 5.3a).

Among developing economies there are also important regional differences (see Figure 5.3b). Since 1960, Asian countries have had the sharpest decline in resource dependency, as these economies have generally become more successful in diversifying their economies and developing labor-intensive manufacturing for exports. Latin America has also seen a decline in the ratio of primary products to total exports, especially in recent decades. But in Africa and the Middle East, resource dependency remains relatively high, around 90 percent for the Middle East and North Africa and 70 percent for Sub-Saharan Africa.

---

[1] For example, Chen and Ravallion (2007) note that the $1-a-day rural poverty rate of 30 percent in 2002 is more than double the urban rate and, although 70 percent of the rural population lives on less than $2 a day, the proportion in urban areas is less than half that figure.

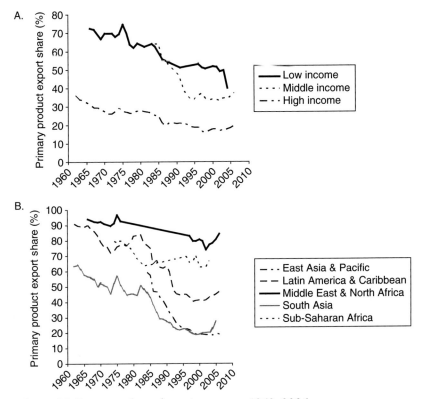

Figure 5.3 Resource dependency in exports, 1960–2006
A. By type of economy
B. Low- and middle-income economies by region
Notes: Primary product export share is the percentage of agricultural raw material, food, fuel, ore, and metal commodities to total merchandise exports. High-income economies are those in which 2006 income per capita was $11,116 or more. Middle-income economies are those in which 2006 income per capita was between $906 and $11,115. Low-income economies are those in which 2006 income per capita was $905 or less.
Source: World Bank (2008).

Despite these regional differences, most low- and middle-income economies still remain highly dependent on the exploitation of their natural resource endowments for commercial, export-oriented economic activities. For these economies, primary product exports – and often one or two main commodities – account for nearly all export earnings. For example, a study of resource dependency in developing economies indicates that seventy-two out of ninety-five low- and middle-income economies have 50 percent or more of their exports from primary products, and thirty-five countries have an export concentration in primary commodities of 90 percent or more.[2]

In sum, developing regions may be the last reservoirs of much of the world's relatively undisturbed ecosystems and biodiversity but poor economies also face intense pressures to develop rather than conserve such areas. Resource-dependent economic development, rural poverty, and population growth, and the concentration of the rural poor and populations in less-favored areas, are the source of much of this pressure to develop natural environments and convert ecological landscapes. These forces are both symptomatic of underdevelopment and mutually reinforcing. For example, Box 5.1 illustrates that, among low- and middle-income countries today, countries with higher levels of resource dependency tend to have lower levels of GDP per capita, a higher degree of rural poverty, and more of their population living in fragile environments.

Table 5.2 confirms this pattern of resource use for eighty-one developing economies that have at least 20 percent of their total populations living on fragile lands, grouping them by the degree of resource dependency of the economy, as measured by the share of primary commodities in total merchandise exports. The figure in parentheses by each country also indicates the share of the rural population living below the national rural poverty line.

The pattern across countries is striking. Sixty-two of the eighty-one developing economies have a primary product export share of 50% or more, and could therefore be considered highly resource dependent.

---

[2] See Barbier (2005, ch. 1 and Appendix 1). Note that in this study, as in Figure 5.3, transition economies, such as the low- and middle-income economies of the former Soviet bloc are excluded for lack of data. For all the low- and middle-income countries, the average export share of GDP is 31.4%. For those countries with a primary product share of 50% or more, the export share of GDP is 29.6%. As the importance of exports across low- and middle-income economies is fairly stable across these countries, around 30% of GDP, this suggests that the percentage share of primary products to total exports is a fairly good indicator of the degree of resource dependency of these economies. In fact, the importance of exports increases slightly with the degree of resource dependency. For economies with an export concentration in primary products of 70% or more, the export share of GDP is 30.7%; for those countries with a primary product export concentration of 90% or more, the export share rises to 34.6%.

Box 5.1 Resource dependency, fragile land populations, and rural poverty

The majority of developing economies have tended to remain resource dependent, in terms of a high concentration of primary products to total merchandise exports. In addition, the performance of these economies, whether measured in terms of levels of income per capita or poverty indices, tends to decline with their degree of resource dependency. The following graphs illustrate that resource dependency in developing economies is negatively correlated with GDP per capita and positively correlated with the degree of rural poverty and the share of population living in "fragile" environments. In these graphs, developing economies are all economies from East Asia and the Pacific, Latin America and the Caribbean, Middle East and North Africa, South Asia, and Sub-Saharan Africa with 2006 per capita income of $11,115 or less, following World Bank (2008).

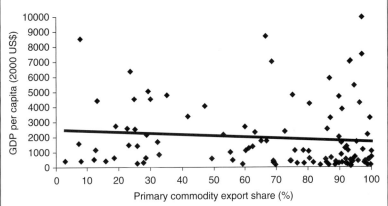

Box figure 5.1a
Notes: Primary product export share is the percentage of agricultural raw material, food, fuel, ore, and metal commodities to total merchandise exports, latest year (average = 68.5%, median = 80.1%).
GDP per capita in constant $ (2000), latest year (average = $1,932, median = $1,069).
Correlation coefficient, $r = -0.110$. Number of observations = 107.
Source: World Bank (2008).

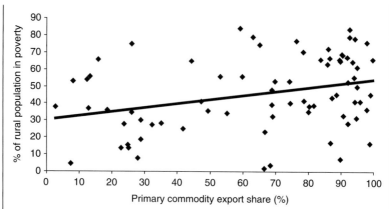

Box figure 5.1b

Notes: Primary product export share is the percentage of agricultural raw material, food, fuel, ore, and metal commodities to total merchandise exports, latest year (average = 65.4%, median = 75.5%).
Poverty headcount ratio at rural poverty line as percentage of rural population), latest year (average = 45.7%, median = 42.6%).
Correlation coefficient, $r = 0.322$. Number of observations = 76.
Source: World Bank (2008).

All of these economies also show high incidence of rural poverty; on average, they have a rural poverty rate of 53.4%, and in almost all economies 20% or more of their rural population is poor. Of the remaining nineteen countries that have at least 20% of their populations on marginal lands but are less resource dependent (primary product export share ≤50%), most still have a high incidence of rural poverty. Only five countries – China, Malaysia, Jordan, Sri Lanka, and Tunisia – have rural poverty rates less than 20%.

Table 5.2 also corroborates the correlation between the concentration of populations in fragile environments and resource dependency. Over 70% of the sixty-two highly resource dependent economies has at least 30% of their populations located in marginal rural areas. Fifteen of these economies have at least 50% of their populations concentrated in fragile environments. In contrast, more than half of the nineteen less resource dependent economies have 20–30% of their populations living on fragile lands, and only one economy (Swaziland) has 50% or more of its population located in marginal areas.

Table 5.2 *Low- and middle-income economies and patterns of resource use*

	Share of population on fragile land > 50%	Share of population on fragile land 30–50%	Share of population on fragile land 20–30%
Primary product export share > 90%	Burkina Faso (52.4) Congo Dem. Rep. (NA) Mali (75.9) Papua New Guinea (41.3) Somalia (NA) Sudan (NA) Yemen Rep. (45.0)	Algeria (16.6) Angola (NA) Belize (NA) Benin (33.0) Cameroon (49.9) Chad (67.0) Equatorial Guinea (NA) Lao PDR (41.0) Mauritania (61.2) Nigeria (36.4) Sierra Leone (79.0) Solomon Islands (NA) Vanuatu (NA)	Bolivia (83.5) Burundi (64.6) Ecuador (69.0) Guinea-Bisseau (65.7) Liberia (NA) Mozambique (55.3) Myanmar (NA) Zambia (78.0)
Primary product export share 50–90%	Afghanistan (NA) Bhutan (NA) Cape Verde (NA) Egypt (23.3) Eritrea (53.0) Namibia (55.8) Niger (66.0) Zimbabwe (48.0)	Central Af. Rep. (84.0) Comoros (NA) Ethiopia (45.0) Gambia (63.0) Grenada (NA) Guatemala (74.5) Guinea (40.0) Guyana (39.2) Iran (7.2) Kenya (53.0) Rwanda (65.7) St Vincent & Gren. (NA) Senegal (40.4) Syria (NA) Tanzania (38.7) Uganda (41.7)	Côte d'Ivoire (38.4) Dominican Rep. (55.7) Ghana (39.2) Honduras (70.4) Indonesia (34.4) Madagascar (76.7) Mongolia (43.4) Panama (64.9) Peru (72.1) Togo (32.3)

Table 5.2 *(cont.)*

	Share of population on fragile land > 50%	Share of population on fragile land 30–50%	Share of population on fragile land 20–30%
Primary product export share < 50%	Swaziland (75.0)	Botswana (55.7) Haiti (66.0) Morocco (27.2) Nepal (34.6) Pakistan (35.9) South Africa (34.1) Tunisia (13.9)	Cambodia (38.0) China (4.6) El Salvador (64.8) India (30.2) Jamaica (25.1) Jordan (18.7) Malaysia (15.5) Mexico (27.9) Sri Lanka (7.9) Vietnam (35.6)

Notes: Primary product export share is the percentage of agricultural raw material, food, fuel, ore, and metal commodities to total merchandise exports, latest year, from World Bank (2008). Share of population on fragile land is from World Bank (2003, Table 4.3). Figure in parenthesis is the percentage of the rural population in poverty, from World Bank (2008). Total countries = 81, of which 62 with 50% or more primary product export share (average rural poverty rate = 53.4%), and 19 with less than 50% primary product export share (average rural poverty rate = 35%).

To conclude, many of the poor countries that contain some of the world's most important ecosystems are facing intense development, population, and poverty pressures. Economic development in the majority of these countries is still highly dependent on expanding primary product exports. The result is that there is a tradeoff between increased development activities, the products of which are often sold on world markets, and the conservation of ecological landscapes. Although agricultural raw material, food, fuel, ore, and metal commodities are important to the development efforts of poor economies, usually a single developing country's exports of these commodities are small relative to the overall world market. Thus, changes in world commodity prices can affect significantly the terms of trade of such small open economies, and thus their decision to develop or conserve remaining ecological landscapes. On the other hand, the growing interest in international payments for ecosystem services is seen as a way of compensating poor economies for increasing their conservation efforts. By extending the natural asset model to allow for such open economy conditions, it is possible to examine further the effects of trade and the international payment of ecosystem services on the decision to conserve rather than convert an ecological landscape.

The open economy natural asset model

The natural asset model developed in Chapter 3 can easily incorporate some open economy conditions. The two conditions are trade and international payment for ecosystem services. The model is extended in the most straightforward way possible, following Barbier and Rauscher (1994). Thus the model developed here is an abstraction from more sophisticated open economy models that consider land conversion.[3]

As in the natural asset model of Chapter 3, A_0 is denoted as the landscape area associated with an ecosystem that is subject to continuous irreversible conversion to provide land for a development activity. However, following Barbier and Schulz (1997), it is also assumed that, given this competing land use, retaining more of the ecological landscape would mean less land available for development activities, thus restricting aggregate production, q, from these activities. Assuming decreasing marginal productivity of q through landscape conversion, then the aggregate production function is

$$q = f\big(A(t)\big), \quad f' < 0, \quad f'' < 0. \tag{5.1}$$

Aggregate output q is sufficiently large with respect to the entire economy that it can either be exported or consumed domestically, and the export earnings are used to import domestic consumption goods from abroad. However, the economy's exports and imports are sufficiently small with respect to world markets that the terms of trade for the economy are given. Denoting exports of aggregate output as x, then domestic consumption from land conversion activities is $q-x$. Imported consumption goods are m. With given world prices p^x for the economy's exports and p^m for its imports, then the balance of trade for the small open economy is

---

[3] See, for example, Barbier and Schulz (1997); Bulte and Barbier (2005); Hartwick *et al.* (2001); Jinji (2006); Polasky *et al.* (2004); and Smulders *et al.* (2004).

$$px = m, \quad p = \frac{p^x}{p^m} \tag{5.2}$$

where p represents the terms of trade for the economy's exports of aggregate production from development activities that depend on land conversion.

Social welfare is indicated by the utility of an infinitely lived representative consumer, whose welfare depends on domestic consumption, $q-x$, imported goods, m, and the benefit flows of ecosystem services, $B(A)$, less the costs of converting landscape, $C(c)$. The economy's objective is therefore to choose land conversion, c, and exports, x, so as to maximize the welfare function

$$W = \int_0^\infty \left[U(q - x, m) + B(A) - C(c) \right] e^{-rt} dt \tag{5.3}$$

subject to (5.1), (5.2), and the rate of conversion of the ecological landscape as represented by equation (3.4), i.e., $\dot{A} = -c(t)$. It is assumed that the utility function, U, is additively separable and has the standard partial derivative properties, $U_i > 0$ and $U_{ii} < 0$ ($i = 1,2$).[4]

The current value Hamiltonian of the problem is

$$H = U(f(A) - x, px) + B(A) - C(c) - \mu c. \tag{5.4}$$

The key necessary conditions for this problem are

$$\frac{\partial H}{\partial x} = 0 \rightarrow U_1 - p U_2 = 0 \tag{5.5}$$

$$\frac{\partial H}{\partial c} = 0 \rightarrow \mu = -C'(c) \tag{5.6}$$

$$-\frac{\partial H}{\partial A} = \dot{\mu} - r\mu \rightarrow \dot{\mu} = r\mu - B'(A) - U_1 f'(A). \tag{5.7}$$

Condition (5.6) is the same as (3.7) for the natural asset model of Chapter 3. Condition (5.7) is similar to (3.8), although now the

---

[4] Note that, since the objective function is social welfare, r should be interpreted as the social discount rate in this problem rather than the average rate of interest in the economy. Under certain conditions, the two may be the same, of course.

opportunity cost of holding on to landscape is not foregone rents but the reduced utility from less domestic consumption derived from development based on land conversion, $U_1 f'(A)$. The new condition is (5.5), which is the standard small open economy result that the relative marginal value of domestic to imported consumption must equal the fixed terms of trade.

As before, from (5.6) and (5.7)

$$-\mu(t) = -\frac{U_1 f'(A)}{r} - \frac{B'(A) + \dot{\mu}}{r} = P(D) - P(A) = C'(c). \quad (5.8)$$

Thus, the open economy model yields a similar result as the natural asset model. The difference between the capitalized marginal value of developed land and land retained as ecological landscape is the marginal cost of converting landscape, which also represents the difference in land prices between developed and ecological land.

As in the basic model, in the long-run steady state, $\dot{A} = \dot{\mu} = 0$. It follows that both landscape conversion and the marginal value of an additional unit of ecosystem landscape approach zero asymptotically, i.e., $c = 0$ and $\lim_{t \to \infty} \mu(t) = C_c(0) = 0$. The wedge between land prices will disappear, $P(D(t)) = P(A(t))$, and ecosystem landscape area will converge to a steady state level A^*. If the initial ecological landscape area is large $A(0) > A^*$, then along the transition path to the long-run steady state, the marginal value of an additional unit of ecosystem landscape is negative $\mu < 0$, and optimal landscape conversion c is at first very large. But along the optimal path, as land conversion proceeds until the steady state is reached, $\mu(t)$ will rise and c fall.

The outcome for the optimal landscape conversion path for the open economy, which is similar to the natural asset model of Chapter 3, is depicted in Figure 5.4. However, in the case of the open economy model, we can now explore what effect a change in the terms of trade might have on the optimal land conversion path of the economy. To do this, it is necessary to examine the effects on both the steady state outcome and the transition path.

A change in the terms of trade

In the open economy version of the model, a change in the economy's terms of trade p will now have an impact on both the long-run steady state level of ecological landscape A^* and the transition path to this equilibrium.

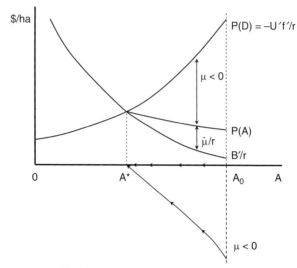

Figure 5.4 Optimal landscape conversion in the open economy model

The steady state is determined by (5.5) and, from (5.7), $B'(A^*) + U_1 f'(A^*) = 0$, which are defined at the equilibrium level of ecological landscape A^* and exports x^*. The comparative static effects of a change in p on these equilibrium values are

$$\frac{dx^*}{dp} = \frac{(1+\eta)\delta}{\Delta} > 0, \quad \frac{dA^*}{dp} = -\frac{(1+\eta)\gamma}{\Delta} < 0,$$

$$\eta = \frac{U_{22}px}{U_2}, \quad -1 < \eta < 0, \quad \Delta = \alpha\delta - \gamma\beta < 0, \tag{5.9}$$

where $\alpha = -(U_{11} + p^2 U_{22}) > 0$, $\beta = U_{11}f'(A) > 0$, $\gamma = -U_{11}f'(A) < 0$ and $\delta = U_1 f''(A) + (f'(A))^2 U_{11} + B''(A) < 0$. Note that Δ is the determinant of the Hessian matrix of coefficients of the totally differentiated equilibrium system. This determinant is negative if $\alpha\delta < \beta\gamma$ or $-\dfrac{\alpha}{\gamma} < -\dfrac{\beta}{\delta}$, which turns out to be a necessary condition for the equilibrium to be locally stable (a saddle point).[5] Finally, η is the elasticity of the marginal utility with respect to imported goods, which reflects the degree of import dependency of the economy. As (5.9) shows, under normal

---

[5] See Barbier and Rauscher (1994) for a proof.

import dependency conditions, with $|\eta| < 1$, then we would get the result that a rise in the terms of trade would lead to more export from development activities in the long run and a lower steady state level of ecological landscape.

The effect of a change in p on the transition path can be determined qualitatively through the impact on the slope of the optimal conversion path. The slope of the path in the open economy is similar to that of the basic model

$$\frac{\partial \mu}{\partial A} = \frac{\dot{\mu}}{\dot{A}} = \frac{r\mu - B'(A) - U_1 f'(A)}{-c(\mu)} < 0. \tag{5.10}$$

Although p does not appear directly in (5.10), it does have an influence on this slope. From totally differentiating (5.5) one gets $dp = \frac{\alpha}{1+\eta} dx + \frac{\beta}{1+\eta} dA$, which implies that a change in terms of trade has a positive influence on exports and ecological landscape levels, given normal import dependency conditions. From totally differentiating (5.7) $d\dot{\mu} = rdu - \gamma dx - \delta dA$. It follows from (5.10) that the slope of the optimal landscape conversion trajectory becomes less negative, or flatter, due to a rise in p. That is, $\mu(t)$ will rise less quickly and c fall more slowly as a result of the change in the terms of trade.

In addition, the isocline locus $B'(A^*)'$ shifts to the right, but the isocline $-U_1 f'(A^*)$ shifts leftward even more, ensuring that equilibrium landscape level A^* falls.[6] The changes in the slope of the optimal land conversion path and in the long-run amount of landscape conservation ensure that the initial value of μ must decrease (i.e., becomes more negative). As indicated by (5.8), a decrease in μ_0 (which means its absolute value rises) corresponds to an increase in c_0. Conversion starts higher initially, and then decreases slowly over time. Because landscape area is still fixed at A_0, more conversion of ecological landscape occurs in the long run.

These effects of a rise in the terms of trade on both the steady state outcome for landscape area and the transition path are depicted in Figure 5.5, with the changes represented by the dotted lines in the figure. The new long-run ecological landscape area is A^{**}.

---

[6] Note that $\dfrac{B''}{r}\dfrac{dA^*}{dp} > 0$ and $-U_{11}\left(f'\right)^2 \dfrac{dA^*}{dp} < 0$.

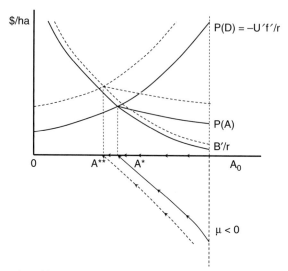

Figure 5.5 The effects of a change in the terms of trade

Payment for ecosystem services

Now consider the possibility that the economy receives international payments for foregoing the export earnings that could otherwise be earned from development activities that require landscape conservation. Such compensatory transfers serve indirectly as *payment for ecosystem services*, because they essentially subsidize the open economy to conserve rather than convert ecological landscape, thus generating a greater flow of ecosystem services. Payments for the conservation of standing forests or wildlife habitat are the most frequent type of compensation programs used in developing countries, and they have been mainly aimed at paying landowners for the opportunity costs of preserving ecological landscapes that provide one or more diverse services: carbon sequestration, watershed protection, biodiversity benefits, wildlife protection, and landscape beauty.[7]

In the open economy model, such international compensation payments can be represented by an increase in foreign exchange available

---

[7] See, for example, Alix-Garcia *et al.* (2008); Barbier (2008); Bulte *et al.* (2008); Grieg-Gran *et al.* (2005); Pagiola *et al.* (2005); Wunder (2008); and Zilberman *et al.* (2008).

to supplement export earnings and thus allow additional imports of consumer goods; i.e., (5.2) becomes

$$px + s = m, \tag{5.11}$$

and the economy's welfare function is

$$W = \int_0^\infty \left[U(q - x, px + s) + B(A) - C(c) \right] e^{-rt} dt. \tag{5.12}$$

The first-order conditions and the long-run steady state equations are unchanged for the open economy. But a change in international payments s has the following comparative static effects on the equilibrium level of ecological landscape A^* and exports x^*

$$\frac{dx^*}{ds} = \frac{pU_{22}\delta}{\Delta} < 0, \quad \frac{dA^*}{ds} = -\frac{\gamma pU_{22}}{\Delta} > 0. \tag{5.13}$$

The effect of an increased payment for ecosystem services is to reduce long-run exports but increase landscape conservation. The payments substitute for exports and thus reduce the pressure in the long run to convert more ecological landscape for development.

The slope of the optimal conversion path in the open economy is still determined by (5.10) and, as before, $d\mu = rdu - \gamma dx - \delta dA$. But now, from differentiating (5.5) but keeping the terms of trade unchanged, one obtains $ds = \dfrac{\alpha}{pU_{22}} dx + \dfrac{\beta}{pU_{22}} dA$, which indicates that an increase in international payments has a negative influence on exports and ecological landscape. From (5.10), the slope of the optimal landscape conversion trajectory becomes more negative, or steeper, due to a rise in s. That is, $\mu(t)$ will rise more quickly and c fall more rapidly as a result of the increase in payments.

In addition, the isocline locus $B'(A^*)'$ shifts to the left, but the isocline $-U_1 f'(A^*)$ shifts even more to the right, and the equilibrium landscape level A^* rises.[8] The changes in the slope of the optimal land conversion path and in the long-run amount of landscape conservation ensure that the initial value of μ must increase (i.e., becomes less negative). An increase in μ_0 (which means its absolute value falls) corresponds to a decline in c_0. Conversion starts lower initially, and then

---

[8] Note that $\dfrac{B''}{r} \dfrac{dA^*}{ds} < 0$ and $-U_{11}(f')^2 \dfrac{dA^*}{ds} > 0$.

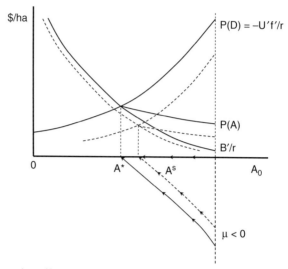

Figure 5.6 The effects of a rise in international payments for ecosystem services

decreases rapidly over time. Because of the fixed landscape area A_0, less conversion of ecological landscape occurs in the long run.

These effects of a rise in international payments for ecosystem services on the steady state ecological landscape area and the transition path are depicted in Figure 5.6, with the changes represented by the dotted lines in the figure. The new long-run ecological landscape area is A_s.

Policy implications

It might be tempting to conclude that, if the world community wants to induce the small open economy to conserve more ecological landscape, it could either provide more payment for ecosystem services, or alternatively, employ trade interventions that lowered the economy's terms of trade. However, recall that the effects of a change in p require that the economy have normal import dependency conditions. If instead $|\eta| > 1$, then trade interventions that lower p could actually produce counter-productive results and lead to more landscape conversion. More complex open economy models that consider land conversion often indicate that trade interventions have ambiguous impacts on conserving natural habitat and ecosystems.[9]

A second difficulty in employing trade interventions to influence conservation policies in natural-resource exporting countries is the complexity of the relationship between global commodity markets and natural resource exploitation. For example, Sohngen *et al.* (1999) model how rising global demand and prices in global timber markets may affect forest management and conservation. They find that higher future demand is expected to increase prices, investments in regeneration, and establishment of plantations as the principal means of expanding global timber supply. Although the total volume is low in both tropical and boreal forests, small price changes can have a substantial impact on harvest from those regions. The harvests in these forests are also sensitive to interest rate increases, access costs, management intensity, and plantation costs. Yet, generally, despite rising demand and prices, the model predicts that large areas of remote forests are likely to remain inaccessible for timber exploitation for the foreseeable future. But the authors note two important caveats to their results. First, to the extent that greater forest protection for biodiversity conservation or carbon sequestration in one region of the world leads to upward pressure on timber prices, it could lead to greater exploitation of previously inaccessible forests in tropical and boreal regions. Second, regardless of the effects of global timber market and price trends, deforestation may still occur in boreal and tropical ecosystems because of the demand for agricultural land conversion, lack of effective tenure and property right regimes, and government subsidies and other policy failures.

Macroeconomic influences and trade policy also have complicated impacts on land conversion in developing countries, making it difficult for trade interventions to work effectively to alter land use change. Depreciation in the real exchange rate increases deforestation in developing countries, and short-term macroeconomic policy, institutional factors, and their interactions are potentially important determinants of environmental conservation outcomes (Arcand *et al.*

[9] See, for example, Barbier and Schulz (1997); Bulte and Barbier (2005); Hartwick *et al.* (2001); Jinji (2006); Polasky *et al.* (2004); and Smulders *et al.* (2004).

2008). An analysis by López and Galinato (2005) indicates that trade openness and economic growth promote three key factors behind deforestation in Brazil, Indonesia, Malaysia, and the Philippines: poverty, agricultural land expansion, and road building. In addition, economic growth has a negative and relatively large direct impact on forest cover in all four countries. Similarly, Naidoo (2004) finds that from 1960 to 1999, economic growth in over seventy developing economies is positively associated with tropical deforestation.

Finally, a number of studies point to the complex interactions that occur between corruption and terms of trade changes to affect natural capital depletion in developing countries. For example, a statistical analysis of agricultural land expansion in 101 developing economies over 1960–1999 indicates that a rise in terms of trade, an increase in agricultural export share, and greater corruption lead directly to more agricultural land expansion (Barbier 2004). However, both greater corruption and increased agricultural export share tend to dissipate, rather than augment, the influence of a rise in the terms of trade on agricultural expansion. One possible explanation is that improved terms of trade and a more corruptible government will lead to higher bribes being paid for any given level of land conversion, thus slowing additional conversion. In addition, improved terms of trade coupled with a higher agricultural export share will lead to greater foreign exchange earnings for any given level of land conversion, also slowing conversion. According to Wunder (2003, 2005), there may also be another interaction effect between corruption and terms of trade changes for those tropical countries that also export oil. For example, if the terms of trade appreciation is due to an oil boom, then the result is usually higher rents in the oil and nontrade goods sectors. Corruptible officials will therefore be able to enrich themselves by diverting more resources away from non-oil primary product sectors, including agriculture, that are mainly responsible for deforestation. The result is again a slowing down of agricultural land expansion and forest conversion. For a broad range of natural capital stocks – fossil fuel energy stocks, metals and minerals, and forest resources – corruption is an important conduit through which natural resource use, trade, and geography in African and Asian countries influences indirectly long-run growth performance (Barbier 2010). Such a result confirms similar findings of how corruption and other institutional factors are important "transmission channels" between trade, natural resource abundance, and long-run growth across economies.[10]

Given such complications associated with trade interventions, payments for ecosystem services seem to be a preferred option for encouraging ecological landscape conservation. However, current efforts to establish international payments for ecosystem services have some limitations, too, as an effective mechanism for spurring global ecosystem conservation.

As noted above, such markets to establish "payment" for providing ecosystem services in developing regions have largely focused on forest systems, and mainly four services from such systems: carbon sequestration, watershed protection, biodiversity benefits, and landscape beauty (Barbier 2008; Grieg-Gran *et al.* 2005; Pagiola *et al.* 2005; Wunder 2008). Beginning in the 1990s, payment for ecosystem services started principally in Latin America, but in recent years it has been adopted in Sub-Saharan Africa and Asia. Hydrological services from watershed protection tend to predominate, although carbon sequestration schemes through the Clean Development Mechanism (CDM) of the Kyoto Protocol have expanded in recent years. One reason that countries and companies are increasingly eager to finance forestry sector CDM projects in developing countries to meet Kyoto obligations is that carbon sequestration costs in tropical regions are significantly lower compared to other locations; e.g., forest CDM projects in Europe cost around $777 per tonne of carbon sequestered whereas in the tropics the most expensive projects cost $128 per tonne of carbon sequestered (van Kooten *et al.* 2007).

There are three principal ways in which market mechanisms for ecosystem services might also alleviate poverty. First, if payments for ecosystem services are made directly to poor rural households to maintain or enhance these services, then they provide needed cash income. Second, whether or not the rural poor receive direct payments, they may benefit indirectly from any resulting improvement in the provision of ecosystem services. Third, the rural poor may also gain from any additional economic opportunities created by payment schemes,

---

[10] See, for example, Aidt (2009); Brunnschweiler (2008); Brunnschweiler and Bulte (2008a, 2008b); Bulte *et al.* (2005); Isham *et al.* (2005); López *et al.* (2007); Papyrakis and Gerlagh (2004); van der Ploeg and Poelhekke (2009, 2010).

such as the employment created by reforestation or other conservation investments. However, in all these instances, there appears to be limits on the success of payment schemes in alleviating poverty.

To date, the main purpose of introducing payment for ecosystem services is to influence land use decisions by enabling landholders to capture more of the value of these environmental services than they would have done in the absence of the mechanism. While in some cases participants in such schemes do not have to demonstrate formal land titles to be eligible for payments, many of the rural poor in developing regions lack not only formal but also actual access to land. Others are near-landless or have holdings so small that they would have difficulty in participating in forest protection or planting schemes on their land. In Latin America, the land users who receive payments for preserving the hydrological services of watersheds tend to be wealthier households, and in at least one case, such as Costa Rica's program, many participants were urban dwellers with substantial nonagricultural income (Pagiola *et al.* 2005). Similarly, the payment for forest ecosystem services in Mexico is specifically targeted to community-owned forests, and although 86.3 percent of the hectares enrolled belong to poor communities, only 31 percent of the participating households are classified as being below the poverty line (Alix-Garcia *et al.* 2008).

Programs paying for ecological services may have unintended side effects for the poor, both positive and negative. In Indian watersheds, community cooperation in managing forest commons was enhanced for villages participating in payment schemes. But the livelihoods of the landless who could not participate, such as women and herders, were harmed if their access to forest commons for gathering non-timber products was restricted by the schemes (Kerr 2002). In Latin America, some programs are thought to have improved tenure security by granting legal status to idle forest land and providing protection against squatting or land invasions. However, by increasing the value of marginal land, some payment schemes for ecosystem services have created incentives for more wealthy groups to appropriate the land, especially if tenure and ownership are in dispute (Engle *et al.* 2008; Grieg-Gran *et al.* 2005; Jack *et al.* 2008; Pagiola *et al.* 2005; Wunder 2008). Finally, payment programs can also have mixed effects on employment opportunities for the landless poor. Ecosystem service schemes that result in considerable replanting or afforestation in rural areas can generate significant demand for unskilled labor; alternatively, if the introduced schemes set aside large areas of local forests that would otherwise have been logged or converted to agriculture, then there may be less work for the landless poor (Grieg-Gran *et al.* 2005).

In sum, because their primary aim is to provide incentives to landowners for protecting critical ecosystems and habitat, payment programs for ecosystem services cannot always be targeted to areas of high poverty. Nor can such schemes always guarantee high participation rates by the rural poor or that their livelihoods will be significantly improved. By definition, the landless and near landless are often excluded. Nevertheless, wherever possible, the payment schemes should be designed to enhance the participation of the poor, to reduce any negative impacts on nonparticipants while creating additional job opportunities for rural workers, and to provide technical assistance, access to inputs, credit, and other support to encourage poor smallholders to adopt the desired land use practices. More effort must be devoted to designing projects and programs that include the direct participation of the landless and near landless, given the high concentration of the rural poor in "fragile environments" that contain many important global ecosystems (Barbier 2008).

The case of REDD

A good example of an international scheme designed to pay for global ecosystem services is the current efforts to establish a financial mechanism to reduce emissions from deforestation and forest degradation (REDD) in developing countries. The 1992 Kyoto Protocol for controlling global greenhouse gas (GHG) emissions excluded emission reduction credits for avoided deforestation by developing countries.[11] To redress this problem, the United Nations Framework Convention on Climate Change (UNFCC) has made progress in developing a REDD mechanism. The UNFCC's Conference of the Parties in Bali, Indonesia in December 2007, endorsed the implementation of a pilot

---

[11] Under the Clean Development Mechanism (CDM) established by the Kyoto Protocol, it is possible for a developing country to gain credits for carbon emission reduction through an afforestation or reforestation project. However, Karsenty (2008) maintains that only one such project out of 1,132 registered CDM projects has been successfully implemented.

phase for a REDD scheme up to 2012, when the Kyoto Protocol expires, in anticipation that an international financial mechanism will become part of a post-2012 climate agreement to reduce global carbon emissions.

In September 2008, a pilot initiative was established by several UN agencies as the United Nations collaborative program on Reducing Emissions from Deforestation and forest Degradation (UN-REDD) in developing countries. UN-REDD currently has funding of $75 million from Norway, Denmark, and Spain (UN-REDD 2010). It operates in nine pilot countries, and provides technical assistance on the measurement, reporting, and verification of carbon emissions and flows, remote sensing, and greenhouse gas inventories.[12] The program also offers guidance on how to design and implement REDD schemes that promote carbon storage, biodiversity conservation, and other environmental benefits of forests. Other areas of work include support for national forest assessments, monitoring policy and institutional change, and facilitating consultation with stakeholders, including indigenous peoples and local communities. The overall aim of the program is to promote REDD financing as a means to reduce carbon emissions through forest conservation and management, and to help prepare developing countries for a future global REDD mechanism.

Several studies indicate that a fully developed and properly designed REDD mechanism could yield considerable benefits in terms of reducing global deforestation and carbon emissions (Bosetti *et al.* 2009; Ebeling and Yasué 2008; Kindermann *et al.* 2008; Strassburg *et al.* 2009). Forest degradation and deforestation currently contribute around 12 percent of global greenhouse gas emissions from human activities (van der Werf *et al.* 2009). The remaining tropical forests may contain up to two-thirds of all species (Dirzo and Raven 2003). Evidence from Panama also suggests that REDD schemes that compensate poor rural households for forest conservation potentially offer significantly more benefits and incentives to households compared to small-scale afforestation and reforestation projects currently allowed under the CDM of the Kyoto Protocol (Coomes *et al.* 2008).[13]

---

[12] The nine pilot countries participating in UN-REDD are Bolivia, Democratic Republic of Congo, Indonesia, Panama, Papua New Guinea, Paraguay, Tanzania, Vietnam, and Zambia.

[13] For example, Coomes *et al.* (2008, p. 211) find that, for a typical CDM afforestation or reforestation project, "the primary impediments for adoption

Thus, it is widely believed that a global REDD financing mechanism could serve as an important incentive to conserve forests in developing countries, thus lessening GHG emissions, biodiversity loss, and ecological degradation.

For example, one prediction is that a successful REDD scheme could reduce 90 percent of global deforestation at an annual cost of $30 billion (Strassburg *et al.* 2009). Alternatively, Kindermann *et al.* (2008) suggest that a REDD program that lessens global deforestation by 10 percent from 2005 to 2030 could provide 0.3–0.6 gigatonnes (Gt) in carbon dioxide (CO_2) equivalent GHG emission reductions at an annual cost of $0.4–1.7 billion for thirty years. A 50 percent reduction in global deforestation could yield 1.5–2.7 Gt in GHG emission reductions at a cost of $17.2–28.0 billion per year. In addition to a stand-alone scheme, REDD could be implemented as part of a post-2012 global climate agreement. Bosetti *et al.* (2009) examine the effects of combining a REDD mechanism within a global policy to stabilize GHG emissions at 550 parts per million per volume by 2050. Introducing REDD reduces global forestry emissions by 64% to 88%, lowers the total costs of the climate policy by 10% to 25%, and decreases carbon prices by 8% to 26%. Similarly, Ebeling and Yasué (2008) estimate that reducing global deforestation rates in developing economies through linkage with a global carbon market could generate annual carbon credit financing for developing countries of $2.2–13.5 billion.

However, monitoring and verifying changes in deforestation rates in developing countries and their impacts on carbon emissions could increase substantially the transaction costs of implementing a REDD scheme. Transaction costs for avoided deforestation and afforestation projects in developing countries currently range from $0.03–4.05 per tonne of CO_2 equivalent GHG emissions abated (Kindermann *et al.* 2008). Establishing deforestation and carbon storage baselines is also problematic, and potentially expensive on a large scale, although

by asset-poor households are more economic in nature than financial – high labor demands, sunk costs and illiquidity, and production and price risk – in absolute terms and, importantly, relative to the best alternate land use, i.e., pasture and cattle raising." In comparison, an avoided deforestation project "has the potential advantages for households of positive financial returns, low labor investment, positive insurance value (sell trees if contract fails) and high perceived equity as well as conserved ecological integrity."

new methods of creating reference scenarios show promise (Olander *et al.* 2008). But solving the baseline problem is not simply a technical issue. A successful global REDD mechanism requires international agreement on how to construct a baseline for tropical deforestation and its carbon emissions across countries. This would most likely require using past rates of deforestation and emissions to predict future trends or to set quantitative national targets for deforestation. But as emphasized by Karsenty (2008, p. 455), "robust predictions of future deforestation seem unlikely given the complex interactions of factors commanding the pace of deforestation," such as changing agricultural prices and poor forest governance, in many developing countries containing tropical forests. The risk of poor targets and baselines is the ultimate transaction cost: countries will be rewarded with carbon credits for "fake emission reductions" from avoided deforestation, "which would flood the main carbon market and ruin collective efforts to maintain a sufficiently high price of emission permits in the energy and industrial sector."

A second concern is that a carbon market for avoided deforestation may not necessarily preserve biodiversity and other forest ecosystem services (Ebeling and Yasué 2008; Grainger *et al.* 2009; Levin *et al.* 2008; Venter *et al.* 2009). As summarized by Ebeling and Yasué (2008, p. 1921), "carbon markets value carbon not biodiversity and are designed to focus on the lowest cost options for generating emission reductions. They will thus favour areas with low land-use opportunity costs which may not coincide with areas of high conservation priorities." For example, one analysis shows that, if a global REDD scheme focuses solely on cost-effectively reducing carbon emissions, its biodiversity benefits are low, protecting only slightly more vertebrate species than if funds were allocated randomly among tropical forest countries (Venter *et al.* 2009). Others argue that "recognition of forests under the climate regime could detract from more encompassing policies that aim to protect all ecosystem services of forests, and could potentially lead to policy fragmentation and further preclude a global regime on forests" (Levin *et al.* 2008, p. 547).

Some suggest that these possible conflicts between conservation and carbon storage goals could be reconciled through incorporating explicit rules and targets for biodiversity within REDD. For example, Grainger *et al.* (2009, p. R975) maintain that "the UNFCCC does not have a mandate to protect biodiversity, but mitigating climate change should not harm biodiversity," which could be achieved through including within REDD financial support to sustain existing protected areas or create new ones and requiring mandatory assessments of the biodiversity and ecosystem service impacts of all projects. Venter *et al.* (2009) show that, if potential REDD funds were carefully targeted to protect biodiversity as well, ecosystem benefits could be doubled while incurring just a 4–8 percent reduction in carbon storage. The key to the outcome is explicitly including biodiversity values into carbon payments under REDD.

Finally, there is the concern that the global scale of REDD could have an impact on world agricultural production and markets. For example, the cost estimates by Kindermann *et al.* (2008), which suggest that a 50 percent reduction in global deforestation through REDD could cost $17–28 billion per year, comprise considerable losses in foregone agricultural and timber values. However, others maintain that such opportunity costs may be over-estimated. For example, Angelsen (2010) argues that, "the relatively low cost opportunity costs of avoided deforestation, particularly for the initial reductions, suggest the conflict between production and conservation is modest."

In sum, REDD is seen by many as the ideal way of overcoming the chronic problem of inadequate forest conservation funding in developing countries. International funding for all forestry initiatives currently amounts to around $1.1 billion annually, with the amount spent on forest protection comprising a much lower amount of this total. In comparison, reducing global deforestation by 10 percent could, through a REDD scheme, attract $2.2–13.5 billion in annual carbon finance (Ebeling and Yasué 2008). However, the many complications associated with negotiating, designing, implementing, and verifying global REDD financing have led some to conclude that developing an alternative mechanism to tackle deforestation directly would be more appropriate. For example, Karsenty (2008) argues that a more effective approach would be to establish an international fund to support policies and measures to reduce deforestation directly, which should be targeted towards local actors causing deforestation, protecting remaining forest areas, and policies to develop better land tenure systems, agricultural organization and practices, and good forest governance.

Do we really care about global ecosystems?

As the quote from David Pearce at the beginning of this chapter indicates, perhaps the biggest obstacle to developing an international system for payment of global ecosystem services is insufficient economic incentives. That is, do we really care enough about global ecosystem services to design an international payment mechanism to cover the considerable opportunity, implementation, and monitoring costs involved?

Pearce clearly thinks that the answer is "no." He cites as evidence that, at best, the world spends around $10 billion annually on ecosystem conservation, yet the benefits of such conservation are more likely in the range of "hundreds of billions" of dollars (Pearce 2007). What is more, although the number of protected areas in the world continue to grow, they are seriously underfunded, perhaps as much as 40% globally and as high as 100% in Africa, 140% in Latin America, 450% in North Africa and the Middle East, and 500% in Asia (James *et al.* 1999).

Yet, in theory, an international system for payment of global ecosystem services could overcome this funding gap. For example, Farley *et al.* (2010) argue that some of the funds raised through a global cap and auction system for GHG emissions among wealthy nations could be diverted to fund international payment for ecosystem services, with the financing apportioned to targeted countries in accordance with how well they meet specific criteria for the provision of global ecosystem services. Similarly, as we saw above in the case of REDD, the annual cost of reducing global deforestation by 10 percent may be around $0.4–1.7 billion but the additional financing through carbon markets could earn developing countries $2.2–13.5 billion annually (Ebeling and Yasué 2008; Kindermann *et al.* 2008).

If the global benefits of ecosystems exceed the costs of conservation, and if an international system to pay for these services can provide billions of dollars in the extra funding needed for ecosystem protection, why hasn't the international community set up such a system? Again, there appear to be strong disincentives to negotiating and implementing such an agreement.

The incentive problem can be illustrated simply, from drawing on insights on past negotiations towards international agreements for global biodiversity and tropical forest conservation (Barbier 2001;

Barrett 1994; Sandler 1993). For example, Sandler (1993) shows that one important incentive in favor of tropical forest conservation is that the international community is bargaining over ways to save a rapidly "shrinking" resource and, as a result, they will want to negotiate an agreement fairly quickly. Reaching an agreement in the near term may mean that developed countries pay more for tropical forest preservation, thus reducing their net share of global benefits. Nevertheless, such an outcome might be preferred to the two alternatives: first, holding out for a later agreement that reduces costs, but which leads to much less forest conservation and global benefits, or second, no agreement at all. However, Sandler also identifies two incentives that could work against an early agreement. First, free-riding may occur within the developed country coalition. Even though all countries will gain from the global benefit, given the high costs of forest conservation, some wealthy countries may try to forego contributing to these costs in the hope that other developed countries will cover them fully. Second, any negotiated agreement involves substantial transaction costs for a signatory. Each country must expend resources to reach and enforce a bargained outcome.

Barrett (1994) demonstrates that these two disincentives are not trivial, and explains why it has been so difficult to establish international financing for implementing the 1992 Convention on Biological Diversity. In particular, because each developed country has an incentive to free-ride on the compensation payments made by other wealthy nations, an international agreement must be self-enforcing, but such an agreement is less likely, the larger the number of countries involved in the negotiations. On the other hand, if a developed country finds that its costs of negotiating and implementing a global biodiversity conservation fund are small relative to the benefits gained, then it will have an incentive to reach an agreement. But given the substantial transaction costs involved, the realized net benefits to a single country may not be substantially higher than in the absence of such an agreement. In other words, a single country may find its net benefits to be just as large if it acts unilaterally to conserve biodiversity, either within its own country or perhaps by funding conservation in other countries, rather than negotiating and contributing to a global biodiversity conservation fund. Of particular concern, however, is the situation in which developed countries have weak incentives to conserve biodiversity unilaterally, yet greater global benefits would arise if more

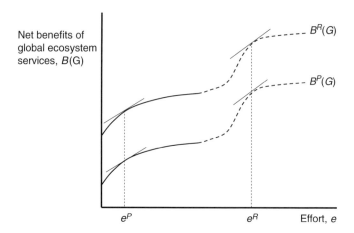

Notes: *R* = Rich (developed) countries
P = Poor (developing) countries

Figure 5.7 The provision of global ecosystem services
Notes: R = Rich (developed) countries
P = Poor (developing) countries
Source: Adapted from Barbier (2001, Figure 2).

biodiversity were protected. Under such a scenario, unfortunately, an international agreement for financing global biodiversity conservation is unlikely.

Barbier (2001) incorporates aspects of both the analysis by Barrett (1994) and Sandler (1993) to examine further the incentives for funding global biodiversity conservation.[14] The analysis is also applicable to the process of establishing a system of international payments for ecosystem services. The outcome is depicted in Figure 5.7.

As indicated in Figure 5.7, assume that there are two coalitions concerned with global ecosystem services, one composed of rich (or developed) countries, *R*, and the other of poor (or developing) countries, *P*. The horizontal axis depicts the amount of effort that each coalition invests in provision of global ecosystem services, *G*. These services are diverse, and could include the informational content of genetic material of species that could be used for medicines or crop

---

[14] As indicated by Barbier (2001), the original inspiration for the analysis is the two-agent model of common property resource management developed by Baland and Platteau (1997).

breeding; ecotourism and other international recreational benefits; transboundary services, such as carbon storage, climate stabilization, watershed protection, and support for marine fisheries; and various nonuse values. The benefits – or willingness to pay – for these various global ecosystem services are likely to be higher for wealthy as opposed to poor nations.[15]

However, as indicated in Figure 5.7, the net benefits of global ecosystem services to both sets of countries are convex, due to the presence of ecological thresholds and feedback effects that can increase the risk of ecological collapse (see Chapters 2 and 6). That is, large shocks or sustained disturbances to ecosystems can set in motion a series of interactions that can breach ecological thresholds, causing the systems to "flip" irreversibly from one functioning state to another.[16] Large-scale landscape conversion is considered one type of irreversible, sustained disturbance that can increase the threat of ecosystem collapse (Busing and White 1993; Dobson *et al.* 2006; Lotze *et al.* 2006; Peterson *et al.* 1998; Turner *et al.* 1993). As shown in Figure 5.7, if less effort is devoted to protecting the world's remaining ecosystems, and thus more large-scale conversion and degradation occurs, then there is likely to be a discontinuous fall in the global net benefits provided to all countries.

In addition, global ecosystems are clearly a shrinking resource, as the evidence discussed earlier suggests. Because of the continuing threats of landscape conversion and ecosystem degradation, there is no guarantee that the higher levels of global net benefits provided by ecosystem services can be attained in the future. Hence, the higher levels of $B^R(G)$ and $B^P(G)$ are indicated as dotted lines in Figure 5.7.

Figure 5.7 suggests that there are two possible outcomes in the provision of global ecosystem services.

First, in the absence of any incentive by the rich countries to invest any additional effort in conserving the world's remaining ecosystems,

---

[15] Although there are relatively few cross-country comparisons of the willingness to pay (WTP) for global ecosystem services, valuation studies generally show that the WTP of individuals from developing countries for such services is generally lower than for individuals from richer countries, or at the very least, that most such services are positively correlated with per capita income. See, for example, Hanley and Barbier (2009) for a review.

[16] See, for example, Batabayal *et al.* (2003); Dasgupta and Mäler (2003); Elmqvist *et al.* (2003); Holling (1973); Levin (1999); May (1975); Murray (1993); Perrings (1998); Pimm (1984); Scheffer *et al.* (2001).

protection would fall mainly to the poor countries, who would contribute only effort level e^P. Although they may be supported through multilateral and bilateral assistance, as shown in the figure, this level of effort is low – perhaps corresponding to the $10 billion annually that the world spends on ecosystem conservation, mainly in developing countries (Pearce 2007). Currently, as long as the remaining ecosystems exist, more global net benefits from their services are provided. But the risk is that, as population and development pressures cause more ecosystem loss and degradation, only the lower levels of global net benefits can be assured of protection.

Second, under certain conditions, the incentive of a shrinking resource could also produce a different outcome. As shown in Figure 5.7, if rich countries are sufficiently concerned about the loss and degradation of the world's remaining ecosystems, and given that developed countries benefit the most from global ecosystem services, they may be willing to contribute sufficient funds to finance a large international effort to maintain and protect ecosystems, e^R. Although all countries gain from the additional global benefits provided, it is the wealthier nations that are now financing the increased effort, which would presumably be in the form of a major international payment for an ecosystem services scheme to compensate developing countries for extra ecosystem protection.

But suppose that developed countries are still undecided as to whether or not to fund the additional effort level e^R, and thus only poor countries are contributing to ecosystem protection. At this level of conservation effort, e^P, the net benefits of global ecosystem services are relatively low. Although global net benefits would be higher if rich countries decided to fund e^R, and disappearing ecosystems give them an incentive to do so, wealthy nations may still not agree to finance and implement an international payment scheme for ecosystem services. For one, the developed countries may have different preferences for global ecosystem services. The net benefits $B^R(G)$ in Figure 5.7 represent the median level across all rich countries in the coalition. Individual countries may vary considerably in their preferences of global ecosystem services, as well as their willingness to pay for the costs of conservation. If there are a number of developed countries that have weak incentives to protect global ecosystems, reaching an agreement among the coalition to finance increasing protection effort is unlikely; or, if such an agreement can be negotiated, it will fund a collective effort well below e^R. Even if all developed countries derive similar net benefits from global ecosystem services, there is still the free-rider problem. Any rich country that refuses to cooperate in providing the full e^R level of protection would still gain if others provided this protection instead. If only a few rich countries are willing to cooperate to provide financing of e^R, they may not wish to subsidize the larger number of non-cooperating (and free-riding) developed countries. Once again, the most likely outcome is an international payments scheme that is underwritten by only a handful of rich countries, but provides a level of protection much lower than e^R, or no agreement on a scheme at all.

Final remarks

Much of the world's remaining ecosystems are located in the tropics. As the developing economies in this region expand their economic activities, combat poverty, and absorb growing populations, greater ecosystem loss and degradation will ensue. But many of these economies are also highly dependent on exploiting their natural resource endowments to provide primary products for world markets. By using trade interventions to influence the terms of trade for the primary product exports of small open economies, it may be possible to deter them from converting more ecosystems. But, as shown in this chapter, this is an undesirable way of controlling ecosystem degradation in small open economies. Alternatively, international payments for ecosystem services compensate developing economies for conserving rather than converting ecological landscapes.

By extending the natural asset model to apply to a small open economy, this chapter was able to explore how the effects of trade, changes in terms of trade, and the international payment of ecosystem services influence ecological landscape conversion. The open economy model confirms the findings of many empirical studies that there are complications in using trade interventions to coerce developing economies to conserve rather than convert more ecological landscape. Although compensating developing countries to encourage more ecosystem conservation appears to be theoretically more straightforward, current efforts at establishing payments for ecosystem services in developing countries need to overcome some limitations if they are to become an effective global conservation mechanism.

For one, the range of ecosystem services must be extended to cover more than carbon sequestration, watershed protection, biodiversity benefits, and landscape beauty. In addition, schemes must be reformed and expanded to enhance their potential to alleviate rural poverty. Either more payments need to be made directly to the rural poor, or they should benefit in other ways, such as from the improved ecosystem services, from greater technical assistance, inputs, credit, and other support, or from the generation of employment opportunities. In addition, projects and programs need to find ways of benefiting the landless and near landless.

Although progress has been made in establishing international payments for global ecosystem services, most notably a nascent financial mechanism to reduce emissions from deforestation and forest degradation (REDD), several important concerns have arisen. Monitoring and verifying changes in deforestation rates in developing countries and their impacts on carbon emissions could increase substantially the transaction costs of implementing a REDD scheme on a global scale. In addition, a carbon market for avoided deforestation may not necessarily be the best way of protecting forests that yield other global ecosystem services. There is also concern over the high opportunity costs faced by many developing countries from losses in foregone agricultural and timber benefits. These issues need to be resolved if there is to be a successful REDD financial mechanism implemented on a global scale.

Currently, the UN pilot REDD program has attracted just $75 million in funding from three developed countries – Norway, Denmark, and Spain. And, at best, total global spending on ecosystem conservation amounts to around $10 billion annually. Although the number of protected areas around the world continues to grow, they are underfunded, especially in developing regions. Given the essential goods and services provided by ecosystems worldwide, including many important global services, and the growing problem of ecological scarcity, more international financing to boost efforts to protect the world's remaining ecosystems is urgently required. Yet, as we explored in this chapter, there are important economic incentives that deter the establishment of large-scale international financial mechanisms for payment of ecosystem services.

Unfortunately, what this implies is that the best outcome that we can hope for currently is an international payments scheme that is underwritten by only a handful of rich countries, and which is capable of providing a level of global ecosystem protection that is only slightly more than current efforts. Although they may be supported through multilateral and bilateral assistance, developing countries will continue to bear the direct and opportunity costs of ecosystem conservation for the foreseeable future. Clearly, this is an unsustainable state of affairs, especially given the growing problem of ecological scarcity globally. But to overcome the economic disincentives that are reinforcing such an outcome, the international community needs to think more creatively as to how to agree, design, implement, and verify international mechanisms for payment of ecosystem services. This is an issue that we will return to in the final chapter of this book.

References

Aidt, T.S. 2009. "Corruption, institutions, and economic development." *Oxford Review of Economic Policy* 25(2):271–291.

Alix-Garcia, J., A. De Janvry, and E. Sadoulet. 2008. "The role of deforestation risk and calibrated compensation in designing payments for environmental services." *Environment and Development Economics* 13:375–394.

Angelsen, A. 2010. "Policies for reduced deforestation and their impact on agricultural production." *Proceedings of the National Academy of Sciences* 107(46):19639–19644.

Arcand, J-L., P. Guillaumont, and S. Guillaumot Jeanneney. 2008. "Deforestation and the real exchange rate." *Journal of Development Economics* 86:242–262.

Baland, J.-M. and J.-P. Platteau. 1997. "Wealth, inequality and efficiency in the commons; part 1: the unregulated case." *Oxford Economic Papers* 49:451–482.

Barbier, E.B. 2001. "Biodiversity, trade and international agreements." *Journal of Economic Studies* 27(1/2):55–74.

2004. "Explaining agricultural land expansion and deforestation in developing countries." *American Journal of Agricultural Economics* 86(5):1347–1353.

2005. *Natural Resources and Economic Development*. Cambridge University Press.

2008. "Poverty, development, and ecological services." *International Review of Environmental and Resource Economics* 2:1–27.

2009. "Ecosystems as natural assets." *Foundations and Trends in Microeconomics* 4(8):611–681.

2010. "Corruption and the political economy of resource-based development: a comparison of Asia and Sub-Saharan Africa." *Environmental and Resource Economics* 46:511–537.

2011. *Scarcity and Frontiers: How Economies Have Developed Through Natural Resource Exploitation.* Cambridge University Press.

Barbier, E.B. and M. Rauscher. 1994. "Trade, tropical deforestation and policy interventions." *Environmental and Resource Economics* 4:75–90.

Barbier, E.B. and C.E. Schulz. 1997. "Wildlife, biodiversity and trade." *Environment and Development Economics* 2:145–172.

Barrett, S. 1994. "The biodiversity supergame." *Environmental and Resource Economics* 4:111–122.

Batabayal, A.A., J.R. Kahn, and R.V. O'Neil. 2003. "On the scarcity value of ecosystem services." *Journal of Environmental Economics and Management* 46:334–352.

Beddington, J.R., D.J. Agnew, and C.W. Clark. 2007. "Current problems in the management of marine fisheries." *Science* 316:1713–1716.

Bellon, M.R., D. Hodson, D. Bergvinson *et al.* 2005. "Targeting agricultural research to benefit poor farmers: relating poverty mapping to maize environments in Mexico." *Food Policy* 30:476–492.

Bosetti, V., R. Lubowski, A. Golub, and A. Markandya. 2009. "Linking reduced deforestation and a global carbon market." Fondazione Eni Enrico Mattei Working Paper Series 56. Fondazione Eni Enrico Mattei, Milan, Italy.

Brunnschweiler, C. 2008. "Cursing the blessings? Natural resource abundance, institutions, and economic growth." *World Development* 36(3):399–419.

Brunnschweiler, C. and E.H. Bulte. 2008a. "Linking natural resources to slow growth and more conflict." *Science* 320:616–617.

2008b. "The resource curse revisited and revised: a tale of paradoxes and red herrings." *Journal of Environmental Economics and Management* 55(3):248–264.

Bulte, E.H. and E.B. Barbier. 2005. "Trade and renewable resources in a second-best world: an overview." *Environmental and Resource Economics* 30:423–463.

Bulte, E.H., R. Damania, and R.T. Deacon, 2005. "Resource intensity, institutions and development." *World Development* 33:1029–1044.

Bulte, E.H., R.B. Boone, R. Stringer, and P.K. Thornton. 2008. "Elephants or onions? Paying for nature in Amboseli, Kenya." *Environment and Development Economics* 13:395–414.

Busing, R.T. and P.S. White. 1993. "Effects of area on old-growth forest attributes: implications for equilibrium landscape concept." *Landscape Ecology* 8:119–126.

Chen, S. and M. Ravallion. 2007. "Absolute poverty measures for the developing world, 1981–2004." *Proceedings of the National Academy of Sciences* 104(43):16757–16762.

Collier, P. 2007. "Poverty reduction in Africa." *Proceedings of the National Academy of Sciences* 104(43):16763–16768.

Comprehensive Assessment of Water Management in Agriculture. 2007. *Water for Food, Water for Life: A Comprehensive Assessment of Water Management in Agriculture.* London, Earthscan; and International Water Management Institute, Colombo, Sri Lanka.

Coomes, O., F. Grimard, C. Potvin, and P. Sima. 2008. "The fate of the tropical forest: carbon or cattle?" *Ecological Economics* 65(2): 207–212.

Dasgupta, P.S. and K.-G. Mäler. 2003. "The economics of non-convex ecosystems: an introduction." *Environmental and Resource Economics* 26:499–525.

Dasgupta, S., U. Deichmann, C. Meisner, and D. Wheeler. 2005. "Where is the poverty-environment nexus? Evidence from Cambodia, Lao PDR, and Vietnam." *World Development* 33(4):617–638.

Dercon, S. 2006. "Economic reform, growth and the poor: evidence from rural Ethiopia." *Journal of Development Economics* 81:1–24.

Dirzo, R. and P.H. Raven. 2003. "Global state of biodiversity and loss." *Annual Review of Environment and Resources* 28:137–167.

Dobson, A., D. Lodge, J. Alder *et al.* 2006. "Habitat loss, trophic collapse, and the decline of ecosystem services." *Ecology* 87:1915–1924.

Ebeling, J. and M. Yasué. 2008. "Generating carbon finance through avoided deforestation and its potential to create climatic, conservation and human development benefits." *Philosophical Transactions of the Royal Society B* 363:1917–1924.

Elmqvist, T., C. Folke, M. Nyström *et al.* 2003. "Response diversity, ecosystem change, and resilience." *Frontiers in Ecology and the Environment* 1:488–494.

Engel, S., S. Pagiola, and S. Wunder. 2008. "Payments for environmental services in theory and practice: an overview of the issues." *Ecological Economics* 65:663–674.

Farley, J., A. Aquino, A. Daniels *et al.* 2010. "Global mechanisms for sustaining and enhancing PES schemes." *Ecological Economics* 69:2075–2084.

Food and Agricultural Organization (FAO) of the United Nations. 2006. *Global Forest Resources Assessment 2005, Main Report: Progress Towards Sustainable Forest Management.* FAO Forestry Paper 147. FAO, Rome.

2007. *The World's Mangroves 1980–2005.* FAO Forestry Paper 153. FAO, Rome.

2009. *The State of World Fisheries and Aquaculture 2008*. FAO, Rome.

Grainger, A., D.H. Boucher, P.C. Frumhoff *et al*. 2009. "Biodiversity and REDD at Copenhagen." *Current Biology* 19(21):R974–R976.

Grieg-Gran, M.-A., I. Porras, and S.Wunder. 2005. "How can market mechanisms for forest environmental services help the poor? Preliminary lessons from Latin America." *World Development* 33:1511–1527.

Gustafsson, B. and W. Zhong. 2000. "Why has poverty in China changed? A study based on microdata for 1988 and 1995." *The China Quarterly* 164:983–1006.

Halpern, B. S., S. Walbridge, K.A. Selkoe *et al*. 2008. "A global map of human impacts on marine ecosystems." *Science* 319:948–952.

Hanley, N. and E.B. Barbier. 2009. *Pricing Nature: Cost-Benefit Analysis and Environmental Policy-Making*. Edward Elgar, London.

Hartwick, J., N. von Long, and H. Tian. 2001. "Deforestation and development in a small open economy." *Journal of Environmental Economics and Management* 41:235–251.

Holling, C.S. 1973. "Resilience and stability of ecological systems." *Annual Review of Ecological Systems* 4:1–23.

Isham, J., M. Woolcock, L. Pritchett, and G. Busby. 2005. "The varieties of resource experience: natural resource export structures and the political economy of economic growth." *World Bank Economic Review* 19(2):141–174.

Jack, B.K., C. Kousky, and K.R.E. Sims. 2008. "Designing payments for ecosystem services: lessons from previous experience with incentive-based mechanisms." *Proceedings of the National Academy of Sciences* 105:9465–9470.

Jackson, J.B.C., M.X. Kirby, W.H. Berger *et al*. 2001. "Historical over-fishing and the recent collapse of coastal ecosystems." *Science* 293: 629–638.

Jalan, J. and M. Ravallion. 2002. "Geographic poverty traps? A micro model of consumption growth in rural China." *Journal of Applied Econometrics* 17:329–346.

James, A., K. Gaston, and A. Balmford. 1999. "Balancing the Earth's accounts." *Nature* 401:323–324.

Jinji, N. 2006. "International trade and terrestrial open-access renewable resources in a small open economy." *Canadian Journal of Economics* 39:790–808.

Kam, S-P., M. Hossain, M.L. Bose, and L.S. Villano. 2005. "Spatial patterns of rural poverty and their relationship with welfare-influencing factors in Bangladesh." *Food Policy* 30:551–567.

Strassburg, B., R.K. Turner, B. Fisher, R. Shaeffer, and A. Lovett. 2009. "Reducing emissions from deforestation – the 'combined incentives' mechanism and empirical simulations." *Global Environmental Change* 19:265–278.

Turner, M.G., W.H. Romme, R.H. Gardner, R.V. O'Neill, and T.K. Kratz. 1993. "A revised concept of landscape equilibrium: disturbance and stability on scaled landscapes." *Landscape Ecology* 8:213–227.

United Nations Collaborative Programme on Reducing Emissions from Deforestation and Forest Degradation (UN-REDD). 2010. *UN-REDD: Supporting countries to get ready for REDD.* August 2010 Fact Sheet, UN-REDD, New York.

United Nations Environment Programme (UNEP). 2006. *Marine and Coastal Ecosystems and Human Wellbeing: A Synthesis Report Based on the Findings of the Millennium Ecosystem Assessment.* UNEP, Nairobi.

Valiela, I., J.L. Bowen, and J.K. York. 2001. "Mangrove forests: one of the world's threatened major tropical environments." *BioScience* 51:807–815.

van der Werf, G.R., D.C. Morton, R.S. DeFries *et al.* 2009. "CO_2 emissions from forest loss." *Nature Geoscience* 2:737–738.

van der Ploeg, R. and S. Poelhekke. 2009. "Volatility and the natural resource curse." *Oxford Economic Papers* 61:727–760.

2010. "The pungent smell of 'red herrings': subsoil assets, rents, volatility and the resource curse." *Journal of Environmental Economics and Management* 60:44–55.

van Kooten, G. Cornelius, and B. Sohngen. 2007. "Economics of forest ecosystem carbon sinks: a review." *International Review of Environmental and Resource Economics* 1:237–269.

Venter, O., W.F. Laurance, T. Iwamura *et al.* 2009. "Harnessing carbon payments to protect biodiversity." *Science* 324:1368.

World Bank. 2003. *World Development Report 2003.* World Bank, Washington, DC.

2008. *World Development Indicators.* World Bank, Washington, DC.

Worm, B., E.B. Barbier, N. Beaumont *et al.* 2006. "Impacts of biodiversity loss on ocean ecosystem services." *Science* 314:787–790.

Worm, B., R. Hilborn, J.K. Baum *et al.* 2009. "Rebuilding global fisheries." *Science* 325:578–585.

Wunder, S. 2003. *Oil Wealth and the Fate of the Forest: A Comparative Study of Eight Tropical Countries.* Routledge, London.

2005. "Macroeconomic change, competitiveness and timber production: a five-country comparison." *World Development* 33(1):65–86.

2008. "Payments for environmental services and the poor: concepts and preliminary evidence." *Environment and Development Economics* 13:279–297.

Zedler, J.B. and S. Kercher. 2005. "Wetland resources: status, trends, ecosystem services, and restorability." *Annual Review of Environment and Resources* 20:39–74.

Zilberman, D., L. Lipper, and N. McCarthy. 2008. "When could payments for environmental services benefit the poor?" *Environment and Development Economics* 13:255–278.

6 | Ecological collapse

An important observation here is that, although an order of magnitude loss in habitat only leads to a 50% reduction in species number, this represents a change in community structure equivalent to an average of one trophic level decline in the average trophic position of the species persisting in the community ... We would thus expect to see an initial sequential reduction in economic goods and services as natural systems are degraded, followed by a more rapid sequential collapse of goods and services.

(Dobson *et al.* 2006, p. 1921)

Introduction

As we have seen throughout this book, the tendency of the risk of ecological collapse to rise with landscape conversion can play a pivotal role in determining ecosystem conservation decisions. A number of ecological studies confirm that irreversible landscape conversion increases the threat of ecosystem collapse (Busing and White 1993; Dobson *et al.* 2006; Lotze *et al.* 2006; Peterson *et al.* 1998; Turner *et al.* 1993). That is, the ability of an ecosystem to survive may be linked to how much of its landscape size or scale remains. Biological productivity, ecosystem functioning, biodiversity, and ecological resilience appear to be affected by the spatial scale of an ecosystem (Dobson *et al.* 2006; Halpern *et al.* 2005; Peterson *et al.* 1998; Wellnitz and Poff 2001). As the ecological landscape declines or is degraded, essential processes and components are disturbed, and the system becomes vulnerable to collapse.

Ecologists are beginning to measure how such linkages unfold. For example, Dobson *et al.* (2006) find that the proportion of surviving species, species diversity, and the trophic level of ecosystems tend to fall exponentially as the fraction of remaining ecosystem habitat declines. The loss of habitat causes first a thinning of species throughout the food web of an ecosystem, followed by rapid loss of the top trophic levels in the web. As food webs and trophic levels largely define ecosystems, this process of trophic implosion can easily trigger ecosystem collapse. The consequence, as the above quote by the authors indicates, is that the declining proportion of habitat area is linked directly to rapid declines in ecosystem goods and services and a higher risk of overall collapse.

Field studies for coastal ecosystems, such as mangroves and salt marsh, also provide evidence in support of such a relationship. For these systems, positive interactions among ecological functions, trophic cascades and linkages, and biodiversity appear to be positively correlated with landscape scale.[1] The implication is that the probability of ecological collapse is likely to increase with a diminishing size of the ecological landscape.

Landscape losses and degradation of ecosystem processes and functions can also lead to unpredictable and sudden increases in the risk of ecological collapse, due to the presence of ecological thresholds and feedback effects. That is, large shocks or sustained disturbances to ecosystems lead to further interactions that can contravene ecological thresholds, causing the systems to "flip" irreversibly from one functioning state to another.[2] Large-scale landscape conversion is one type of irreversible, sustained disturbance that can trigger such a process.[3] Thus the *resilience* or *robustness* of an ecosystem – its ability to absorb large shocks or sustained disturbances and still maintain internal integrity and functioning – may be an important attribute determining the extent to which landscape conversion affects the risk of ecological collapse.

To explore some of these issues further, the following chapter extends the natural asset model to consider some possible effects of landscape conversion on the risk of ecological collapse. We first incorporate the risk of collapse into the basic model developed in

[1] See, for example, Elliott *et al.* (2007); Farnsworth (1998); Halpern *et al.* (2007); Petersen *et al.* (2003); Rilov and Schiel (2006); and Silliman and Bertness (2002).
[2] See, for example, Batabayal *et al.* (2003); Dasgupta and Mäler (2003); Elmqvist *et al.* (2003); Holling (1973); Levin (1999); May (1975); Murray (1993); Perrings (1998); Pimm (1984); Scheffer *et al.* (2001).
[3] See, for example, Busing and White (1993); Dobson *et al.* (2006); Lotze *et al.* (2006); Peterson *et al.* (1998); and Turner *et al.* (1993).

Chapter 3. We then apply a similar approach to the spatial model of Chapter 4, and use the case study of conversion of a mangrove landscape to shrimp farming to simulate the key insights of the model. The chapter ends by discussing the growing interest of ecologists and economist in analyzing the importance of ecological robustness or resilience to ensuring the survival of ecosystems, and showing how such considerations can lead to both theoretical and empirical measurement of the value of ecosystem resilience to external disturbance or stress.

Extending the natural asset model to allow for ecological collapse

One straightforward way of extending the basic natural asset model of Chapter 3 to include the risk of collapse is to adopt the hazard rate function approach of Reed and Heras (1992). This approach has been used in economics for a variety of problems in which environmental use could lead to an irrevocable change in the system, such as a fishery collapse, biological invasion, pollution, species extinction, and risk of forest fire or pest damage.[4] In the following approach, the risk of ecosystem collapse is modeled as a hazard rate function, where the hazard is defined as the probability at any time t that the ecosystem will collapse given that it has not collapsed up until that time period. Following Reed and Heras (1992), such a stochastic optimization problem can be converted to a more tractable deterministic control problem and solved for the conditions determining the risk of collapse. As a result, we can easily see how incorporating this risk influences the optimal landscape conversion of the ecosystem as well as the long-run outcome for the amount of landscape conserved.

Consider that the ecosystem is vulnerable to random catastrophic collapse as its landscape is converted irreversibly for development. Up until the collapse (if it occurs), the ecological landscape can still be converted to development activity or left to generate periodic ecosystem service flow. Thus, the net benefit flows of the allocation of ecological landscape at time t is

---

[4] See, for example, Amacher *et al.* (2009); Clarke and Reed (1994); Knowler and Barbier (2005); Reed (1988); Reed and Heras (1992); Tsur and Zemel (1994, 2007).

$$W(A,c,t) = R(A(t)) - C(c(t)) + B(A(t)). \tag{6.1}$$

As in the basic model, landscape conversion is governed by (3.4), i.e., $\dot{A} = -c(t)$. If the instantaneous discount rate is r, then the expected net present value of the benefit flow gained up until the time of collapse is

$$J = E\left\{ \int_0^\tau W(A,c,t) e^{-rt} dt \right\} \tag{6.2}$$

where the expectation is taken with respect to the random variable ô. Maximizing (6.2) with respect to the rate of landscape conversion $\dot{A} = -c(t)$ is a stochastic optimization problem. Following Reed and Heras (1992), it is possible to transform the maximization into a problem of deterministic control by expressing the probability of collapse as a hazard rate function and introducing a new state variable linked to the hazard function.

The likelihood of collapse can be characterized by a hazard rate function that specifies the probability that the ecosystem collapses at time t, given that it has survived so far up to that time. Formally, the hazard rate can be defined as

$$h(t) = \lim_{\Delta t \to 0} \Pr(t \le T < t + \Delta t \,|\, T \ge t)/\Delta t = \frac{f(t)}{S(t)} \tag{6.3}$$

where $f(t)$ is the corresponding density function of the probability distribution of the duration T of the ecosystem $F(t) = \Pr(T < t)$. The survivor function $S(t)$ is the upper tail of this probability distribution, and it is the probability that the random variable T will equal or exceed the value t, or $S(t) = 1 - F(t) = \Pr(T \ge t)$. Note that the latter survival probability is also related to the hazard function, i.e., $S(t) = \exp\left\{ -\int_0^t h(u)du \right\}$. The latter expression can be used to introduce a new state variable

$$y(t) = -\ln S(t) = \int_0^t h(u)du. \tag{6.4}$$

The probability of ecosystem collapse, and therefore the hazard rate function, depends inversely upon the remaining ecological landscape that is not converted, i.e., from (6.4)

$$\dot{y} - h(t) = \psi(A(t)), \quad \psi' < 0, y(0) = 0. \tag{6.5}$$

Evaluating (6.2) in terms of $y(t)$ yields

$$J = \int_0^\infty W(A,c,t) e^{-rt-y(t)} dt. \tag{6.6}$$

The objective function (6.6) can now be maximized subject to $\dot{A} = -c(t)$ and also the new dynamic constraint (6.5). This is a standard problem of deterministic control similar to one that arises if there is no possibility of collapse, except for the inclusion of a new state variable $y(t)$ related to the survival function and which operates as a premium added to the discount rate. Note that $e^{-y(t)}$ is simply $S(t)$ and is often referred to as the survival probability term.

The current value Hamiltonian is

$$H = W(A,c) e^{-y(t)} - \mu_1 c + \mu_2 \psi(A), \tag{6.7}$$

which can be transformed into a conditional current value Hamiltonian by dividing H by the survival probability $e^{-y(t)}$

$$\tilde{H} = W(A,c) - \rho_1 c + \rho_2 \psi(A) \tag{6.8}$$

where $\rho_i = e^{y(t)} \mu_i$ and $\tilde{H} = He^{y(t)}$.

The first-order conditions for maximization are

$$\frac{d\tilde{H}}{dc} = \frac{dHe^{y(t)}}{dc} = 0 \rightarrow -C'(c) = \rho_1 \tag{6.9}$$

$$\dot{\rho}_1 - (\delta + \psi)\rho_1 = -\frac{d\tilde{H}}{dA} = -\frac{dHe^{y(t)}}{dA} \rightarrow$$
$$\dot{\rho}_1 = [r + \psi(A)]\rho_1 - \rho_2 \psi'(A) - R'(A) - B'(A) \tag{6.10}$$

$$\dot{\rho}_2 - (\delta + \psi)\rho_2 = -\frac{d\tilde{H}}{dy} = -\frac{dHe^{y(t)}}{dy} = W(A,c) \rightarrow$$
$$\dot{\rho}_2 = [\delta + \psi(A)]\rho_2 + R(A) + B(A) - C(c). \tag{6.11}$$

The optimal conversion path $c^*(t)$ maximizes the conditional current-value Hamiltonian at all t, and can be found by solving the system given by conditions (6.9) to (6.10) and the dynamic equations $\dot{A} = -c(t)$ and (6.5). The costate variable ρ_1 is the shadow value of an additional unit of ecological landscape at time t conditional on the ecosystem not having yet collapsed at this time. As shown by Reed and Heras (1992), the costate variable ρ_2 is defined as $\rho_2 = e^{rt+y(t)} \dfrac{\partial J^*}{\partial y} = -V(A^*,t)$, where J^* represents the optimal value of (6.6). For the above problem, ρ_2 is therefore the negative of the expected present value at time t of the remaining optimally managed ecological landscape, given that the ecosystem has not yet collapsed. Thus $V(A^*, t)$ represents the "value" of the functioning ecosystem at time t with its landscape area at level A^*.

Interpretation of the first-order conditions is facilitated by comparing them to the case where there is no risk of ecosystem collapse. From (6.11)

$$\rho_2 = \frac{\dot{\rho}_2 - W(A,c)}{\tilde{r}}, \quad \tilde{r} = (r + \psi(A)). \tag{6.12}$$

As indicated, by definition, $\rho_2 < 0$ so (6.12) must be negative. Any change in the costate variable over time must be less than the benefit flows of the ecological landscape at time t as represented by $W(A,c,t) = R(A(t)) - C(c(t)) + B(A(t))$. Both of the values on the right-hand side of (6.12) are adjusted by the effective discount rate $\tilde{r}$, which includes the risk "premium" for the threat of collapse $\psi(A)$. Note that this premium implies that the effective discount rate rises as more ecological landscape is converted over time.

From (6.9) and (6.10) and using $-R'(A) = R'(D)$ for annual periodic rent from developed land use

$$-R'(A) - \tilde{r}C(c) = R'(D) - \tilde{r}C(c) = B'(A) + \dot{\rho}_1 + \rho_2\psi'(A) \tag{6.13}$$

and

$$-\rho_1 = \frac{R'(D)}{\tilde{r}} - \left[\frac{B'(A) + \dot{\rho}_1}{\tilde{r}} + \frac{\rho_2\psi'(A)}{\tilde{r}} \right] = P(D) - P(A)$$
$$= C'(c). \tag{6.14}$$

Expression (6.13) indicates that, once again, along the optimal landscape conversion path the returns from the two competing land uses must be equal. The marginal profits from development less conversion costs $R'(D) - \tilde{r}C(c)$ must just equal the marginal benefit of holding on to the ecological landscape $B'(A) + \dot{\rho}_1 + \rho_2\psi'(A)$. Of course now, the risk premium for collapse raises the effective discount rate and thus marginal conversion costs, $\tilde{r}C'(c)$, as more landscape is converted. In addition, the benefits of holding on to landscape include the impact of more conversion on raising the risk of collapse, $\rho_2\psi'(A)$. The latter impact is positive, implying that one would want to avoid converting more ecological landscape because it would increase the risk of collapse, which is valued in terms of the expected present value at time t of the remaining functioning ecosystem ρ_2. The change in the (conditional) shadow value of a unit of landscape $\dot{\rho}_1$ is positive and is also augmented by the growing risk of collapse from landscape conversion, since $\rho_1 = e^{y(t)}\mu_1$. Overall, (6.13) implies that, with the threat of collapse posed by irreversible development of ecological landscape, along the optimal path of landscape conversion more of the ecological landscape will be preserved compared to when the threat is absent.

Expression (6.14) indicates that the difference between the capitalized marginal value of developed land and land retained as ecological landscape is again the marginal cost of converting landscape. However, the capitalized value of both land uses is determined by the effective discount rate, and thus lowered by the risk premium due to the threat of ecosystem collapse. In addition, the "price" of ecological landscape includes an additional term that, as in (6.13), reflects the impact of conversion on the increasing probability of collapse $\rho_2\psi'(A)$. The effect of this additional term plus the change in the (conditional) shadow value of a unit of landscape $\dot{\rho}_1$ is to increase the value of ecological landscape, $P(A)$. The result is that the difference in land prices between developed and ecological land will be lower than in the case without the threat of ecosystem collapse, and thus the optimal path for land conversion $c^*(t)$ is lower.

In the long run, $\dot{\rho}_1 = \dot{\rho}_2 = \dot{A} = 0$. It follows from $\dot{A} = -c(t)$ and (6.9) that both landscape conversion and the marginal (conditional) value of an additional unit of ecosystem landscape approach zero asymptotically, i.e., $c = 0$ and $\lim_{t\to\infty} \rho_1(t) = C_c(0) = 0$ The wedge between land prices will disappear, $P(D(t)) = P(A(t))$, and ecosystem landscape area will converge to a steady state level A^*. However, from (6.14), this steady-state outcome implies

$$P\left(D^*\right) = P\left(A^*\right) = \left[\frac{B'\left(A^*\right)}{\tilde{r}} + \frac{\rho_2 \psi'\left(A^*\right)}{\tilde{r}}\right], \quad \rho_2 = -W\left(A^*\right). \qquad (6.15)$$

Assume once again that the initial ecological landscape area is large $A(0) > A^*$. From (6.9), along the transition path to the long-run steady state, the marginal value of an additional unit of ecological landscape, conditional on the ecosystem not yet collapsed, is negative $\rho_1 < 0$. As in the case of no threat of collapse, this conditional shadow value is rising, i.e., $\dot{\rho}_1 > 0$. Thus, optimal landscape conversion is initially large but falls over time. However, (6.13) and (6.14) indicate that, along the optimal path of landscape conversion, more of the ecosystem will be preserved compared to when the threat of collapse is absent, and thus the optimal path for land conversion $c^*(t)$ is lower due to the presence of the hazard. Finally, the steady-state level of ecological landscape A^* is also larger compared to the case of no ecosystem collapse, as indicated by (6.15) .

The outcome for the optimal landscape conversion path with a risk of ecological collapse is depicted in Figure 6.1.

Risk of ecological collapse in the spatial landscape model

As noted above, increasingly ecological studies have linked the threat of ecological collapse to an ecosystem's overall landscape size or scale (Busing and White 1993; Dobson *et al.* 2006; Lotze *et al.* 2006; Peterson *et al.* 1998; Turner *et al.* 1993). For example, as Dobson *et al.* (2006, p. 1921) conclude, because "species drive ecosystem processes" in most ecological landscapes, as habitat size decline, "we would thus expect to see an initial sequential reduction in economic goods and services as natural systems are degraded, followed by a more rapid sequential collapse of goods and services." Such a relationship may be especially pronounced in coastal ecosystems, such as mangroves and salt marsh, as positive interactions among ecological functions, trophic cascades and linkages, and biodiversity appear to be positively correlated with scale (Elliott *et al.* 2007; Farnsworth

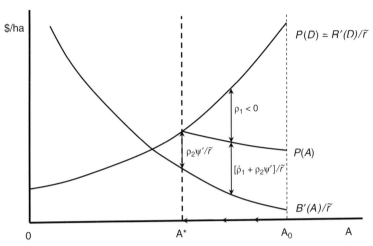

Figure 6.1 Optimal landscape conversion over time with a risk of ecological collapse

1998; Halpern *et al.* 2007; Petersen *et al.* 2003; Rilov and Schiel 2006; Silliman and Bertness 2002). The implication is that the probability of ecological collapse is likely to increase with a diminishing size of the ecological landscape.

In Chapter 4, we used a spatial model of a coastal landscape to characterize the problem of allocating land uses between preservation and development. This model can be easily extended to allow for a greater risk of collapse with diminishing landscape spatial scale (i.e., as measured by a smaller width across the landscape, *a*).

Recall that the basis of the model is the spatial production of ecosystem services. We begin by summarizing the main results of the model from Chapter 4, and then show the effects of including the risk of ecological collapse.

Assume that 0 denotes one ecologically defined boundary (e.g., the seaward edge of a coastal ecosystem) and *A* denotes the distance across to the furthest boundary of the ecological landscape (e.g., the furthest landward edge of the coastal ecosystem). *A* is predetermined by the biophysical characteristics of the landscape. Let *a* denote any specific location along the width [0,*A*] of the coastal landscape. Based on the above ecological evidence on declining wave attenuation and fish density, it is assumed that ecological production of ecosystem services $s(a)$ at any location a varies spatially according to

$$s = s(a), \quad s' < 0. \tag{6.16}$$

That is, spatial production of ecosystem services is highest at the seaward boundary, $a = 0$, and declines for locations further inshore. Denoting v as the value of a unit of ecosystem services and m as the cost of maintaining that service, then the net benefit of these services is simply $(v - m)s(a)$. The total rents earned from use of the remaining landscape for development are therefore $R(A - a)$, $R' > 0$, and the social planner's decision is to choose the optimal width of the coastal landscape, a^*, that maximizes

$$\underset{a}{Max}\; W(a) = \int_0^a (v - m)s(i)\,di + R(A - a). \tag{6.17}$$

The result is the optimal land use allocation decision

$$(v - m)s(a^*) = R'(A - a^*). \tag{6.18}$$

The optimal width of coastal landscape to preserve is where the marginal ecosystem service benefits of an additional distance inward from the seaward boundary just equals the opportunity cost of foregone development rents at that location.

Now let us introduce the threat of collapse. Assume that over the spatial distance $[0, A]$ that defines the ecological landscape, the probability of ecological collapse rises as a declines. Let a^c represent the critical spatial width of the landscape scale that leads to collapse of the ecosystem. However, as this critical size is unknown, a^c is a random variable. It follows that the expected total net benefits from the two landscape uses up to the critical size that will cause ecological collapse a^c is

$$J = E\left\{ \int_0^{a^c} (v - m)s(i)\,di + R(A - a^c) \right\}. \tag{6.19}$$

The *spatial survival rate function* is the probability that the ecosystem survives at a landscape of slightly larger spatial distance than a, given that it has not yet collapsed up to that size of landscape. This function is defined as $z(a) = \lim_{\Delta a \to 0} \Pr\left(a \le a^* \le a + \Delta a \middle| a^* \ge a\right)\middle/\Delta a > 0$.

Thus, by introducing a new variable

$$y(a) = \int_0^a z(u)\,du \text{ and } \frac{\partial y}{\partial a} = z(a) = \frac{\partial Z(a)/\partial a}{Z(a)} \tag{6.20}$$

the new (deterministic) maximization problem is

$$\underset{a}{Max}\ J = e^{y(a)}\left[\int_0^a (v-m)s(i)di + R(A-a)\right],\ e^{y(a)} = z(a). \tag{6.21}$$

Note that the exponential term $e^{y(a)} = Z(a)$ has a special meaning; it represents the survival probability of the ecosystem of spatial extent a.

The first-order condition is

$$\frac{\partial J}{\partial a} = z(a)e^{y(a)}W(a) + e^{y(a)}\left[(v-m)s(a) - R'(A-a)\right] = 0 \tag{6.22}$$

which rearranging yields

$$(v-m)s(a) + z(a)W(a) = R'(A-a). \tag{6.23}$$

This new optimal land use condition can be directly compared to the previous condition (6.18) that ignores the risk of collapse. Thus for any landscape size associated with $0 < a < A$, there is an additional benefit for holding on to more ecological landscape, $z(a)W(a)$. As can be seen from (6.17), the total value of allocating the ecological landscape to conversion and preservation, $W(a)$, consists of the rents from converting $(A - a)$ of the ecological landscape and the net benefits of ecosystem services $(v - m)s(a)$ from the remaining landscape of width a. This value is weighted by the spatial survivor rate function, $z(a)$, which is positive. In other words, the additional benefit of holding on to more landscape includes the impact of conservation on avoiding ecological collapse, $z(a)$, which is valued in terms of the expected total benefits of the subsequent survival of the ecosystem, $W(a)$.

Figure 6.2 shows the likely impact of this additional benefit of conservation on the optimal landscape size of the ecosystem. For expediency of illustration, the only case shown is when the foregone

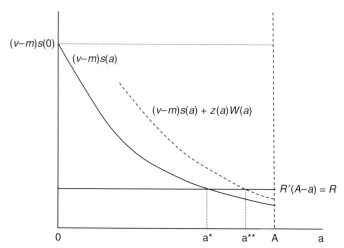

Figure 6.2 Optimal coastal landscape allocation with risk of collapse

marginal rents across the landscape are constant, i.e., $R'(A - a^*) = R$. As the figure indicates, with the additional benefit of holding on to more landscape to reduce the risk of collapse, the result is more preservation (i.e., $a^{**} > a^*$).

As with the basic spatial landscape model of Chapter 4, the above model with the risk of collapse can be simulated using empirical estimates applied to a mangrove ecosystem. Recall from Chapter 4 that it is assumed that the ecosystem comprises a mangrove forest extending 1,000 m seaward along a 10 km coastline, which corresponds to a 10 sq. km mangrove landscape. Each location, a, in the landscape represents a hectare along the 1,000 m distance from the seaward edge inland, where $a = 0$ is the seaward edge and $A = 1000$ is the maximum distance inward of the mangrove landscape from the seaward edge. Since the entire ecosystem contains an area of 10 sq. km, which is equivalent to 1,000 ha, each 1,000 m location a across the landscape from the seaward edge to its inshore boundary comprises a one hectare unit of land.

In the simulation of Chapter 4, the services of the mangrove ecosystem consist of three benefits: the role of mangroves as natural "barriers" to periodic damaging coastal storm events, their role as nursery and breeding habitats for offshore fisheries, and the exploitation of mangrove forests by coastal communities for a variety of wood and nonwood products. The total value for all three mangrove services at the seaward edge, $vs(0)$, amounts to \$18,978 per ha. The spatial production function (6.16) is assumed to apply to storm protection and habitat-fishery linkages. In the case of storm protection, ecological production amounts to a value of \$9,632 per ha at the seaward edge, but is assumed to decline exponentially, $s(a) = vs(0)e^{-\delta a}$, with $\delta = -0.014$ (see Figure 4.1). For habitat-fishery linkages, spatial production is simulated by the fish density estimates shown in Figure 4.2. The first 25 meters of mangroves on the seaward edge have the highest habitat-fishery linkage value of \$2,117 per ha, but this declines to three-fifths of this value for mangroves located 30–50 meters inshore, and to zero for the remaining mangroves located inland. The value of wood and nonwood products is constant across the mangrove landscape at \$864 per ha.

Maintenance costs m of mangrove ecosystems and their services are assumed to be zero. It is also assumed that the marginal economic net return to shrimp farming, which represents $R'(A - a^*) = R$, is constant across the landscape at \$1,220 per ha.

Based on these assumptions for the value of ecosystem services and costs, it is possible to estimate $W(a)$ for any location a in the coastal landscape. However, to incorporate the risk of ecological collapse in the model simulation, it is necessary to stipulate a specific functional form for the cumulative density function $F(a) = \Pr(a^* < a)$, the probability that the critical spatial distance associated with ecosystem collapse is less than some spatial distance across the ecological landscape, a. Recall that Dobson *et al.* (2006) find evidence that the proportion of species remaining, species diversity, and the trophic level of ecosystems tend to fall exponentially as the proportion of ecosystem habitat remaining declines. This suggests that the probability of ecological collapse will also decline exponentially as the proportion of habitat remaining becomes larger. A functional form that corresponds to this relationship is $F(a) = 1 - \left(\dfrac{a}{A}\right)^{\gamma}$. Using this specific relationship for the risk of collapse, it is possible to derive the resulting survival probability $Z(a) = \left(\dfrac{a}{A}\right)^{\gamma}$, and the survival rate function $z(a) = \dfrac{\partial Z(a)/\partial a}{Z(a)} = \dfrac{\gamma}{a}$.

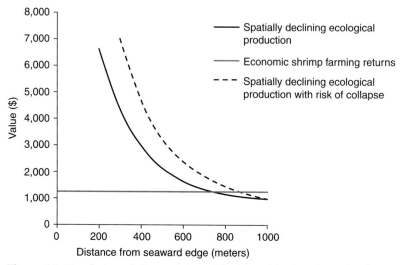

Figure 6.3 Simulation of the spatial model with a risk of ecological collapse

With these functional forms it is possible to show how incorporating the risk of collapse affects the optimal landscape allocation, which is depicted in Figure 6.3. As indicated in the figure, the reference outcome for this simulation is the optimal landscape condition (6.18), in which the value of spatially declining production of ecosystem services equals the marginal economic returns foregone from converting the mangrove landscape to shrimp aquaculture. According to the simulation of (6.18) depicted in Chapter 4, this base case result suggests it is optimal to preserve mangroves up to 746 meters from the seaward edge and convert the remaining mangroves located inland (see also Figure 4.6). However, as depicted by condition (6.23), the additional benefit of holding onto more landscape to avoid ecosystem collapse, $z(a)W(a)$, increases the overall net benefits of preserving the mangrove ecosystem. The result is that it is now optimal to preserve mangroves up to 864 meters from the seaward boundary, and convert only the landward fringe of the coastal landscape to shrimp ponds.

The simulation confirms that incorporating the risk of ecological collapse is also extremely important to the landscape conservation decision. If the survival of the ecosystem is positively influenced by the scale of the landscape conserved, then there is an additional benefit of holding onto more landscape to ensure ecosystem survival. If the additional benefit of conserving more landscape to ensure ecosystem survival is sufficiently large, then it will lead to more preservation of the landscape than the case where there is no risk of ecological collapse, and in some cases, to preservation of the entire ecosystem.

Ecosystem resilience

Ecological collapse appears to be a sequential process, which is initiated first by the loss of species throughout the food web of an ecosystem, followed by the decline in the web itself accompanied by the loss of key ecological functions, and then culminating in "a more rapid sequential collapse of goods and services" provided by the ecosystem (Dobson *et al.* 2006). Given the ecological evidence suggesting that landscape conversion can be a major instigator of this sequential process of collapse, we have so far focused on how conversion may influence such a threat of collapse.

However, ecologists have also examined threats to ecosystem functioning and stability from another perspective. There is mounting evidence for a number of ecosystems that, under pressure from external disturbances, they may switch abruptly to a contrasting alternative stable state, or *ecological regime* (Folke *et al.* 2004; Scheffer *et al.* 2001). Although a variety of disturbances may trigger the regime shift, what determines whether an ecosystem will change to an alternative state depends on its *resilience* or *robustness* – the ecosystem's ability to absorb large shocks or sustained disturbances and still maintain internal integrity and functioning.

Because ecologists use resilience (or robustness) to describe a special stability property of ecosystems, it is often misinterpreted. According to Levin and Lubchenco (2008, p. 28), "the concepts of robustness and resilience are widely used in the scientific literature, although there is considerable confusion about their meaning … it is clear that the notion of resilience is sometimes interpreted in the general literature in the narrower sense of recovery from disturbance, and at other times in the broader sense of the maintenance of functioning in the face of disturbance." Levin and Lubchenco (2008, p. 29) clearly favor the wider definition: "we use the term *robustness* and *resilience* interchangeably to mean the capacity of a system to absorb stresses and continue functioning." Similarly, Walker *et al.* (2004) define resilience as "the capacity of a system to absorb disturbance and reorganize while undergoing change so as to still retain essentially the same function, structure, identity, and feedbacks." This view of ecosystem resilience is due originally to Holling (1973), who argues that this property "does not depend on whether a system is at or near some equilibrium. It assumes that ecosystems are characterized by multiple locally stable equilibria, and the measure of a system's resilience in any one locally stable domain is the extent of the shocks it can absorb before being displaced into some other local stability domain" (Perrings 1998, p. 505).[5]

Evidence of how diminishing ecological resilience influences regime shifts exists for deserts, coral reefs, forests, lakes, and oceans (see Table 6.1).[6] Although the triggering events that lead to shifts in these ecosystems from one state to another can have natural causes, the factors that influence the resilience of the systems to such events often have a human origin, such as land use, fishing, pollution, and overexploitation. As summarized by Folke *et al.* (2004, p. 573),

regime shifts in ecosystems are, to a large extent, driven by human actions. A combination of top-down impacts, such as fishing down food webs and losing response diversity and functional groups of species, and bottom-up impacts, such as accumulation of nutrients, soil erosion, or redirection of water flows, as well as altered disturbance regimes, such as suppression of fire and increased frequency and intensity of storms, have shifted several ecosystems into less desired states with diminished capacity to generate ecosystem services.

Clearly, then, human uses and impacts on ecosystems are the most important disturbances, or stresses, on these systems, and are also factors in affecting their resilience to these stresses. One possible reason, as argued by Peterson *et al.* (1998, pp. 12–13), is that "the resilience of ecological processes, and therefore of the ecosystems they maintain, depends upon the distribution of functional groups

---

[5] As pointed out by Perrings (1998, p. 505), the alternative interpretation of ecosystem resilience (or stability) in the ecology "refers to the properties of the system near some stable equilibrium (i.e. in the neighbourhood of a stable focus or node). This definition, due to Pimm (1984), takes the resilience of a system to be a measure of the speed of its return to equilibrium." However, the consensus view of most ecologists is that ecosystems are complex, adaptive systems that are not characterized by a single, stable equilibrium (Levin 1999).

[6] See also Folke *et al.* (2004), who document regime shifts to alternative states in an even wider variety of terrestrial and aquatic ecosystems.

Table 6.1 *Major ecosystem state shifts and their causes*

Ecosystem	State I	State II	Trigger events	Factors affecting resilience
Arid lands	Perennial vegetation	Bare soil with ephemeral plants	Climatic events	Overgrazing, land use
Coral reefs	Corals	Fleshy brown macroalgae	Hurricanes, pathogens	Climate change, fishing, nutrient accumulation
Lakes	Clear with submerged vegetation	Turbid with phytoplankton	Herbicides, pesticides, water levels	Nutrient accumulation
Forests	Woodlands	Herbaceous vegetation	Fires, tree cutting	Climate change, land use, overgrazing, overharvesting
Marine	Various	Various	Climatic events	Climate change, fishing, pollution

Source: Adapted from Scheffer *et al.* (2001, Table 1).

within and across scales ... Ecological resilience does not derive from redundancy in the traditional engineering sense; rather, it derives from overlapping function within scales and reinforcement of function across scales." In other words, a well-functioning natural landscape or ecosystem is also an indicator of a more resilient, integrated, and healthy ecosystem. As ecological landscapes become converted and fragmented, the functioning of ecosystem services becomes disrupted, which compromises not only the delivery of ecosystem services but also the resilience of ecosystems to further stresses and shocks.

Although several attributes of ecosystems may contribute to their resilience, the most fundamental may be *diversity*.[7] Biologists and

---

[7] Levin (1999) identifies several essential elements that underlie an ecosystem's resilience: diversity and heterogeneity, redundancy and degeneracy, modularity, and the tightness of feedback loops. Levin and Lubchenco (2008)

Box 6.1 Diversity and adaptability of ecosystems

From Levin and Lubchenco (2008, p. 30):

It is well established that, at least in some circumstances, lowered diversity exposes ecosystems to catastrophic change ... Diversity and heterogeneity capture the adaptive capacity of a system, its ability to alter its composition in a changing environment. In evolutionary theory, Fisher's fundamental theorem of natural selection states that the rate of evolutionary change is proportional both to the selective differential and to the genic variation in the population. Without variance, there can be no adaptation; and without this adaptive capacity, populations are at risk. The same applies to changes at higher levels of organization – without variation, there can be no adaptive response.

---

ecologists use the term biological diversity – or biodiversity for short – to refer to the range of variation or differences in living organisms and their environment. As a result, "biodiversity" is often applied to describe the degree of diversity at one or more levels of biological hierarchy: genes, populations, species, communities, and ecosystems. Increasingly, evidence suggests that biodiversity has a pivotal role in ecosystem functioning (Duffy 2009; Duffy *et al.* 2007). The consequence, as described in Box 6.1, is that diversity and heterogeneity are also critical to the adaptability of an ecosystem, and "lowered diversity exposes ecosystems to catastrophic change."

For example, in coastal and marine systems, the loss of biodiversity increases an ecosystem's susceptibility to abrupt change as well as reduces the provision of ecosystem services. In ocean systems, more highly diverse large-scale marine ecosystems contain a smaller fraction of collapsed commercial fisheries, and a higher rate of recovery of collapsed fisheries, than large marine ecosystems with less diversity (Worm *et al.* 2006). In marine intertidal and subtidal communities, species redundancy and complementarity are important to ecosystem resistance to disturbance and recovery (Palumbi *et al.* 2008).

In terrestrial systems, conservation of biodiversity is also viewed as essential insurance to maintain more resilient ecosystems and provision

describe how all these elements interact in the support of the resilience of marine ecosystems.

of ecosystem goods and services (Bengtsson *et al.* 2003; Duffy 2009; Duffy *et al.* 2007; Gross *et al.* 2009; Tilman *et al.* 2001). One impact is that biological productivity is greater at higher diversity because of "niche complementarity" among particular combinations of species and the greater chance of occurrence of such combinations at higher diversity (Tilman *et al.* 2001). Food-web stability may also be enhanced when species at a higher trophic level feed on multiple prey species and when species at an intermediate trophic level are fed upon by multiple predator species (Gross *et al* 2009). Finally, Bengtsson *et al.* (2003, p. 391) cite theoretical and empirical evidence showing that "lower diversity and more synchronized ecosystem dynamics in managed and fragmented landscapes are likely to lead to a lower capacity to recover naturally after disturbances, such as pest attacks or extreme climatic events."

As we saw in Chapter 1, just as landscape conversion and alteration is the major cause of ecosystem loss, it is also the main factor behind biodiversity decline. For example, habitat loss and degradation are the most important threat to species richness, affecting 91 percent of threatened plants, 88 percent of threatened amphibians, and 86 percent of threatened birds and mammals (Baillie *et al.* 2004; Hilton-Taylor 2000). The primary factors behind habitat modification are agricultural activities, extraction activities, such as mining, fishing, logging, and harvesting, and the development of infrastructure, such as human settlements, industry, roads, dams, and power lines. As a result of these land use and commercial development pressures, especially in tropical developing countries, over the next fifty years, the rate of global biodiversity loss is expected to accelerate, leading to the extinction of at least 500 of the 1,192 currently threatened bird species and 565 of the 1,137 mammal species (Dirzo and Raven 2003).

Extending the natural asset model to allow for ecosystem resilience

Given the increasing recognition of the importance of ecosystem resilience, a number of integrated ecological–economic models have explored the theoretical implications of this property.[8] By adopting an

[8] See, for example, Batabayal *et al.* (2003); Brock and Starrett (2003); Common and Perrings (1992); Dasgupta and Mäler (2003); Mäler (2008); Perrings (1998); and Perrings and Brock (2009).

approach inspired by Common and Perrings (1992), it is also possible to extend the basic natural asset model of Chapter 3 to account for ecosystem resilience. Following Common and Perrings (1992), define a time varying k-vector of stochastic system "parameters", $z(t)$, which has a joint probability density function at time t denoted as

$$z(t) = \Pr\big[z(t)\big]. \tag{6.24}$$

The vector of parameters describes the organizational structure and normal functioning of the ecosystem, such as photosynthesis, productivity, diversity, nutrient cycling, etc. Let $d(t)$ represent a disturbance, or perturbation, to the ecosystem due to some form of economic activity. It is assumed that this perturbation affects some of the stochastic system parameters, but not others. Denote as $\bar{z}(t)$ those parameters of the ecosystem that are undisturbed by the economic activity. It is assumed that $\bar{z}(t)$ is a nonstationary random process, and that the effect of the economic activity is to change both the mean and variance of the system parameters that it disturbs. It therefore follows that $z(t)$ is a function of 1) the undisturbed organizational structure of the ecosystem; and 2) the perturbance due to economic activity at time t. Formally

$$z(t) = h\big(d(t), \bar{z}(t)\big). \tag{6.25}$$

The stability (resilience) of the ecosystem implies that the time derivative of $z(t)$ with respect to economic perturbations $d(t)$ is nonpositive. That is,

$$\dot{z}(t) = h_d \dot{d}(t) \le 0. \tag{6.26}$$

If $\dot{z}(t) \le 0$ is in the neighborhood of the unperturbed parameters of the system, then the function $h\big(d(t), \bar{z}(t)\big)$ is a Lyapunov function and the neighborhood may be said to be a stable region. It is asymptotically stable if $\dot{z}(t) < 0$. If the probability density function of the system parameters $z(t)$ is a Lyapunov function as dictated by condition (6.26), not only is the system resilient as defined by Holling (1973) but also locally stable. That is, if the rate of change of the ecosystem parameters with respect to a disturbance caused by economic activity is nonpositive, then the economic process does not have a destabilizing effect on the ecosystem, and the system is still able to maintain its organizational integrity and normal functioning.

In the natural asset model, the disturbance caused by economic activity is the allocation of some of the ecological landscape for development, $D(t)$. As before, landscape conversion is defined by state equations (3.4) and (3.5), i.e., $\dot{D} = -\dot{A} = c(t)$. Thus, in the natural asset model, the condition governing ecosystem resilience can be characterized as

$$z(t) = h\big(D(t), \bar{z}(t)\big), \quad \dot{z}(t) = h_D c(t) \le 0. \tag{6.27}$$

If land conversion has a diminishing (i.e., nonpositive) impact on ecosystem structure and functioning, then the system is not destabilized and resilience is maintained.

Finally, the flow of beneficial ecosystem goods and services also depend on the organization and normal functioning of the system. That is, the periodic ecosystem benefit from the remaining landscape area is $B(A(t), z(t))$, $B_A = \partial B/\partial A(t) > 0$, $B_z = \partial B/\partial z(t) > 0$. The decision maker determining landscape use maximizes the present value of net returns from the land, V, by choosing optimal levels of land to convert, $c(t)$

$$\underset{c(t)}{Max}\, V = \int_0^\infty \big[R(D) - C(c) + B(A, z)\big] e^{-rt}\, dt \tag{6.28}$$

subject to (3.4), (3.5), and (6.27).

Note that (6.27) is an inequality constraint on the problem, which can be rewritten as $-\dot{z}(t) = -h_D c(t) \ge 0$. Since landscape conversion cannot be negative, $c(t) \ge 0$, the inequality constraint implied by (6.27) requires that $h_D = \partial h(D)/\partial D \le 0$, which in turn means that $h_A = \partial h(A)/\partial A = -h_D \ge 0$. Conserving a larger landscape area enhances the resilience of the system.

Thus, a Lagrangean expression can be formed from the current value Hamiltonian of the problem plus the inequality constraint implied by (6.27) $L = R(A) - C(c) + B(A, h(A)) - \mu c - \lambda h_D c$, where ì is the shadow value of ecological landscape, and we make use of the fact that $D(t) = D_0 + A_0 - A(t)$.

Two of the first-order conditions are

$$\frac{\partial L}{\partial c} = 0 \rightarrow \mu = -C'(c) - \lambda h_D, \ \lambda \ge 0, \ -h_D c \ge 0, \ -\lambda h_D c = 0 \tag{6.29}$$

$$-\frac{\partial L}{\partial A} = \dot{\mu} - r\mu \rightarrow \dot{\mu} = r\mu - B_A - R'(A) - B_z h_A. \tag{6.30}$$

Combining (6.29) and (6.30) yields

$$-\mu(t) = \frac{R'(D)}{r} - \frac{B_A + \dot{\mu} + B_z h_A}{r} = P(D) - P(A) = C'(c) + \lambda h_D, \tag{6.31}$$

where $-R'(A) = R'(D)$ is annual periodic rent from developed land use. Expression (6.31) once again shows that the difference between the capitalized marginal value of developed land and land retained as ecological landscape is the marginal cost of converting landscape. However, now the cost of landscape conversion includes an additional cost, λh_D, which reflects the disturbance caused by conversion to the stability of ecosystem organization and functioning. In addition, the "price" of ecological landscape includes an additional term that reflects the fact that conserving more of the landscape assists stability, and thus yields additional ecosystem benefits, $B_z h_A$.

The complementary slackness condition of (6.29) influences the optimal landscape conversion path $c(t)$ that satisfies (6.31). There are two cases. If the constraint (6.27) is binding, then $h_D c = 0$ and $\lambda > 0$. Alternatively, if the constraint is not binding, then $h_D c < 0$ and $\lambda = 0$.

With regard to the first case, along the transition path to the long-run steady state, landscape conversion is positive, $c(t) > 0$. Thus, in order for the binding constraint $h_D c = 0$ to hold, it follows that $h_D = 0$. Converting landscape for development has no impact on the structure and functioning of the ecosystem. But that implies that condition (6.31) becomes $P(D) - P(A) = \dfrac{R'(D)}{r} - \dfrac{B_A + \dot{\mu}}{r} = C'(c)$, which is exactly the same outcome for the basic natural asset model of Chapter 3. If there is no impact of landscape conversion on the resilience of the ecosystem, then optimal conversion should proceed at the same rate over time as in the basic natural asset model of Chapter 3. However, as discussed in the previous section, this outcome is unrealistic, given the ecological evidence that habitat loss and landscape conversion are major disturbances, or stresses, on the functioning and structure of most ecosystems.

The second case of a nonbinding constraint, i.e., $h_D c < 0$ and $\lambda = 0$, is consistent with $c(t) > 0$ along the transition to the long-run steady state. The implication is that $h_D < 0$ and thus $h_A < 0$. Retaining more ecological landscape assists the resilience of the ecosystem. Condition (6.31) determining the optimal conversion path is $P(D) - P(A) = \dfrac{R'(D)}{r} - \dfrac{B_A + \dot{\mu} + B_z h_A}{r} = C'(c)$. The difference between the "price" of developed and ecological land is still marginal conversion costs, but the benefits of the ecological landscape now include its additional capitalized value in terms of improving the resilience of the ecosystem $B_z h_A / r$. In the long-run steady state $\dot{A} = \dot{\mu} = 0$, and the marginal value of an additional unit of ecosystem landscape approaches zero asymptotically, i.e., $c = 0$ and $\lim_{t \to \infty} \mu(t) = C'(c) = \lambda c h_D = 0$. Because of the additional benefit of conserving more ecological landscape to support ecosystem resilience, compared to the basic natural asset model of Chapter 3, there will be less conversion over time and more landscape conservation in the long run.

Figure 6.4 depicts the new optimal landscape conversion path and steady state. Assume that the initial ecological landscape area is large, $A(0) > A^*$. As shown in the figure, including the additional value of holding onto ecological landscape to assist the resilience of the ecosystem increases its value $P(A)$. Less landscape conversion occurs over time, and in the long run, the area of ecological landscape conserved is larger.

Valuing ecosystem resilience

As the above extension of the natural asset model illustrates, there is clearly an additional benefit of holding on to additional ecological landscape if it supports the overall resilience of an ecosystem. Although a number of theoretical models of threshold effects, regime shifts, and resilience in ecological–economic systems have shown similar results, empirically measuring the additional benefit of ecosystem resilience has proved more difficult. Two different methods have been attempted. The first approach is indirect, focusing on valuing the benefits of avoiding an ecological regime shift (Knowler *et al.* 2002). The second approach is to measure directly the wealth effects of resilience (Mäler 2008; Walker *et al.* 2010).

For example, Knowler *et al.* (2002) estimate the benefits of avoiding the effects of ecological regime shift in the open access Turkish

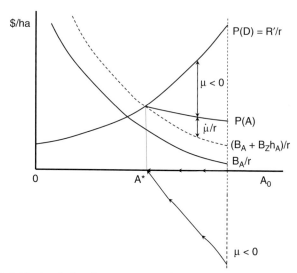

Figure 6.4 Optimal landscape conversion over time with ecosystem resilience

anchovy fishery in the Black Sea. The major cause of the regime shift was the accidental introduction in the 1980s of the comb jellyfish (*Mnemiopsis leidyi*), which preys on anchovy juveniles. However, this biological invasion was facilitated by nutrient enrichment in the Black Sea due to phosphate pollution, as the high nutrient levels helped the jellyfish become established and flourish in the marine system. The authors examine the effects of a 50 percent nutrient abatement policy, if it had been implemented before the *Mnemiopsis* invasion and outbreak, in preventing the ecological regime shift. They find that avoiding the regime change would have increased anchovy catch by nearly 330,000 metric tonnes annually and, at a price of $120 per tonne (in 1989/1990 prices), raised fishing revenues by almost $40 million. Fishing employment would have also increased by around 2,320–3,480 more crew members working. Although in the long run the greatest threat to the Black Sea anchovy fishery continues to be open access harvesting, the analysis shows that implementing a pollution abatement policy could have yielded substantial economic consequences by preventing *Mnemiopsis* establishment and subsequent ecological regime shift.

Box 6.2 summarizes the effort by Walker *et al.* (2010) to value ecosystem resilience for the Goulburn–Broken Catchment (GBC)

Box 6.2 The value of ecosystem resilience in the Goulburn–Broken Catchment of Southeast Australia

Using the inclusive wealth framework of Arrow *et al.* (2003), Mäler (2008) shows that it is possible to add a "resilience stock" to the measure of an economy's wealth. Resilience is interpreted as the probability of the system transitioning to another state (regime). That is, the closer to the threshold, the lower the stock of resilience, and the higher is the probability that the system will flip to the alternative regime. The real value, or shadow price, of the resilience stock is the expected change in future social welfare from a marginal change in resilience today. This value changes as the likelihood of crossing the threshold into the alternative regime increases.

Walker *et al.* (2010) apply this approach to the Goulburn–Broken Catchment (GBC) in Southeast Australia. The GBC includes 300,000 ha in irrigation, of which 80 percent is for dairy pasture. However, the removal of native vegetation for agriculture has led to rising water tables and increased soil salinity. Once the water table rises above 2 meters, however, pasture land is radically changed, and the agro-ecological system shifts to a different regime dominated by degraded and salinized soil. Thus, the resilience of the GBC system is measured by the distance from the water table to the 2 m threshold, and this indicator determines the probability that the system will shift from the nonsaline to saline regime. To demonstrate the impact of resilience on the inclusive wealth of the GBC, Walker *et al.* assume that all other economic assets are constant and only the stock of resilience changes. Between 1991 and 2001, they calculate that the resilience stock increased by 0.5 m due to a water table fall from 3 to 3.5 m. They estimate the value of this change in resilience under two different climate regimes: normal versus drier rainfall and evaporation conditions. The results are depicted in the table below. Under normal climate conditions, the 0.5 m change in ecosystem resilience is valued at about $23 million, or around 7 percent of the total wealth of the GBC in 1991. Under drier climatic conditions, resilience is worth $28 million, or 8.4 percent of total wealth.

Box 6.2 (*cont.*)

Climate scenario	Change in wealth from 1991 to 2001 from 0.5 m change in the resilience stock	Share of 1991 inclusive wealth
Normal conditions	$22,852,650	7.0%
Dry conditions	$28,558,360	8.4%

Source: Walker *et al.* (2010, Table 2).

in Southeast Australia. The GBC is prime agricultural land, most of which is used for dairy pasture. However, the agro-ecosystem is threatened by increased soil salinity due to rising water tables from removal of native vegetation. At the 2 meter water table threshold, the system is in danger of flipping to a different regime dominated by degraded and salinized pasture. The authors estimate resilience as the distance from the current water table to the 2 m threshold. Under normal climate conditions, a 0.5 m change in ecosystem resilience is valued at about $23 million, or around 7 percent of the total wealth of the GBC in 1991. Under drier climatic conditions, resilience is worth $28 million, or 8.4 percent of total wealth.

These two examples of valuing of ecosystem resilience suggest that this value can be considerable. In these highly productive ecosystems supporting economic activity, regime shift can be catastrophic. Or to put it differently, the value of avoiding regime shift by maintaining or enhancing the resilience of ecosystems can be a sizable component of the total economic wealth generated by these systems.

As the above extension of the natural asset model shows, land conversion is often a significant disturbance threatening the stability of an ecosystem. Although to date there are no studies that value either directly or indirectly the benefit of conserving ecological landscape to support ecosystem resilience, Box 6.3 describes how land clearing can "tip the balance" in tropical forest ecosystems in favor of invasion by exotic species. The forest ecosystem is highly vulnerable to the ecological disturbance caused by land clearing. Long before complete conversion of the forest occurs, deforestation will sufficiently disrupt the interspecific competition between invasive and native species so that the latter is eliminated. This result has important implications

Box 6.3 Land clearing and ecological disturbance in tropical forest ecosystems

Ecological evidence indicates that human-induced land use conversion and change, which is widespread in tropical regions, is not only a direct cause of habitat range loss for native species but also contributes indirectly to their loss by aiding interspecific competition by successful invaders (Lozon and MacIsaac 1997; Mack *et al.* 2000; Peterson 2003; Tilman and Lehman 2001). For example, Lozon and MacIsaac (1997) identify 94 cases from the ecological field literature where exotic plants have invaded successfully tropical terrestrial environments. Disturbance of the natural habitat was required for successful establishment of the exotic species in all but one case and for range expansion of the invader in all but five cases.

By combining an ecological model of interspecific competition between a native species and an exotic invader with an economic model of land clearing, Barbier (2007) demonstrates how relative farm prices and access to forest areas influence land clearing and thus ecological regime shift – the complete replacement of native with exotic species in a tropical forest ecosystem. The base case assumes that the land area of the tropical ecosystem is not altered by agricultural conversion. However, an increase in the relative price of agricultural output or in forest access will lead to more land clearing. As the two simulations below show, if relative prices rise by only 20% or if road improvements or other factors increase forest access by 2.75%, then this induces enough land clearing to "tip the balance" in favor of a regime shift that replaces native species (x_{1t}) with invasive species (x_{2t}). Complete forest conversion is not necessary for this outcome. A 20% increase in relative prices causes land clearing to rise by around 23%, whereas a 2.75% increase in forest access induces land clearing to rise by 24% – yet in both cases complete takeover of the forest ecosystem by the invader occurs. This result has important policy implications. If the aim of policy is to control deforestation – i.e., keep agricultural conversion of forest areas low – then clearing around a quarter of the land may seem tolerable. However, if the aim of the policy is to avoid ecological regime shift by biological invasion, then only modest land clearing is acceptable (e.g., 10–13% or less).

Box 6.3 (*cont.*)

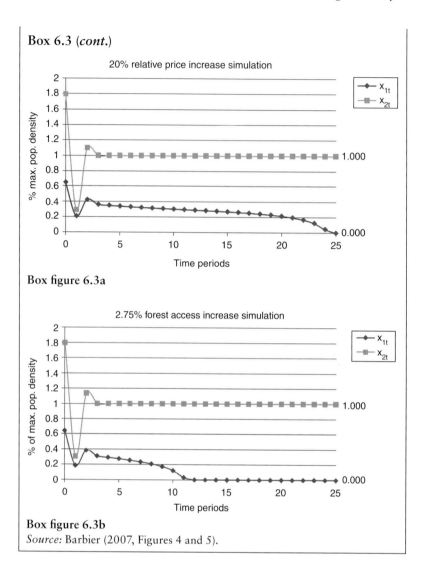

Box figure 6.3a

Box figure 6.3b
Source: Barbier (2007, Figures 4 and 5).

for the management of tropical forest clearance. If the aim is to control agricultural conversion only, then clearing a quarter of the forest landscape may be tolerable. However, if the objective is to avoid ecological disruption leading to a regime shift – i.e., the replacement of native with exotic species – then conversion should be limited to at most 10–13 percent of the land.

Final remarks

Ecological evidence indicates that biological productivity, ecosystem functioning, biodiversity, trophic levels, and ecological resilience appear to be affected by the spatial scale of an ecosystem, and so as ecological landscapes are degraded or disappear, they become vulnerable to collapse. This chapter has examined a number of ways in which such processes can occur. For example, both the basic natural asset model developed in Chapter 3 and the spatial version of Chapter 4 can be easily extended to include the risk of ecological collapse that arises through landscape conversion. The latter extension was also used to revise the case study of spatial conversion of a mangrove conversion to shrimp farms from Chapter 4, to allow for the threat of collapse. The theoretical models and the empirical application illustrate that incorporating the risk of ecological collapse is also extremely important to the landscape conservation decision. If the survival of the ecosystem is positively influenced by the scale of the landscape conserved, then there is an additional benefit of holding onto more landscape to ensure ecosystem survival.

Although ecosystem resilience appears to be a different approach to ecological stability, accounting for resilience also translates into an additional benefit of conserving more ecological landscape. Extending the natural asset model to allow for ecosystem resilience shows this clearly. Including the additional value of holding onto ecological landscape to assist the resilience of the ecosystem increases its capitalized value. Less landscape conversion should therefore occur over time, and in the long run, more of the ecological landscape should be conserved. There are not many examples of valuing ecosystem resilience, but available evidence confirms that the value of maintaining and enhancing resilience, and thus avoiding ecological regime shift, can be considerable.

The similar effects of either avoiding the threat of ecological collapse or the risk of regime shift should not be surprising. In both cases, the economic consequences can be significant, if not catastrophic, especially for highly productive ecosystems that support valuable economic activities such as agriculture or fishing, or if the ecosystem services of the remaining ecological landscape are very beneficial.[9]

---

[9] In fact, the modeling approach to determining the value of ecosystem resilience and the economic benefits of avoiding the risk of ecological collapse can be similar. For example, the approach that Mäler (2008) adopts for

Ecological collapse

Clearly, further research is required to examine the importance of ecosystem functioning and organization on both the provision of ecosystem goods and services and also important system properties, such as resilience and tendency to collapse.

Perhaps the most important lesson from this chapter is that such research requires interdisciplinary collaboration between economists, ecologists, and other environmental scientists. The next chapter explores this and other areas where interdisciplinary collaboration is essential for further progress in managing ecosystems as natural assets.

References

Amacher, G.S., M. Ollikainen, and E. Koskela. 2009. *Economics of Forest Resources*. MIT Press, Cambridge, MA.

Arrow, K.J., P. Dasgupta, and K.-G. Mäler. 2003. "Evaluating projects and assessing sustainable development in imperfect economies." *Environmental and Resource Economics* 26:647–685.

Baillie, J.E.M., C. Hilton-Taylor, and S.N. Stuart, eds. 2004. *IUCN Red List of Threatened Species: A Global Species Assessment*. World Conservation Union, Gland, Switzerland.

Barbier, E.B. 2007. "Land conversion, interspecific competition and bioinvasion in a tropical ecosystem." *Journal of Agricultural and Applied Economics* 39:133–147.

2009. "Ecosystems as natural assets." *Foundations and Trends in Microeconomics* 4(8):611–681.

Batabayal, A.A., J.R. Kahn, and R.V. O' Neil. 2003. "On the scarcity value of ecosystem services." *Journal of Environmental Economics and Management* 46:334–352.

Bengtsson, J., P. Anelstam, T. Elmqvist *et al.* 2003. "Reserves, resilience and dynamic landscapes." *Ambio* 32:389–396.

Brock, W.A. and D. Starrett. 2003. "Nonconvexities in ecological management problems." *Environmental and Resource Economics* 26:575–624.

Busing, R.T. and P.S. White. 1993. "Effects of area on old-growth forest attributes: implications for equilibrium landscape concept." *Landscape Ecology* 8:119–126.

modeling resilience as the probability of the system transitioning to another state (regime) is very similar to the approach of Reed and Heras (1992) that was used in this chapter to incorporate the risk of ecological collapse in the natural asset model.

Clarke, H.R. and W.J. Reed. 1994. "Consumption/pollution tradeoffs in an environment vulnerable to pollution-related catastrophic collapse." *Journal of Economic Dynamics and Control* 18:991–1010.

Common, M. and C. Perrings. 1992. "Towards an ecological economics of sustainability." *Ecological Economics* 6:7–34.

Dasgupta, P.S. and K.-G. Mäler. 2003. "The economics of non-convex ecosystems: an introduction." *Environmental and Resource Economics* 26:499–525.

Dirzo, R. and P.H. Raven. 2003. "Global state of biodiversity and loss." *Annual Review of Environment and Resources* 28:137–167.

Dobson, A., D. Lodge, J. Alder *et al.* 2006. "Habitat loss, trophic collapse, and the decline of ecosystem services." *Ecology* 87:1915–1924.

Duffy, J.E. 2009. "Why biodiversity is important to the functioning of real-world ecosystems." *Frontiers in Ecology and the Environment* 7:437–444.

Duffy, J.E., B.J. Cardinale, K.E. France *et al.* 2007. "The functional role of biodiversity in ecosystems: incorporating trophic complexity." *Ecology Letters* 10:522–538.

Elliott, M., D. Burdon, K.L. Hemingway, and S.E. Apitz. 2007. "Estuarine, coastal and marine ecosystem restoration: confusing management and science – a revision of concepts." *Estuarine Coastal and Shelf Science* 74:349–366.

Elmqvist, T., C. Folke, M. Nyström *et al.* 2003. "Response diversity, ecosystem change, and resilience." *Frontiers in Ecology and the Environment* 1:488–494.

Farnsworth, E.J. 1998. "Issues of spatial, taxonomic and temporal scale in delineating links between mangrove diversity and ecosystem function." *Global Ecology and Biogeography Letters* 7(1):15–25.

Folke, C., S. Carpenter, B. Walker *et al.* 2004. "Regime shifts, resilience, and biodiversity in ecosystem management." *Annual Review of Ecology, Evolution, and Systematics* 35:557–581.

Gross, T., L. Rudolf, S.A. Levin, and U. Dieckmann. 2009. "Generalized models reveal stabilizing factors in food webs." *Science* 325:747–750.

Halpern, B.S., S.D. Gaines, and R.R. Warner. 2005. "Habitat size, recruitment, and longevity as factors limiting population size in stage-structured species." *American Naturalist* 165(1):82–94.

Halpern, B.S., B.R. Silliman, J.D. Olden, J.P Bruno, and M.D. Bertness. 2007. "Incorporating positive interactions in aquatic restoration and conservation." *Frontiers in Ecology and the Environment* 5:153–160.

Hilton-Taylor, C. 2000. *IUCN Red List of Threatened Species.* World Conservation Union, Gland, Switzerland.

Holling, C.S. 1973. "Resilience and stability of ecological systems." *Annual Review of Ecological Systems* 4:1–23.

Knowler, D.J. and E.B. Barbier. 2005. "Importing exotic plants and the risk of invasion: are market-based instruments adequate?" *Ecological Economics* 52:341–354.

Knowler, D.J., E.B. Barbier, and I. Strand. 2002. "An open-access model of fisheries and nutrient enrichment in the Black Sea." *Marine Resource Economics* 16:195–217.

Levin, S.A. 1999. *Fragile Dominion: Complexity and the Commons.* Perseus Books, Reading, MA.

Levin, S.A. and J. Lubchenco. 2008. "Resilience, robustness, and marine ecosystem-based management." *BioScience* 58:27–32.

Lotze, H.K., H.S. Lenihan, B.J. Bourque *et al.* 2006. "Depletion, degradation and recovery potential of estuaries and coastal seas." *Science* 312:1806–1809.

Lozon, J.D. and H.J. MacIsaac. 1997. "Biological invasions: are they dependent on disturbance?" *Environmental Reviews* 5:131–144.

Mack, R.N., D. Simberloff, W.M. Lonsdale *et al.* 2000. "Biotic invasions: causes, epidemiology, global consequences and control." *Ecological Applications* 10(3):689–710.

Mäler, K.-G. 2008. "Sustainable development and resilience in ecosystems." *Environmental and Resource Economics* 39:17–24.

May, R.M. 1975. *Stability and Complexity in Model Ecosystems.* 2nd edn. Princeton University Press, NJ.

Murray, J.D. 1993. *Mathematical Biology.* Springer-Verlag, Berlin.

Palumbi, S.R., K.L. McLeod, and D. Grünbaum. 2008. "Ecosystems in action: lessons from marine ecology about recovery, resistance, and reversibility." *BioScience* 58:33–42.

Perrings, C. 1998. "Resilience in the dynamics of economic-environmental systems." *Environmental and Resource Economics* 11:503–520.

Perrings, C. and W.A. Brock. 2009. "Irreversibility in economics." *Annual Review of Resource Economics* 1:219–238.

Petersen, J.E., W.M. Kemp, R. Bartleson *et al.* 2003. "Multiscale experiments in coastal ecology: improving realism and advancing theory." *BioScience* 53:1181–1197.

Peterson, A.T. 2003. "Predicting the geography of species' invasions via ecological niche modeling." *The Quarterly Review of Biology* 78(4):419–433.

Peterson, G., C.R. Allen, and C.S. Holling. 1998. "Ecological resilience, biodiversity and scale." *Ecosystems* 1:6–18.

Pimm, S.L. 1984. "The complexity and stability of ecosystems." *Nature* 307:321–326.

Reed, W.J. 1988. "Optimal harvesting of a fishery subject to random catastrophic collapse." *IMA Journal of Mathematics Applied in Medicine & Biology* 5:215–235.

Reed, W.J. and H.E. Heras. 1992. "The conservation and exploitation of vulnerable resources." *Bulletin of Mathematical Biology* 54:185–207.

Rilov, G. and D.R. Schiel. 2006. "Seascape-dependent subtidal-intertidal trophic linkages." *Ecology* 87(3):731–744.

Scheffer, M., S. Carpenter, J.A. Foley, C. Folke, and B. Walker. 2001. "Catastrophic shifts in ecosystems." *Nature* 413:591–596.

Silliman, B.R. and M.D. Bertness. 2002. "A trophic cascade regulates salt marsh primary production." *Proceedings of the National Academy of Sciences* 99(16):10500–10505.

Tilman, D. and C. Lehman. 2001. "Human-caused environmental change: impacts on plant diversity and evolution." *Proceedings of the National Academy of Sciences* 98:5433–5440.

Tilman, D., P.B. Reich, J. Knops *et al.* 2001. "Diversity and productivity in a long-term grassland experiment." *Science* 294:843–845.

Tsur, Y. and A. Zemel. 1994. "Endangered species and natural resource exploitation: extinction vs. coexistence." *Journal of Economic Dynamics and Control* 20:1289–1305.

2007. "Bio-economic resource management under threats of environmental catastrophes." *Ecological Research* 22:431–438.

Turner, M.G., W.H. Romme, R.H. Gardner, R.V. O' Neill, and T.K. Kratz. 1993. "A revised concept of landscape equilibrium: disturbance and stability on scaled landscapes." *Landscape Ecology* 8:213–227.

Walker, B., C.S. Holling, S.R. Carpenter, and A. Kinzig. 2004. "Resilience, adaptability and transformability in social-ecological systems." *Ecology and Society* 9(2):5.

Walker, B., L. Pearson, M. Harris *et al.* 2010. "Incorporating resilience in the assessment of inclusive wealth: an example from South East Australia." *Environmental and Resource Economics* 45:183–202.

Wellnitz, T. and N.L. Poff. 2001. "Functional redundancy in heterogeneous environments: implications for conservation." *Ecology Letters* 4:177–179.

Worm, B., E.B. Barbier, N. Beaumont *et al.* 2006. "Impacts of biodiversity loss on ocean ecosystem services." *Science* 314:787–790.

7 | *The way ahead*

Ecosystems are capital assets. Like reproducible capital assets (roads, buildings, and machinery), ecosystems depreciate if they are misused or are overused. But they differ from reproducible capital assets in three ways: (1) depreciation of natural capital is frequently irreversible (or at best the systems take a long time to recover), (2) except in a very limited sense, it isn't possible to replace a depleted or degraded ecosystem by a new one, and (3) ecosystems can collapse abruptly, without much prior warning.

(Dasgupta 2008, p. 3)

Introduction

The above quote by Partha Dasgupta summarizes succinctly the main theme of this book. Ecosystems are a special and unique form of capital asset and, as a result, the various goods and services that they provide us are not routinely reflected in markets and policy decisions. Most importantly, however, the quote reminds us of how much we still do not know about these unique capital assets. Overcoming this gap in knowledge is clearly a major research challenge. Natural science and economics are important to enhancing our understanding of ecosystems as natural assets, but only if these disciplines are applied jointly to the problem. That is, significant progress in the major research questions concerning ecosystems as natural assets can only be achieved through interdisciplinary collaboration between economists, ecologists, and environmental scientists.[1]

---

[1] I use the term "environmental scientist" very broadly, to include not only natural scientists who study various biophysical aspects of the natural environment (e.g., geographers, geomorphologists, hydrologists, soil scientists, etc.) but also scholars from history and social science who also study human interactions with the environment (e.g., anthropologists, environmental historians, political scientists, sociologists, etc.).

The purpose of the following chapter is to point "the way ahead" for such interdisciplinary research. The preceding chapters have pointed to several key research issues that are necessary to make further progress in assessing the contributing of ecosystems to human well-being. These issues are:

- the key advances that will be required to improve economic valuation of ecosystem goods and services;
- the research needed to determine how spatially heterogeneous landscapes influence the provision of ecosystem benefits, thus helping to identify the important biophysical and economic attributes of each landscape parcel in each location to optimize conservation decisions across ecological landscapes;
- the research required to analyze phases of ecological transition and assist restoration of degraded ecosystems;
- the need for more economic empirical and analytical studies to verify the conditions under which an open economy is likely to conserve rather than convert ecological landscapes, thus generating a greater flow of ecosystem services; and
- the research collaboration required to determine how the threat of collapse and the presence of thresholds affects the management of ecosystems as natural assets.

Although all of these issues have been touched on briefly in one or more of the previous chapters, this chapter will discuss these research needs in more detail. But in order to understand the "way ahead," we must first decide in which direction we need to go. And that objective should be to make economic development more sustainable.

Sustainable economic development

Much has been written and said about sustainable development. Fortunately, in economics, progress has been made in recent years to clarify this concept.

Two approaches have emerged in thinking about the role of the environment in sustainable development. The first adopts a *systems approach* to characterize sustainability as the maximization of goals across ecological, economic, and social systems. The second is a *capital approach*, which is more consistent with the theme of this book.

The systems approach can be captured in a Venn diagram (see Box 7.1), which was first proposed by Barbier (1987). The diagram depicts sustainable development as the intersection of the goals attributed to three systems: ecological, economic, and social. Attempting to maximize the goals for just one system does not achieve sustainabilility, because the impacts on the other systems are ignored. For example, achieving greater efficiency, equity, and reduced poverty in economic systems may still generate unintended environmental and social impacts that undermine ecological and social systems. Instead, sustainable development can only be achieved by balancing the trade-offs among the various goals of the three systems. Thus, the economic system should strive for efficiency, equity, and poverty reduction, but at the same time account for the impacts on biological productivity, biodiversity, and ecological resilience as well as the implications for social justice, good governance, and social stability.

Box 7.1 Sustainable development as systems Venn diagram

One popular way of representing sustainable development is to characterize it in a Venn diagram of three interlinked systems: ecological, economic, and social. The Venn diagram representation of sustainable development now has many versions, but was first used by Barbier (1987, Figure 1). The diagram below is adapted from the original.

As argued by Barbier (1987, p. 104), "each system has its own set of human-ascribed goals;" in contrast, "sustainable development involves a *process of trade-offs* among the various goals of the three systems" as "it is not possible to maximize all these objectives all the time." Attempting to maximize the goals for just one system, or even two, does not achieve sustainability because the costs imposed on the other systems are not taken into account. For example, an economic system may be efficient, and even equitable, in the allocation of resources but still generate environmental degradation that threatens biological productivity, biodiversity, and resilience. "The general objective of sustainable economic development, then, is to maximize the goals across all these systems through an adaptive process of trade-offs," which is illustrated by the intersection of the ecological, economic, and social systems.

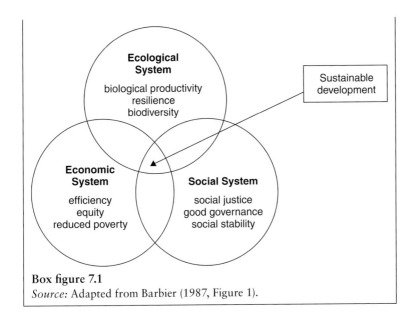

Box figure 7.1
Source: Adapted from Barbier (1987, Figure 1).

The sustainability objective of the systems approach sounds ideal, but it has practical limitations. In particular, there is no guidance as to how the tradeoffs among the goals of the various systems should be made. How should we decide to trade off, for example, more economic efficiency for less biodiversity and ecological resilience? As argued throughout this book, deciding on such tradeoffs is relatively straightforward, provided that we have a common framework of evaluation. The *capital approach* to sustainable development is one such framework, which is now the dominant economic paradigm for thinking about sustainability. This approach is summarized schematically in Figure 7.1.

Economic interpretations of sustainability usually take as their starting point the consensus reached by the World Commission on Environment and Development (WCED). The WCED (1987) defined sustainable development as "development that meets the needs of the present without compromising the ability of future generations to meet their own needs."

Economists are generally comfortable with this broad interpretation of sustainability, as it is easily translatable into economic terms: an increase in well-being today should not have as its consequences a

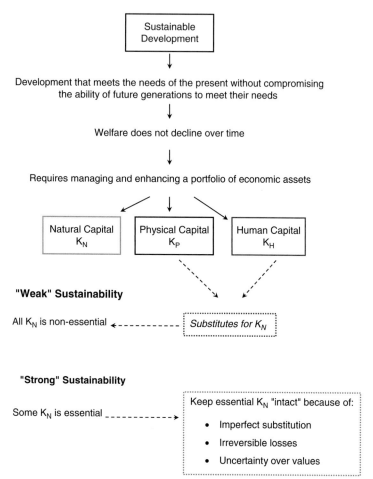

Figure 7.1 The capital approach to sustainable development
Source: Adapted from Pearce and Barbier (2000).

reduction in well-being tomorrow.[2] That is, future generations should be entitled to at least the same level of economic opportunities – and thus at least the same level of economic welfare – as currently available

[2] As Bishop (1993) has pointed out, stated in this way the objective of "sustainability" is different from that of the standard economic goal of "efficiency." That is, there is potentially an infinite number of development paths for an economy, only some of which are sustainable. Efficiency therefore does not guarantee sustainability, as some efficient paths are not sustainable. At the same time, there is no reason why an economy could not be both efficient and sustainable.

to present generations. Consequently, economic development today must ensure that future generations are left no worse off than present generations. Or, as some economists have succinctly put it, per capita welfare should not be declining over time (Pezzey 1989).

As noted in Figure 7.1, it is the *total* stock of capital employed by the economic system, including natural capital, which determines the full range of economic opportunities, and thus well-being, available to both present and future generations. Society must decide how best to use its total capital stock today to increase current economic activities and welfare, and how much it needs to save or even accumulate for tomorrow, and ultimately, for the well-being of future generations.

However, it is not simply the aggregate stock of capital in the economy that may matter but also its composition, in particular whether present generations are using up one form of capital to meet the needs of today. For example, much of the interest in sustainable development has risen out of concern that current economic development may be leading to rapid accumulation of physical and human capital, but at the expense of excessive depletion and degradation of natural capital. The major concern has been that, by depleting the world's stock of natural wealth irreversibly, the development path chosen today will have detrimental implications for the well-being of future generations. In other words, according to this view, current economic development is essentially unsustainable.

From an economic standpoint, the critical issue of debate is not whether natural capital is being irreversibly depleted, but whether individuals today can compensate future generations for the current loss of natural capital and, if that is possible, how much compensation is required for this loss (Mäler 1995). Economists concerned with this problem appear to be divided into two camps over the special role of natural capital in sustainable development. The main disagreement is whether natural capital has a unique or *essential* role in sustaining human welfare, and thus whether special "compensation rules" are required to ensure that future generations are not made worse off by natural capital depletion today. These two contrasting views are now generally referred to as *weak sustainability* versus *strong sustainability* (see Figure 7.1).[3]

---

[3] For further discussion of this distinction between weak and strong sustainability see Barbier *et al.* (1994); Howarth and Norgaard (1995); Pearce

According to the *weak sustainability* view, there is essentially no inherent difference between natural and other forms of capital, and hence the same compensation rules ought to apply to both. As long as the natural capital that is being depleted is replaced with even more valuable physical and human capital, then the value of the aggregate stock – comprising human, physical, and the remaining natural capital – is increasing over time.[4] Maintaining and enhancing the total stock of all capital alone is sufficient to attain sustainable development.

In contrast, proponents of the *strong sustainability* view argue that physical or human capital cannot substitute for all the environmental resources comprising the natural capital stock, or all of the ecological services performed by nature. Consequently, the strong sustainability viewpoint questions whether, on the one hand, human and physical capital, and on the other, natural capital, effectively comprise a single homogeneous total capital stock. Instead, proponents of strong sustainability maintain that some forms of natural capital are essential to human welfare, particularly key ecological goods and services, unique environments and natural habitats, and even irreplaceable natural resource attributes (such as biodiversity). Uncertainty over the true value to human welfare of these important assets, in particular the value that future generations may place on them if they become increasingly scarce, further limits our ability to determine whether we can adequately compensate future generations for irreversible losses in such essential natural capital today. Thus the strong sustainability view suggests that environmental resources and ecological goods and services that are essential for human welfare and cannot be easily substituted by human and physical capital should be protected and not depleted. The only satisfactory compensation rule for protecting the welfare of future generations is to keep essential natural capital intact. That is, maintaining or increasing the value of the total capital

---

et al. (1989); Neumayer (2010); Pearce and Barbier (2000); Toman *et al.* (1995); and Turner (1993).

[4] Note, however, that rapid population growth may imply that the value of the per capita aggregate capital stock is declining even if the total value stays the same. Moreover, even if the per capita value of the asset base were maintained, it may not imply non-declining welfare of the majority of people. These considerations also hold for the "strong sustainability" arguments discussed below.

stock over time in turn requires keeping the nonsubstitutable and essential components of natural capital constant over time.

The debate between weak and strong sustainability perspectives is not easy to reconcile. Nevertheless, it is clear that the *very minimum* criterion for attaining sustainable economic development is ensuring that an economy satisfies *weak sustainability* conditions. That is, as long as the natural capital that is being depleted is replaced with even more valuable physical and human capital, then *the value of the aggregate stock* – comprising human, physical, and the remaining natural capital – should be increasing over time (Barbier *et al.* 1994; Barbier 2005). This in turn requires that the development path of an economy is governed by certain principles.[5] First, environmental and natural resources must be managed efficiently so that the welfare losses from environmental damages are minimized and any resource rents earned after "internalizing" environmental externalities are maximized. Second, the rents arising from the depletion of natural capital must be invested into other productive economic assets.

However, the conditions under which depletion of natural capital may or may not lead to more sustainable development clearly depend on what we include as this form of wealth. This book has argued that ecosystems should and can be viewed as economic assets. But as Dasgupta (2008, p. 3) reminds us, ecosystems are very unique capital assets. The provision of goods and services by many ecosystems are poorly understood, and their values are often unmarketed and unknown. In addition, the presence of ecological thresholds and the threat of collapse mean that we are often unaware of the full ecological and economic consequences of current levels of ecosystem degradation and conversion. Moreover, once converted, ecosystems may not be irreversibly lost, but reparation and restoration could be prohibitively expensive, if not technically infeasible in some cases. Improving our knowledge in all of these areas is a critical task. Better understanding of the complex workings of ecosystems and the value of the

---

[5] These principles are inspired conceptually by Hartwick's rule (Hartwick 1977), which is often also referred to as the Hartwick–Solow rule, in recognition that Solow (1974) first derived the principle that reinvestment of the rents generated from the intertemporally efficient use of exhaustible natural resources can be reinvested in reproducible capital in order to ensure a constant stream of consumption over time. Solow (1993) provides an excellent summary of the implications of Hartwick's rule for economic sustainability.

various goods and services they produce may also help to resolve the weak versus strong sustainability debate over what constitutes essential natural capital. As we have seen throughout this book, overcoming these gaps in our knowledge is also important for improving the management decision to convert or conserve ecological landscapes.

Overcoming valuation challenges

As pointed out in Chapter 2, assessing the nonmarket value of ecosystem goods and services is essential to getting the conservation versus development tradeoff right. Although in recent years substantial progress has been made by economists working with ecologists and other natural scientists in valuing many important ecosystem goods and services, more research progress is still required for many services arising from ecosystem processes and regulatory functions, such as storm protection, water flow regulation, nutrient cycling, erosion control, water purification, and carbon sequestration. How these functions vary temporally and spatially across ecological landscapes can affect significantly the economic benefits that they provide.

For example, Chapter 4 demonstrates the importance of spatial variation in determining conservation decisions. Already, studies have shown how the spatial variability of costs across an ecological landscape influences the decision as to how much land area to protect, which landscapes to include cost-effectively for achieving overall conservation targets, and the selection of alternative possible sites for protected areas (Ando *et al.* 1998; Balmford *et al.* 2003; Carwardine *et al.* 2008; Ferraro 2003, 2004; Naidoo *et al.* 2006; Parkhurst and Shogren 2008; Polasky *et al.* 2001). But as shown in Chapter 4, the spatial variability of ecosystem benefits across a landscape can have a considerable influence on conservation and land use decisions. What is needed is more studies to illustrate this effect, and for more ecosystem services than the mangrove case study analyzed in that chapter.

The value of some ecosystem services can also vary spatially (i.e., distance from one landscape boundary) and temporally (i.e., seasonality). This is of particular importance for recreational and property-related benefits in coastal systems (Coombes *et al.* 2010, Morgan and Hamilton 2010). A study of home values near Pensacola Beach, Florida, found that Gulf-front property owners were willing to pay an annual tax of $5,807 for a five-year beach nourishment project that would improve access and shoreline views; however, the tax payment declines to $2,770 for a property in the next block, $2,540 for a property two blocks away, and $1,684 for a property three blocks away (Morgan and Hamilton 2010). Models of beach visitors in East Anglia, UK, reveal that seasonal differences are important. For example, school holidays and temperatures have the greatest influence on visitor numbers, and the visitors' propensity to visit the coast increases rapidly at temperatures exceeding 15°C (Coombes *et al.* 2010). Spatial characteristics that were also associated with more visitors included wide and sandy beaches, beach cleanliness, the presence of a nature reserve, pier or an urban area behind the beach, and close proximity of an entrance point, car park, and toilet facilities.

Since the seminal contribution by Clark (1976), economists have also sought to develop spatial models of marine ecosystem management in a variety of contexts, including determining optimal harvesting and marine reserve establishment.[6] As noted by Grafton *et al.* (2005, p. 168), there are two key implications that arise from including spatial variability in such models. First, fishers tend to reallocate their effort to areas that generate higher relative rents. The result is the creation of spatial "economic gradients" that might differ from the "biological gradients" generated by larval export and adult migration. Second, including the additional spatial variation in rents may be particularly important in determining the location of marine reserves. Ignoring this spatial effect tends to result in predicted rises in fish stocks that are greater than the actual increases associated with establishing a reserve. For example, in the Californian sea urchin fishery, how divers respond to profits earned in different locations is an important determinant of whether reserve creation leads to higher net benefits (Smith and Wilen 2003).

Spatially explicit models of land use change have also emerged in recent years.[7] Such models have enhanced our understanding of how to manage forest, watersheds, and other ecological landscapes. However, the observation of Albers (1996, p. 92) concerning the effectiveness of such models for tropical forests still holds true for

[6] See, for example, Brown and Roughgarden (1997); Costello and Polasky (2008); Sanchirico (2005); Sanchirico and Wilen (1999, 2002, 2005); Smith and Wilen (2003); and Smith *et al.* (2009).

[7] See, for example, Albers (1996); Albers *et al.* (2008); Alix-Garcia (2007); Irwin and Geoghegan (2001); and Robinson *et al.* (2008).

all landscape applications: "an application of the model to a management decision requires extensive studies on economic valuation and the underlying ecological production functions, but both types of information are limited for tropical forests."

In addition, landscapes generate multiple ecosystem goods and services. These typically range from tourism and recreation benefits to property protection, erosion control, nutrient cycling, water purification, and carbon sequestration to food and raw material products. Where studies are aware of such multiple benefits, the current approach is still to value each service independently, as was done for coastal protection, habitat-fishery linkages, and raw materials for mangroves in Thailand (see Barbier 2007 and Chapter 2). However, as the same ecological processes and functions may influence more than one ecosystem good or service, such ecological interactions are bound to affect the value of multiple benefits arising from a single landscape, which is an important direction for future research.

One approach is simply to account for as many of the important ecosystem values necessary for determining conservation versus development tradeoffs. For example, Johnston *et al.* (2002) estimate the benefits arising from a wide range of ecosystem services provided by the Peconic Estuary in Long Island, New York. The tidal mudflats, salt marshes, and seagrass (eelgrass) beds of the estuary support the shellfish and demersal fisheries. In addition, birdwatching and waterfowl hunting are popular activities. Incorporating production function methods, the authors simulate the biological and food web interactions of the ecosystems to assess the marginal value per acre in terms of gains in commercial value for fish and shellfish, birdwatching, and waterfowl hunting. The aggregate annual benefits are estimated to be $67 per acre for intertidal mud flats, $338 for salt marsh, and $1,065 for seagrass across the estuary system. Using these estimates, the authors calculate the asset value per acre of protecting existing habitats to be $12,412 per acre for seagrass, $4,291 for salt marsh, and $786 for mud flats; in comparison, the asset value of restored habitats is $9,996 per acre for seagrass, $3,454 for marsh, and $626 for mudflats.

A second approach is to develop integrated ecological–economic modeling to determine the complex ecological production underlying multiple ecosystem services (see Tschirhart 2009, for a review). For example, economic studies of large marine ecosystems have extended simple single-species or predator–prey harvesting models to consider multi-species relationships and their impacts on harvesting the commercially valuable species from the ecosystem (Finnoff and Tschirhart 2003a, 2003b; Sanchirico *et al.* 2008). These studies find that the non-commercial species in marine ecosystems have value because they support commercial fisheries indirectly via the effect of total diversity on the productivity of the fisheries and overall ecosystem stability. Finnoff and Tschirhart (2008) extend such a modeling framework to include a second service, tourism, and show how the food web connections between fish and mammals in the marine system are essential to the provision of both commercial harvest and tourism values.[8]

But a word of caution: integrated ecological–economic models may lead to better predictions of how changes in an ecosystem can influence the flow of ecosystem goods and services, yet the result may not always matter to environmental policy. For example, Settle and Shogren (2006) use an integrated model of Yellowstone Lake to show how the predictive risks to native cutthroat trout valued by anglers is affected by the introduction of the exotic lake trout invader. Although the integrated model represents ecological changes more accurately, the authors find little difference between the present value of net benefits for the best and worst case scenarios for cutthroat populations. In addition, valuation experiments that elicit preferences for wildlife scenarios reveal that a park visitor cares more about improving road quality than protecting cutthroat trout. Thus, Settle and Shogren (2006, p. 2) conclude: "Bioeconomic integration matters for species population estimates, but does not matter to the composite visitor, which implies the policy recommendation would be the same regardless of whether one accounts for feedbacks or not: *fix the roads, forget the fish.*"

Ecosystems also do not exist in isolation, but are interconnected. Often, this interlinking of systems results in enhanced values and multiple benefits. For instance, a unique feature of estuarine and coastal ecosystems (ECEs) is that they occur at the interface between the coast, land, and watersheds, which also make them especially valuable. The location of ECEs in the land–sea interface suggests a high

---

[8] See also Nelson *et al.* (2009), who combine integrated ecological–economic modeling with economic valuation methods to analyze land use options in the Willamette Basin, which is discussed in detail in Chapter 2.

degree of *interconnectedness* or *connectivity* across these systems, leading to the linked provision of one or multiple services by more than one ECE.

As Moberg and Rönnbäck (2003) describe for tropical regions, numerous physical and biogeochemical interactions have been identified among mangroves, seagrass beds, and coral reefs that effectively create interconnected systems, or a single *seascape*. By dissipating the force of currents and waves, coral reefs are instrumental for the evolution of lagoons and sheltered bays that are suitable environments for seagrass beds and mangroves. In turn, the control of sedimentation, nutrients, and pollutants by mangroves and seagrasses create the coastal water conditions that favor the growth of coral reefs. This synergistic relationship between coral reefs, seagrasses, mangroves, and even sand dunes, suggests that the presence of these interlinked habitats in a seascape may considerably enhance the ecosystem service provided by one single habitat.

For example, Alongi (2008) suggests that the extent to which mangroves offer protection against catastrophic storm events, such as tsunamis, may depend not only on the relevant features and conditions within the mangrove ecosystem, such as width of forest, slope of forest floor, forest density, tree diameter and height, proportion of above-ground biomass in the roots, soil texture, and forest location (open coast versus lagoon), but also on the presence of foreshore habitats, such as coral reefs, seagrass beds, and dunes. Similar cumulative effects of wave attenuation are noted for seascapes containing coral reefs, seagrasses, and marshes (Koch *et al.* 2009). Each ECE habitat has considerable ability to attenuate waves, and thus the presence of foreshore habitats, such as coral reefs and seagrasses, can reduce significantly the wave energy reaching the seaward edge of mangroves, salt marshes, sand beaches, and dunes. For instance, evidence from the Seychelles documents show how rising coral reef mortality and deterioration have increased significantly the wave energy reaching shores that are normally protected from erosion and storm surges by these reefs (Sheppard *et al.* 2005). In the Caribbean, mangroves appear not only to protect shorelines from coastal storms but may also enhance the recovery of coral reef fish populations from disturbances due to hurricanes and other violent storms (Mumby and Hastings 2008).

ECE habitats are also linked biologically. Many fish and shellfish species utilize mangroves and seagrass beds as nursery grounds, and eventually migrate to coral reefs as adults, only to return to the mangroves and seagrasses to spawn.[9] In addition, the high biological productivity of mangroves, marshes, and seagrasses also produce significant amounts of organic matter that is used directly or indirectly by marine fishes, shrimps, crabs, and other species (Chong 2007). The consequence is that interconnected seascapes contribute significantly to supporting fisheries via a number of ecosystem functions including nursery and breeding habitat, trophic interactions, and predator-free habitat.

For example, studies in the Caribbean show that the presence of mangroves and seagrasses enhance considerably the biomass of coral reef fish communities (Mumby 2006; Mumby *et al.* 2004; Nagelkerken *et al.* 2002). In Malaysia, it is estimated that mangrove forests sustain more than half of the annual offshore fish landings, much of which are from reef fisheries (Chong 2007). In Puerto Rico, maps show fish distributions to be controlled by the spatial arrangement of mangroves, seagrasses, and coral reefs and the relative value of these habitats as nurseries (Aguilar-Perera and Appeldoorn 2008). Stratification of environmental conditions along a marsh habitat gradient, stretching from intertidal vegetated salt marshes, to subtidal marsh creeks, to marsh–bay fringe, and then to open water channels, indicates large spatial and temporal variability in fish migration, nursery habitats, and food webs (Rountree and Able 2007). Finally, indices representing the connectivity of mangroves, salt marshes, and channels explained 30–70 percent of the catch-per-unit effort harvesting yields for commercially caught species in Queensland, Australia (Meynecke *et al.* 2008).

Sanchirico and Mumby (2009) develop an integrated seascape model to illustrate how the presence of mangroves and seagrasses enhance considerably the biomass of coral reef fish communities. A key finding is that mangroves become more important as nursery habitat when excessive fishing effort levels are applied to the reef, because the mangroves can directly offset the negative impacts of fishing effort. Such results support the development of *ecosystem-based management* of fisheries and the design of integrated coastal-marine

---

[9] See, for example, Layman and Silliman (2002); Meynecke *et al.* (2008); Mumby *et al.* (2004); Nagelkerken *et al.* (2002); and Rountree and Able (2007).

reserves that emphasize the importance of conserving and restoring coastal mangroves as nursery sites for reef fisheries (Mumby 2006).

Ecological restoration and transitions

Chapter 3 examined many ecological and economic aspects of ecosystem restoration, focusing in particular on case study examples of forests and wetlands. These issues are becoming more relevant as development proceeds, landscapes disappear, and ecological scarcity ensures that ecosystem goods and services become more valuable with time. But for ecological restoration to occur on a large scale, it must not only be technologically feasible but also be sufficient to justify the costs of restoration.

However, for many ecosystems, ecological restoration is difficult and costly, and requires the right incentives. For example, in Thailand, the full costs of replanting and restoring mangroves in abandoned shrimp ponds is estimated to be around $9,318 per hectare (ha), which nearly accounts for the entire capitalized value of the restored services of $12,392 per ha (Barbier 2007). As discussed in Chapter 3, this suggests that investors in shrimp farms and other coastal developments that cause widespread mangrove destruction should have the legal requirement to replant mangroves and finance the costs, rather than leaving mangrove restoration solely to governments and local communities.

It should be recognized also that *ex post* ecological restoration is no panacea for failed conservation. Such investments are not only costly but risky, and in many cases fall short of recovering the full suite of ecosystem goods and services (Palmer and Filoso 2009). For example, as discussed above, the Johnston *et al.* (2002) study of the Peconic Estuary of Long Island found that the asset value of restored salt marsh and seagrass and tidal mudflats in terms of nursery habitat and recreational services were much lower than for conserving the original habitats. Studies of wetland mitigation programs in the United States reveal that the overall criterion of restoring particular wetland plant community types is not an appropriate goal if the objective is to restore wetlands with a high conservation value or provision of ecosystem services; instead, consideration of hydrological and landscape processes and the appropriate species assemblage in the restored wetlands is essential (Matthews *et al.* 2009). Similar findings have been noted for restoring coastal and estuarine wetlands in the United States, where poor site location with respect to the surrounding landscape and lack of consideration of the appropriate hydrological regime have been common ecological factors in restoration failure (Lewis 2000, 2005; Lewis and Gilmore 2007; Reed and Wilson 2004; Simenstad *et al.* 2006).

In addition to more analysis of the costs and benefits of ecological restoration efforts, as well as the economic incentives determining whether such investments will take place, there need to be more studies of the long-term policy and market trends that influence ecological transitions. As discussed in Chapter 3, a good example is the wider development and policy context that determines whether a *forest transition* occurs. The forest transition literature recognizes that long-term forest land use consists of two distinct phases, an initial phase of forest conversion followed by a new phase where forest recovery becomes technically and economically feasible. Different factors also appear to drive forest decline as opposed to forest recovery.

As we discussed in Chapter 3, for most countries the decline in forest cover is mainly the result of the rapid loss of natural forest cover as agricultural area expands in response to rising demand for food and other commodities as economic development proceeds and populations grow. Agricultural land expansion may eventually taper off as the limits of land suitability are reached, farming modernizes and intensifies following investment in improved technologies, and economies reach an advanced stage of economic development such that the demand for food rises less rapidly. In contrast, as an economy develops further, the increased demand for wood products and nonmarket ecosystem services from forested land may lead to forest replenishment, and perhaps eventually a recovery in the total forest area. International trade may also play an important role in forest land use decisions through its export demand for forest-based products. In addition, if farmland is abandoned but not necessarily converted to other uses, e.g., to satisfy the demand for land for residential housing and urbanization, natural reforestation may also occur (Mather and Needle 1998; Rudel *et al.* 2005).

Attempts have been made to explain the typical paths of forest change that characterize the forest transition. Rudel *et al.* (2005) distinguish between an *economic development path* and a *forest scarcity path.* As economies advance, they create better nonfarm jobs and economic opportunities that attract farmers, rural households, and workers from the agricultural sector, which in turn leads to the abandonment of the less productive and profitable arable land. As the stock of abandoned cropland increases, some of it reverts to forest. Rudel *et al.* (2005) refer to this process as the *economic development path* to the forest transition. Their second hypothesis is that a relative scarcity of forests results in either price signals or political pressures. Forest replenishment occurs as private landowners and the forest products industry increasingly invest in more plantations and the management of secondary forests for commercial timber products as well as tree crops (e.g., oil palm, rubber, cocoa, coffee, etc.). The stimulus for these investments is the rising demand for these products, as per capita incomes increase (Foster and Rosenzweig 2003; Mather 2000; Rudel *et al.* 2005). Rudel *et al.* (2005) refer to this process as the *forest scarcity path* to the forest transition, since it is often signaled through rising prices for timber and tree products in markets and growing concern over the availability of domestic supplies expressed by policymakers and industry. Economic development may also lead to an improvement in domestic institutions that are better able to establish and enforce appropriate land use policies that reduce the previously distorted incentives for excessive forest land conversion. Policymakers may also respond to local and international political pressures arising out of reductions in ecosystem goods and services as forest areas contract and create positive incentives for forest conservation and re-establishment.

In addition, the transition from forest decline to recovery may not necessarily be smooth (Perz and Skole 2003). Long-term forest loss trends may fluctuate, reflecting alternating phases of decline and rise. Forest area may also rise discontinuously after the forest transition, leading to confusion about whether it has happened. Changes in economic and political conditions can contribute to such trends; e.g., Mather and Needle (2000) cite numerous examples of both discontinuous decline and rise in France due to changes in such conditions. Forest can also expand in some parts of a country while deforestation still continues elsewhere. Such evidence of regional forest restoration has been documented by Grainger (2008). For example, in some locations forest can expand through natural forest regeneration on abandoned farmland, e.g., because more productive farmland has been discovered elsewhere. But it is also possible that local wood market forces may come into play as forest is depleted in some parts of a country, and promote forest recovery there. But afforestation could also occur preferentially in some regions of a country in response to world market factors, as happened with pulpwood plantations in Brazil.

International trade and payments for ecosystem services

The example of the forest transition illustrates how international trade can play an important role in influencing land and resource use over time. As we saw in Chapter 5, many of the poor countries that contain some of the world's most important ecosystems are facing intense development, population, and poverty pressures. Economic development in the majority of these countries is still highly dependent on expanding primary product exports. The result is that there is a tradeoff between increased development activities, the products of which are often sold on world markets, and the conservation of ecological landscapes.

However, simply because such a tradeoff exists, it does not mean that the policy response should be to discourage trade in primary products by developing economies. To the contrary, as the literature on the forest transition indicates, forest replenishment often occurs as private landowners and the forest products industry increasingly invest in more plantations and the management of secondary forests for commercial timber products as well as tree crops (e.g., oil palm, rubber, cocoa, coffee, etc.). Similarly, the development of an export-oriented forest products industry can also lead to rational management of the remaining old-growth forests between production and conservation uses. As we discussed in both Chapters 2 and 5, a number of studies point to the complex interactions that occur between corruption and terms of trade changes to affect natural capital depletion in developing countries. Macroeconomic influences and trade policy also have complicated impacts on land conversion in developing countries, making it difficult to determine how trade interventions alter land use change. Nevertheless, the worrying trend is that deforestation, especially in tropical countries, is still occurring at a rapid pace, and that it is both correlated with economic growth, agricultural land expansion, and road building (Barbier 2005; Chomitz *et al.* 2007; López and Galinato 2005; Naidoo 2004; Rudel 2005, 2007).

What is clearly needed are more studies to disentangle the complex relationship between trade, economic policies, good governance, and ecosystem loss, especially in developing countries.

Improving our understanding of the long-term trends behind the continuing decline in major ecosystems would be a start. Box 7.2 summarizes, for example, the preliminary effort by Barbier and Cox (2003) to understand how economic development has affected mangrove loss globally. The results show that shrimp aquaculture and agriculture are associated with mangrove deforestation, especially in low- and middle-income countries with large mangrove areas. But as mangrove-rich countries develop economically and become less dependent on primary sector activities, they incur less mangrove loss. The number of protected areas, length of coastline, and political stability are also important in determining the remaining mangrove area of a country. However, such an analysis is currently limited by data availability on changes in mangrove area over time. Improved data collection and further analysis are needed for determining how long-run economic development affects mangroves and other important global ecosystems.

More studies are also needed on the complex relationship between international commodity markets, natural resource exploitation, and environmental protection. A good example is the study by Sohngen *et al.* (1999), who model how rising global demand and prices in global timber markets may affect forest management and conservation (see Chapter 5). In general, they find that, despite rising demand and prices for forest products, large areas of remote forests are likely to remain inaccessible for timber exploitation for the foreseeable future. But if greater forest protection for biodiversity conservation or carbon sequestration in one region of the world leads to upward pressure on timber prices, it could lead to greater exploitation of previously inaccessible forests in tropical and boreal regions. In addition, deforestation may still occur in boreal and tropical ecosystems because of the demand for agricultural land conversion, lack of effective tenure and property right regimes, and government subsidies and other policy failures.

The idea of paying farmers and landowners to preserve land that yields valuable ecosystem goods and services is gaining ground.

Box 7.2 How does economic development affect mangrove loss?

Mangroves line one-quarter of the world's tropical coastlines, and approximately 117 countries have mangrove resources within their borders. However, as a result of human activities in coastal areas, an estimated 35 percent of the world's mangroves have disappeared (FAO 2007; Valiela *et al.* 2001). To understand better how economic development affects mangrove deforestation Barbier and Cox (2003) analyze the relationship between remaining mangrove area, economic activity, and other important causative factors for a cross-section of 89 countries. The authors find that mangrove loss is associated with expansion of shrimp aquaculture production along coastlines and primary sector (i.e., agricultural) activities generally, but not necessarily in all low- and middle-income countries. Instead, it appears that countries with large mangrove areas are particularly susceptible to mangrove conversion from primary sector activities. There is also evidence that, as a mangrove-rich country develops economically and presumably becomes less dependent on primary sector activities, it may reduce its mangrove deforestation. On the other hand, if the country is politically unstable and has accessible mangrove areas due to improved road networks, then these factors will also contribute to increased mangrove loss. However, increased investment in environmental protection will counteract this loss somewhat. Two important policy implications emerge from the analysis. First, there seems to be considerable scope for countries to reduce mangrove deforestation through mitigating the impacts of all primary sector activities in coastal areas, including shrimp aquaculture, on remaining mangrove areas. Second, if the international community can provide technical and financial assistance to developing economies with large remaining mangrove areas to increase their protection and conservation efforts, then this may be one way of slowing down rates of mangrove loss globally.

Progress has been made in establishing international payments for global ecosystem services, most notably a nascent financial mechanism to reduce emissions from deforestation and forest degradation (REDD). As we saw in Chapter 5, in theory, REDD and other international payment schemes for ecosystem services could help overcome the huge funding gap for global ecosystem conservation (Pearce 2007). For example, the annual cost of reducing global deforestation by 10 percent through a REDD scheme may be around $0.4–1.7 billion but the additional financing through carbon markets could earn developing countries $2.2–13.5 billion annually (Ebeling and Yasué 2008; Kindermann *et al.* 2008).

But as we discussed in Chapter 5, there are also important disincentives that deter the establishment of large-scale international financial mechanisms for payment of ecosystem services (PES). More work needs to be conducted on these issues, to determine how best to design international payment schemes, overcome monitoring and verification concerns, and compensate for the losses in development benefits incurred by poor economies and rural people.

Much more analysis has to be conducted on reconciling payment for ecosystem services with the problem of widespread rural poverty in many developing economies. The main purpose of introducing PES schemes is to influence land use decisions by enabling landholders to capture more of the value of these environmental services than they would have done in the absence of the mechanism. While in some cases participants in such schemes do not have to demonstrate formal land titles to be eligible for payments, many of the rural poor in developing regions lack not only formal but also actual access to land. Others are near-landless or have holdings so small that they would have difficulty in participating in forest protection or planting schemes on their land. In such instances, there are limits on the success of payment schemes in alleviating poverty.

As we argued in Chapter 5, there are three principal ways in which market mechanisms for ecosystem services might also alleviate poverty. First, if payments for ecosystem services are made directly to poor rural households to maintain or enhance these services, then they provide needed cash income. Second, whether or not the rural poor receive direct payments, they may benefit indirectly from any resulting improvement in the provision of ecosystem services. Third, the rural poor may also gain from any additional economic opportunities created by payment schemes, such as the employment created by reforestation or other conservation investments. Clearly, further work needs to be conducted to examine these three ways of designing PES schemes to help boost their alleviation of rural poverty. However, there are limits to trying to use any conservation mechanism, such as PES, as a widespread poverty-alleviation measure. The principle aim of such measures is still fundamentally to compensate land users for foregoing ecological degradation and preserving remaining valuable ecological landscapes instead. As Wunder (2008, p. 295) reminds us: "Poverty reduction is an important PES side objective, and safeguards can be taken to address it properly – but it should never become the primary goal of PES."

Further research is also needed on the incentives for landowners and resource users to participate in PES schemes. To supply ecosystem services, private landowners incur costs. If payments fail to compensate landowners for these costs, then there will be poor enrolment in or compliance with PES schemes. As shown in Box 7.3, the cost-effectiveness of a PES scheme can be considerably enhanced if a reliable supply curve of ecosystem services obtained per dollar spent can be estimated. Such an approach can improve the design of a scheme to target contracts and reduce the tradeoffs between poverty alleviation and the provision of ecosystem services.

Box 7.3 Estimating a supply curve for ecosystem services

To supply ecosystem services, landowners incur costs. Although knowing how much ecosystems services will be supplied per dollar spent can increase the cost-effectiveness of payment for ecosystem services (PES) schemes, obtaining this information is difficult before a scheme is established. To overcome this problem, Jack *et al.* (2009) demonstrate how an auction of payment contracts can be used to reveal private information about the costs of supplying ecosystem services during the design phases of a PES program. With an estimate of the ecosystem-service supply curve from a pilot auction, implementers of the scheme can improve the design of programs devised to protect and enhance ecosystem services. The authors conduct a uniform-price auction for soil conservation contracts in Sumatra, Indonesia, where soil erosion on coffee farms generates downstream ecological impacts and economic cost. The figure below is the supply curve for hectares under soil erosion control, which was estimated by Jack *et al.* (2009) from auction bids for payment contracts for two villages. Just under half of the 82 auction participants received contracts for soil conservation, with

Box 7.3 (*cont.*)

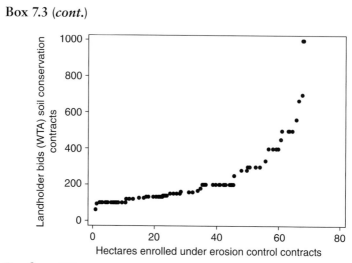

Box figure 7.3
Source: Jack *et al.* (2009, Figure 1).

an average auction price of $171.70 per hectare (ha). The aggregate supply curve in the figure is for both villages, and shows the number of ha enrolled in the program for any given price. Employing this supply curve, Jack *et al.* (2009) demonstrate how conservation targets can be altered by: 1) varying the program budget and thus the price offered per contract; 2) combining bids with measures of erosion per ha to target plots with high erosion-control benefits; and 3) targeting the poorer households.

Thresholds, resilience, and collapse

Chapter 6 emphasized the need for further research to examine the importance of ecosystem functioning and organization on both the provision of ecosystem goods and services and also important system properties, such as ecological resilience and regime shift. Clearly, understanding these processes is an urgent priority, for as Dasgupta (2008, p. 3) points out, "ecosystems can collapse abruptly, without much prior warning."

There is still much uncertainty concerning the complex processes that lead to ecological collapse. For example, Dobson *et al.* (2006) model changes in ecosystem services for large-scale land use change to determine which services tend to decline rapidly with habitat loss and trophic collapse. As discussed in Chapter 6, field studies for coastal ecosystems, such as mangroves and salt marsh, also provide evidence in support of such a relationship. For these systems, positive inter-actions among ecological functions, trophic cascades and linkages, and biodiversity appear to be positively correlated with landscape scale.[10] The implication is that the probability of ecological collapse is likely to increase with a diminishing size of the ecological landscape. But there is still considerable uncertainty surrounding this relationship, and the processes that lead to hysteresis and collapse for many ecosystems.

There is mounting evidence for a number of ecosystems that, under pressure from external disturbances, may switch abruptly to a con-trasting alternative stable state, or *ecological regime* (Folke *et al.* 2004; Scheffer *et al.* 2001). Although a variety of disturbances may trigger the regime shift, what determines whether an ecosystem will change to an alternative state depends on its *resilience* or *robust-ness* – the ecosystem's ability to absorb large shocks or sustained dis-turbances and still maintain internal integrity and functioning. As we discussed in Chapter 6, this concept of resilience can be traced to Holling (1973), who assumes that ecosystems are characterized by multiple locally stable equilibria, and regime shift entails sudden shift from one stable equilibrium to another. Thus, the resilience of an eco-system can be thought of as the extent to which it can sustain shocks or disturbances before the ecosystem "flips" to an alternative stable state, or ecological regime.

As explored in Chapter 6, there is now mounting evidence of how diminishing ecological resilience influences regime shifts in a number of distinct ecosystems, including deserts, coral reefs, forests, lakes, and oceans (see Table 6.1 and Folke *et al.* 2004). There have even been attempts to measure the "capital value" of resilience for agricul-tural systems in Australia (see Walker *et al.* 2010 and Box 6.2) and the benefits of avoiding the effects of ecological regime shift in the Black Sea anchovy fishery (Knowler *et al.* 2002). But clearly much more research is required to examine the importance of ecosystem functioning and organization on ecosystem thresholds, resilience,

---

[10] See, for example, Elliott *et al.* (2007); Farnsworth (1998); Halpern *et al.* (2007); Petersen *et al.* (2003); Rilov and Schiel (2006); and Silliman and Bertness (2002).

and tendency to collapse. Box 7.4 summarizes some of the essential
elements that ecologists believe underlie an ecosystem's resilience,
and the supporting evidence from field studies of coastal and marine
systems.

**Box 7.4 Ecological resilience in coastal and marine
ecosystems**

Levin (1999) identifies several essential elements that underlie
an ecosystem's resilience: *diversity and heterogeneity, redundancy and degeneracy, modularity*, and the *tightness of feedback
loops*. Levin and Lubchenco (2008) describe how all these elements interact in the support of the resilience of coastal and marine ecosystems. For example, diversity and heterogeneity reflect
the adaptive capacity of a system, and assist its ability to alter its
composition in a changing environment. In ocean systems, more
highly diverse large-scale marine ecosystems contain a smaller
fraction of collapsed commercial fisheries, and a higher rate of
recovery of collapsed fisheries, than large marine ecosystems with
less diversity (Worm *et al.* 2006). Redundancy, or degeneracy,
means that multiple, distinct elements in an ecosystem perform
the same function, and are linked to diversity and heterogeneity.
For example, having multiple nitrogen fixers in a system means
that if environmental conditions change so that one is lost, the
others may expand their role and replace it. In marine intertidal
and subtidal communities, species redundancy and complementarity are important to ecosystem resistance to disturbance and
recovery (Palumbi *et al.* 2008). Modularity refers to the compart-
mentalization of the ecosystem in space, time, or organizational
structure. Modularity in the distribution of species in a marine
ecosystem allows species populations and subpopulations to fluctuate independently, buffering against unfavorable environmental
conditions (Ruckelshaus *et al.* 2008). Tight feedback loops allow
the system to respond quickly and adaptively to changing environmental conditions, and may be reflected in critical ecosystem
properties such as food-web stability. As pointed out by Worm
and Duffy (2003, p. 630), "No discussion of ecological feedbacks
would be complete without considering trophic interactions, which

represent perhaps the most important class of feedback phenomena in ecosystems." Food-web stability appears to be enhanced when species at a higher trophic level feed on multiple prey species and when species at an intermediate trophic level are fed upon by multiple predator species (Gross *et al.* 2009). Food web links are especially notable in ocean systems. The openness of marine ecosystems, lack of specialists, long lifespans, and large size changes across the life histories of many marine species make marine food webs more highly connected than terrestrial and freshwater webs (Link 2002). But this high connectivity also means that marine ecosystems are highly vulnerable to "fishing down the food web," which has been a persistent phenomenon for most global fisheries for decades (Pauly *et al.* 1998).

Chapter 2 emphasized the importance of greater understanding of the ecological production underlying the provision of many ecosystem goods and services. As argued by Polasky and Segerson (2009, p. 422), "among the more practical difficulties that arise in either predicting changes in service flows or estimating the associated value of ecosystem services" include the "lack of multiproduct, ecological production functions to quantitatively map ecosystem structure and function to a flow of services that can then be valued." Equally important is understanding the complex interrelationships among biodiversity, productivity, and community stability that seem critical to the normal functioning and processes within ecosystems. Worm and Duffy (2003) hypothesize some of the possible interrelationships (see Figure 7.2).

As indicated in Figure 7.2, based on reviewing field studies, Worm and Duffy (2003) maintain that changes in biodiversity affect community stability, and changes in community stability affect biological diversity. A similar reciprocal relationship occurs between biodiversity and productivity. Worm and Duffy believe that enhanced community stability promotes productivity, and vice versa, but this linkage has yet to be supported by field studies. The authors conclude by suggesting: "Although many of these effects are poorly explored and some are entirely hypothetical, there is much empirical evidence that the loss of species can bring about complex and dramatic reorganizations

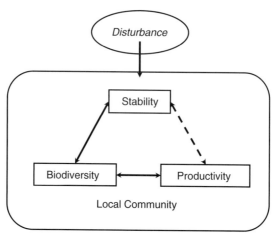

Figure 7.2 Biodiversity, productivity, and stability in ecological communities
Notes: Possible reciprocal relationships among biodiversity (species composition and richness), productivity (the rate of production of organic matter), and stability (temporal constancy) within a local ecological community.
Source: Adapted from Worm and Duffy (2003, Figure 1).

of ecosystems, including trophic cascades, cascading extinctions and rapid shifts to undesirable stable states" (Worm and Duffy 2003, p. 631). More research is clearly needed on these important inter-relationships for a variety of communities and ecosystems.

Further study is also needed to determine what happens to eco-systems after they undergo regime shift. Ecological collapse involves abrupt and large-scale changes from one stable regime to another. Although it is generally assumed that considerable loss of ecosystem goods and services occurs as a result, it is important to determine the resulting ecological and economic impacts. For example, the jelly-fish invasion of the Black Sea severely impaired the commercial value of the anchovy fishery, but it did not lead to its complete collapse. However, because of the ecological regime shift, the open access exploitation of the fishery became a major threat to its sustainability (Knowler *et al.* 2002). Similarly, salinization of the irrigated pasture land of the Goulburn–Broken Catchment in Southeast Australia may lead to irreversible soil degradation, but some livestock rearing is still possible in the region after the regime shift, albeit at a highly dimin-ished rate (Walker *et al.* 2010 and Box 6.2). Carpenter and Brock (2004) find that, in the lake region of Wisconsin in the United States, local collapses of fish populations evoke spatial shifts of angling effort that can lead to serial collapses in neighboring fisheries and degraded fisheries in most or all of the lakes. The authors conclude that, in lake fisheries, habitat protection adds an important dimension to policy design, and can be a critical element in facilitating both ecological resilience and the sustainability of the economic uses of the lakes.

Final remarks

The more we learn about ecosystems, the more we appreciate what unique economic assets they are. Ecosystems are special forms of natural wealth, and the key to managing them properly lies in understanding better their distinct attributes.

There is clearly much more we need to know about how ecosystems produce the goods and services that we value and, equally important, how ecosystems respond to the persistent demands and disturbances caused by human beings and their economic activities. In keeping with the main topics discussed in this book, this chapter has focused on several important areas where economic and ecological analysis is urgently needed in the near future: overcoming valuation challenges; ecological restoration and transitions; international trade and payments for ecosystem services; and thresholds, resilience, and collapse.

As more progress is made in these areas, we are learning how different ecosystems are from other forms of capital in our economy. Dasgupta (2008, p. 3) summarizes this difference succinctly: compared to other economic assets that are largely reproducible, such as physical and human capital, ecosystems are frequently degraded irreversibly, are difficult to replace once depleted, and they can collapse abruptly without any warning. In fact, many ecosystems are a strong candidate for the essential component of natural capital that we should consider keeping intact, as the proponents of strong sustainability maintain (see Figure 7.1).

However, as Chapter 1 illustrates, the problem of global ecological scarcity is becoming more acute, not less. If we believe that ecosystems are essential natural assets, and that we should be formulating policies and management strategies to conserve more ecosystems rather than allowing them to disappear, humankind is clearly doing a poor job of it. As Pearce (2007) has pointed out, the global benefits of ecosystem goods and services are likely to be "hundreds of billions of dollars" yet currently the world spends at most $10 billion annually on ecosystem conservation.

The final chapter of this book addresses this policy challenge: if we really care about ecosystem conservation, what do we need to do to tackle the global problem of ecological scarcity more effectively?

References

Aguilar-Perera, A. and R.S. Appeldoorn. 2008. "Spatial distribution of marine fishes along a cross-shelf gradient containing a continuum of mangrove-seagrass-coral reefs off southwestern Puerto Rico." *Estuarine, Coastal and Shelf Science* 76:378–394.

Albers, H.J. 1996. "Modeling ecological constraints on tropical forest management: spatial interdependence, irreversibility and uncertainty." *Journal of Environmental Economics and Management* 30:73–94.

Albers, H.J., A.W. Ando, and X. Chen. 2008. "A spatial-econometric analysis of attraction and repulsion of private conservation by public reserves." *Journal of Environmental Economics and Management* 56: 33–49.

Alix-Garcia, J. 2007. "A spatial analysis of common property deforestation." *Journal of Environmental Economics and Management* 53:141–157.

Alongi, D.M. 2008. "Mangrove forests: resilience, protection from tsunamis, and responses to global climate change." *Estuarine, Coastal and Shelf Science* 76:1–13.

Ando, A.W., J. Camm, S. Polasky, and A. Solow. 1998. "Species distributions, land values, and efficient conservation." *Science* 279:2126–2128.

Balmford, A., K.J. Gaston, S. Blyth, A. James, and V. Kapos. 2003. "Global variation in terrestrial conservation costs, conservation benefits, and unmet conservation needs." *Proceedings of the National Academy of Sciences* 100:1046–1050.

Barbier, E.B. 1987. "The concept of sustainable economic development." *Environmental Conservation* 14(2):101–110.

    2005. *Natural Resources and Economic Development*. Cambridge University Press, Cambridge and New York.

    2007. "Valuing ecosystems as productive inputs." *Economic Policy* 22:177–229.

    2008. "Ecosystems as natural assets." *Foundations and Trends in Microeconomics* 4(8):611–681.

Barbier, E.B. and M. Cox. 2003. "Does economic development lead to mangrove loss? A cross-country analysis." *Contemporary Economic Policy* 21(4):418–432.

Barbier, E.B., J.C. Burgess, and C. Folke. 1994. *Paradise Lost? The Ecological Economics of Biodiversity*. Earthscan Publications, London.

Bishop, R.C. 1993. "Economic efficiency, sustainability and biodiversity." *Ambio* 22(2–3):69–73.

Brown, G. and J. Roughgarden. 1997. "A metapopulation model with a common pool." *Ecological Economics* 22:65–71.

Carpenter, S.R. and W.A. Brock. 2004. "Spatial complexity, resilience and policy diversity: fishing on lake-rich landscapes." *Ecology and Society* 9(1):8. www.ecologyandsociety.org/vol9/iss1/art8, accessed April 6, 2011.

Carwardine, J., K.A. Wilson, G. Ceballos *et al.* 2008. "Cost-effective priorities for global mammal conservation." *Proceedings of the National Academy of Sciences* 105:11446–11450.

Chomitz, K.M. with P. Buys, G. De Luca, T.S. Thomas, and S. Wertz-Kanounnikoff. 2007. *At Loggerheads? Agricultural Expansion, Poverty Reduction, and Environment in the Tropical Forests*. The World Bank, Washington, DC.

Chong, V.C. 2007. "Mangrove-fishery linkages – the Malaysian perspective." *Bulletin of Marine Science* 80:755–772.

Clark, C.W. 1976. *Mathematical Bioeconomics*. Wiley Interscience, New York.

Coombes, E.G., A.P. Jones, I.J. Bateman *et al.* 2010. "Spatial and temporal modeling of beach use: a case study of East Anglia, UK." *Coastal Management* 37(1):94–115.

Costello, C. and S. Polasky. 2008. "Optimal harvesting of stochastic spatial resources." *Journal of Environmental Economics and Management* 56:1–18.

Dasgupta, P. 2008. "Nature in economics." *Environmental and Resource Economics* 39:1–7.

Dobson, A., D. Lodge, J. Alder *et al.* 2006. "Habitat loss, trophic collapse, and the decline of ecosystem services." *Ecology* 87:1915–1924.

Ebeling, J. and M. Yasué. 2008. "Generating carbon finance through avoided deforestation and its potential to create climatic, conservation and human development benefits." *Philosophical Transactions of the Royal Society B* 363:1917–1924.

Elliott, M., D. Burdon, K.L. Hemingway, and S.E. Apitz. 2007. "Estuarine, coastal and marine ecosystem restoration: confusing management and science – a revision of concepts." *Estuarine Coastal and Shelf Science* 74:349–366.

Farnsworth, E.J. 1998. "Issues of spatial, taxonomic and temporal scale in delineating links between mangrove diversity and ecosystem function." *Global Ecology and Biogeography Letters* 7(1):15–25.

Ferraro, P.J. 2003. "Assigning priority to environmental policy interventions in a heterogeneous world." *Journal of Policy Analysis and Management* 22:27–43.

——— 2004. "Targeting conservation investments in heterogeneous landscapes: a distance-function approach and application to watershed management." *American Journal of Agricultural Economics* 86:905–918.

Finnoff, D. and J. Tschirhart. 2003a. "Protecting an endangered species while harvesting its prey in a general equilibrium ecosystem model." *Land Economics* 70:160–180.

——— 2003b. "Harvesting in an eight-species ecosystem." *Journal of Environmental Economics and Management* 45:589–611.

——— 2008. "Linking dynamic economic and ecological general equilibrium models." *Resource and Energy Economics* 30:91–114.

Folke, C., S. Carpenter, B. Walker *et al.* 2004. "Regime shifts, resilience, and biodiversity in ecosystem management." *Annual Review of Ecology, Evolution, and Systematics* 35:557–581.

Food and Agricultural Organization (FAO) of the United Nations. 2007. *The World's Mangroves 1980–2005*. FAO Forestry Paper 153. FAO, Rome.

Foster, A. and M. Rosenzweig. 2003. "Economic growth and the rise of forests." *Quarterly Journal of Economics* 118:601–637.

Grafton, R.Q , T. Kompas, and V. Schneider. 2005. "The bioeconomics of marine reserves: a selected review with policy implications." *Journal of Bioeconomics* 7:161–178.

Grafton, R.Q., T. Kompas, and P.V. Ha. 2009. "Cod today and none tomorrow: the economic value of a marine reserve." *Land Economics* 85:454–469.

Grainger, A. 2008. "Difficulties in tracking the long-term global trend in tropical forest area." *Proceedings of the National Academy of Sciences* 105: 818–823.

Gross, T., L. Rudolf, S.A. Levin, and U. Dieckmann. 2009. "Generalized models reveal stabilizing factors in food webs." *Science* 325:747–750.

Halpern, B.S., B.R. Silliman, J.D. Olden, J.P Bruno, and M.D. Bertness. 2007. "Incorporating positive interactions in aquatic restoration and conservation." *Frontiers in Ecology and the Environment* 5:153–160.

Hartwick, J. 1977. "Intergenerational equity and the investing of rents from exhaustible resources." *American Economic Review* 67:972–974.

Holling, C.S. 1973. "Resilience and stability of ecological systems." *Annual Review of Ecological Systems* 4:1–23.

Howarth, R.B. and R.B. Norgaard 1995. "Intergenerational choices under global environmental change." In D. Bromley, ed. *The Handbook of Environmental Economics*. Basil Blackwell, Oxford, pp. 111–138.

Irwin, E.G. and J. Geoghegan. 2001. "Theory, data, methods: developing spatially explicit models of land use change." *Agriculture, Ecosystems & Environment* 85:7–23.

Jack, B.K., B. Leimona, and P.J. Ferraro. 2009. "A revealed preference approach to estimating supply curves for ecosystem services: use of auctions to set payments for soil erosion control in Indonesia." *Conservation Biology* 23:359–367.

Johnston, R.J., T.A. Grigalunas, J.J. Opaluch, M. Mazzotta, and J. Diamantedes. 2002. "Valuing estuarine resource services using economic and ecological models: the Peconic Estuary system." *Coastal Management* 30: 47–65.

Kindermann, G., M. Obersteiner, B. Sohngen *et al.* 2008. "Global cost estimates of reducing carbon emissions through avoided deforestation." *Proceedings of the National Academy of Sciences* 105(30):10302–10307.

Knowler, D.J., E.B. Barbier, and I. Strand. 2002. "An open-access model of fisheries and nutrient enrichment in the Black Sea." *Marine Resource Economics* 16:195–217.

Koch, E.W., E.B. Barbier, B.R. Silliman *et al.* 2009. "Non-linearity in ecosystem services: temporal and spatial variability in coastal protection." *Frontiers in Ecology and the Environment* 7:29–37.

Layman, C.A. and B.R. Silliman. 2002. "Preliminary survey of the fish fauna in Fresh Creek, Andros, Bahamas." *Bulletin of Marine Science* 70: 199–210.

Levin, S.A. 1999. *Fragile Dominion: Complexity and the Commons.* Perseus Books, Reading, MA.

Levin, S.A. and J. Lubchenco. 2008. "Resilience, robustness, and marine ecosystem-based management." *BioScience* 58:27–32.

Lewis, R.R. III. 2000. "Ecologically based goal setting in mangrove forest and tidal marsh restoration in Florida." *Ecological Engineering* 15:191–198.

2005. "Ecological engineering for successful management and restoration of mangrove forests." *Ecological Engineering* 24:403–418.

Lewis, R.R. III and R.G. Gilmore, Jr. 2007. "Important considerations to achieve successful mangrove forest restoration with optimum fish habitat." *Bulletin of Marine Science* 3:823–837.

Link, J. 2002. "Does food web theory work for marine ecosystems?" *Marine Ecology Progress Series* 230:1–9.

López, R. and G.I. Gallinato. 2005. "Trade policies, economic growth, and the direct causes of deforestation." *Land Economics* 81(2): 145–169.

Mäler, K.-G. 1995. "Economic growth and the environment." In C.A. Perrings, K.-G. Mäler, C. Folke, C.S. Holling, and B.-O. Jansson, eds. *Biodiversity Loss: Economic and Ecological Issues.* Cambridge University Press, pp. 213–224.

Mather, A.S. 2000. "South-North challenges in global forestry." In M. Palo, and H. Vanhanen, eds. *World Forests from Deforestation to Transition?* Kluwer, Dordrecht, pp. 25–40.

Mather, A.S. and C.L. Needle. 1998. "The forest transition: a theoretical basis." *Area* 30:117–124.

2000. "The relationships of populations and forest trends." *Geographic Journal* 166(1):2–13.

Matthews, J.W., A.L. Peralta, D.N. Flanagan *et al.* 2009. "Relative influence of landscape vs. local factors on plant community assembly in restored wetlands." *Ecological Applications* 19(8):2108–2123.

Meynecke, J.-O., S.Y. Lee, and N.C. Duke. 2008. "Linking spatial metrics and fish catch reveals the importance of coastal wetland connectivity to inshore fisheries in Queensland, Australia." *Biological Conservation* 141:981–996.

Moberg, F. and P. Rönnbäck. 2003. "Ecosystem services of the tropical seascape: interactions, substitutions and restoration." *Ocean and Coastal Management* 46:27–46.

Morgan, O.A. and S.E. Hamilton. 2010. "Estimating a payment vehicle for financing nourishment of residential beaches using a spatial-lag hedonic property price model." *Coastal Management* 38:65–75.

Mumby, P.J. 2006. "Connectivity of reef fish between mangroves and coral reefs: algorithms for the design of marine reserves at seascape scales." *Biological Conservation* 128:215–222.

Mumby, P.J. and A. Hastings. 2008. "The impact of ecosystem connectivity on coral reef resilience." *Journal of Applied Ecology* 45:854–862.

Mumby, P.J., A.J. Edwards, J.E. Arias-Gonzalez *et al.* 2004. "Mangroves enhance the biomass of reef fisheries in the Caribbean." *Nature* 427:533–536.

Nagelkerken, I., C.M. Roberts, G. van der Velde *et al.* 2002. "How important are mangroves and seagrass beds for coral-reef fish? The nursery hypothesis tested on an island scale." *Marine Ecology Progress Series* 244:299–305.

Naidoo, R. 2004. "Economic growth and liquidation of natural capital: the case of forest clearance." *Land Economics* 80(2):194.

Naidoo, R., A. Balmford, P.J. Ferraro *et al.* 2006. "Integrating economic costs into conservation planning." *TRENDS in Ecology and Evolution* 21:681–687.

Nelson, E., S. Polasky, D.J. Lewis *et al.* 2008. "Efficiency of incentives to jointly increase carbon sequestration and species conservation on a landscape." *Proceedings of the National Academy of Sciences* 105(28):9471–9476.

Nelson, E., G. Mendoza, J. Regetz *et al.* 2009. "Modeling multiple eco-system services, biodiversity conservation, commodity production, and tradeoffs at landscape scales." *Frontiers in Ecology and the Environment* 7(1):4–11.

Neumayer, E. 2010. *Weak versus Strong Sustainability: Exploring the Limits of Two Opposing Paradigms.* 3rd edn. Edward Elgar, Cheltenham, UK.

Palmer, M.A. and S. Filoso. 2009. "Restoration of ecosystem services for environmental markets." *Science* 31:575–576.

Palumbi, S.R., K.L. McLeod, and D. Grünbaum. 2008. "Ecosystems in action: lessons from marine ecology about recovery, resistance, and reversibility." *BioScience* 58:33–42.

Parkhurst, G.M. and J.F. Shogren. 2008. "Smart subsidies for con-servation." *American Journal of Agricultural Economics* 90:1192–1200.

Pauly, D., V. Christensen, J. Dalsgaard, R. Froese, and F. Torres, Jr. 1998. "Fishing down marine food webs." *Science* 279:860–863.

Pearce, D.W. 2007. "Do we really care about biodiversity?" *Environmental and Resource Economics* 37:313–333.

Pearce, D.W. and E.B. Barbier. 2000. *Blueprint for a Sustainable Economy.* Earthscan Publications, London.

Pearce, D.W., A. Markandya, and E.B. Barbier. 1989. *Blueprint for a Green Economy.* Earthscan Publications, London.

Perz, S.G. and D.L. Skole. 2003. "Secondary forest expansion in the Brazilian Amazon and the refinement of forest transition theory." *Society and Natural Resources* 16: 277–294.

Petersen, J.E., W.M. Kemp, R. Bartleson *et al.* 2003. "Multiscale experi-ments in coastal ecology: improving realism and advancing theory." *BioScience* 53:1181–1197.

Pezzey, J.C.V. 1989. "Economic analysis of sustainable growth and sus-tainable development." Environment Department Working Paper No. 15. The World Bank, Washington, DC.

Polasky, S. and K. Segerson. 2009. "Integrating ecology and economics in the study of ecosystem services: some lessons learned." *Annual Review of Resource Economics* 1:409–434.

Polasky, S., J.D. Camm, and B. Garber-Yonts. 2001. "Selecting biological reserves cost-effectively: an application to terrestrial vertebrate con-servation in Oregon." *Land Economics* 77:68–78.

Reed, D.J. and L. Wilson. 2004. "Coast 2050: a new approach to res-toration of Louisiana coastal wetlands." *Physical Geography* 25:4–21.

Rilov, G. and D.R. Schiel. 2006. "Seascape-dependent subtidal-intertidal trophic linkages." *Ecology* 87(3):731–744.

Robinson, E.J.Z., H.J. Albers, and J.C. Williams. 2008. "Spatial and temporal modeling of community non-timber forest extraction." *Journal of Environmental Economics and Management* 56:234–245.

Rountree, R.A. and K.W. Able. 2007. "Spatial and temporal habitat use patterns for salt marsh nekton: implications for ecological functions." *Aquatic Ecology* 41:25–45.

Ruckelhaus, M., T. Klinger, N. Knowlton, and D.P. DeMaster. 2008. "Marine ecosystem-based management in practice: scientific and governance challenges." *BioScience* 58:53–63.

Rudel, T.K. 2005. *Tropical Forests: Regional Paths of Destruction and Regeneration in the Late 20th Century*. Columbia University Press, New York.

2007. "Changing agents of deforestation: from state-initiated to enterprise driven process, 1970–2000." *Land Use Policy* 24:35–41.

Rudel, T.K., O.T.Coomes, E. Moran *et al*. 2005. "Forest transitions: towards a global understanding of land use change." *Global Environmental Change* 15:23–31.

Sanchirico, J.N. 2005. "Additivity properties in metapopulation models: implications for the assessment of marine reserves." *Journal of Environmental Economics and Management* 49:1–25.

Sanchirico, J.N. and J.E. Wilen. 1999. "Bioeconomics of spatial exploitation in a patchy environment." *Journal of Environmental Economics and Management* 37:129–150.

2002. "The impacts of marine reserves on limited-entry fisheries." *Natural Resource Modeling* 15:291–310.

2005. "Optimal spatial management of renewable resources: matching policy scope to ecosystem scale." *Journal of Environmental Economics and Management* 50:23–46.

Sanchirico, J.N. and P.J. Mumby. 2009. "Mapping ecosystem functions to the valuation of ecosystem services: implications of species-habitat associations for coastal land-use decisions." *Theoretical Ecology* 2:67–77.

Sanchirico, J.N., M.D. Smith, and D.W. Lipton. 2008. "An empirical approach to ecosystem-based fishery management." *Ecological Economics* 64:586–596.

Scheffer, M., S. Carpenter, J.A. Foley, C. Folke, and B. Walker. 2001. "Catastrophic shifts in ecosystems." *Nature* 413:591–596.

Settle, C. and J.F. Shogren. 2006. "Does integrating economic and biological systems matter for public policy? The case of Yellowstone Lake." *Topics in Economic Analysis and Policy* 6:1(9). www.bepress.com/bejeap/topics/vol6/iss1/art9, accessed April 4, 2011.

Sheppard, C., D.J. Dixon, M. Gourlay, A. Sheppard, and R. Payet. 2005. "Coral mortality increases wave energy reaching shores protected by reef flats: examples from the Seychelles." *Estuarine, Coastal and Shelf Science* 64:223–234.

Silliman, B.R. and M.D. Bertness. 2002. "A trophic cascade regulates salt marsh primary production." *Proceedings of the National Academy of Sciences* 99(16):10500–10505.

Simenstad, C., D. Reed, and M. Ford. 2006. "When is restoration not? Incorporating landscape-scale processes to restore self-sustaining ecosystems in coastal wetland restoration." *Ecological Engineering* 26:27–39.

Smith, M.D. and J.E. Wilen. 2003. "Economic impacts of marine reserves: the importance of spatial behavior." *Journal of Environmental Economics and Management* 46:183–206.

Smith, M.D., J.N. Sanchirico, and J.E. Wilen. 2009. "The economics of spatial-dynamic processes: applications to renewable resources." *Journal of Environmental Economics and Management* 57:104–121.

Sohngen, B., R. Mendelsohn, and R. Sedjo. 1999. "Forest management, conservation, and global timber markets." *American Journal of Agricultural Economics* (February):1–13.

Solow, R.M. 1974. "Intergenerational equity and exhaustible resources." *Review of Economic Studies*, Symposium on the Economics of Exhaustible Resources, 29–46.

1993. "Sustainability: an economist's perspective." In R. Dorfman and N.S. Dorfman, eds. *Economics of the Environment: Selected Readings*. 3rd edn. Norton, New York, pp. 179–187.

Toman, M.A., J.C.V. Pezzey, and J. Krautkramer. 1995. "Neoclassical economic growth theory and 'sustainability'". In D. Bromley, ed. *The Handbook of Environmental Economics*. Basil Blackwell, Oxford, pp. 139–165.

Tschirhart, J. 2009. "Integrated ecological-economic models." *Annual Review of Resource Economics* 1:381–407.

Turner, R.K. 1993. "Sustainability principles and practice." In R.K. Turner, ed. *Sustainable Environmental Management: Principles and Practice*. 2nd edn. Belhaven Press, London, pp. 3–36.

Valiela, I., J.L. Bowen, and J.K. York. 2001. "Mangrove forests: one of the world's threatened major tropical environments." *BioScience* 51: 807–815.

Walker, B., L. Pearson, M. Harris *et al.* 2010. "Incorporating resilience in the assessment of inclusive wealth: an example from South East Australia." *Environmental and Resource Economics* 45:183–202.

World Commission on Environment and Development (WCED). 1987. *Our Common Future*. Oxford University Press, Oxford and New York.

Worm, B. and J.E. Duffy. 2003. "Biodiversity, productivity and stability in real food webs." *TRENDS in Ecology and Evolution* 18:628–632.

Worm, B., E.B. Barbier, N. Beaumont *et al.* 2006. "Impacts of biodiversity loss on ocean ecosystem services." *Science* 314:787–790.

Wunder, S. 2008. "Payments for environmental services and the poor: concepts and preliminary evidence." *Environment and Development Economics* 13:279–297.

8 | Policies in the Age of Ecological Scarcity

The rationales for conserving natural capital are several. It accounts for the lack of substitutability for many environmental functions, for uncertainty, and for resilience. It is consistent with many equity concerns, especially in the poorer parts of the world.

(Pearce *et al.* 1989, p. 48)

Introduction

Chapter 1 pointed to a number of trends in global ecosystem degradation and loss that indicate that *ecological scarcity* is becoming a major challenge for the world. Given the scale of the problem, it is in fact possible to characterize the current global era as the "Age of Ecological Scarcity" (Barbier 2011).

This final chapter explores the major policy challenges that need to be overcome in order to avert the worsening global ecological scarcity problem. These challenges fall into three areas.

First, as highlighted in Chapter 1, ecological scarcity arises through a fundamental tradeoff in our use of the natural environment (see Figure 1.1). Economic development leads to important benefits for humankind, but the result has been profound alterations to the world's major ecosystems and the valuable benefits that they provide. The continuing loss of these benefits as global development proceeds constitutes increasing ecological scarcity. As outlined in Chapter 1, the reason for this growing scarcity is straightforward. We use natural capital because it is valuable, but we are losing natural capital because it is free. Convincing global policymakers that economic development must take into account the worsening ecological scarcity that it causes remains the paramount challenge facing the world today.

Second, there remains a huge gap between the global benefits that humankind receives from ecosystems and what we are willing to pay to maintain and conserve them. For example, Pearce (2007) estimates

269

that the global benefits of ecosystem goods and services are likely to be "hundreds of billions of dollars," yet currently the world spends at most $10 billion annually on ecosystem conservation. Overcoming this funding gap is critical if we are to stop the current decline in global ecosystems and the benefits they provide. But as we saw in Chapter 5, there are a number of economic disincentives that have so far prevented successful international negotiation and agreement to halt biodiversity loss and ecosystem degradation worldwide. Financing and implementing international mechanisms to combat this global problem is a second critical challenge facing the world today.

Finally, global ecosystem loss is an equity issue. Increasing ecological scarcity disproportionately affects the world's poor, who depend critically on many ecosystem goods and services for their livelihoods (Barbier 2008b and 2010; MEA 2005; TEEB 2010; Wunder 2008). As we saw in Chapter 5, most developing countries, and certainly the majority of the populations living within them, depend directly on natural resources. Much of the world's rural poor continue to be concentrated in the less favored areas of developing regions, and their livelihoods are intricately linked with exploiting fragile environments and ecosystems. The clustering of rural populations in less-favored areas and fragile environments is also likely to continue into the foreseeable future, given current global rural population and poverty trends. Thus, finding ways to halt ecosystem loss and enhance the livelihoods of the poor is also an important challenge for global policymakers.

These three policy challenges are the focus of this final chapter. Overcoming them should be the main policy goal in the Age of Ecological Scarcity.

Sustainability challenge

Current global economic development is unsustainable. An important source of natural capital, which should be kept intact, is being irreversibly degraded, which is putting current and future generations at risk.

An important indicator of the growing ecological scarcity was provided by the MEA (2005), which found that over 60 percent of the world's major ecosystem goods and services were degraded or used unsustainably (see Table 8.1). Some important benefits to humankind fall into this category, including fresh water, capture fisheries, water

Table 8.1 *Global status of key ecosystem goods and services*

Condition globally has been enhanced	Condition globally has been degraded	Condition globally is mixed
Crops	Capture fisheries	Timber
Livestock	Wild foods	Cotton, hemp, silk,
Aquaculture	Wood fuel	and other fiber
Global climate	Genetic resources	crops
regulation	Biochemicals, natural	Water regulation
	medicines and	Disease regulation
	pharmaceuticals	Recreation and
	Fresh water	ecotourism
	Air quality regulation	
	Regional and local climate	
	regulation	
	Erosion regulation	
	Water purification and waste	
	treatment	
	Pest regulation	
	Pollination	
	Natural hazard regulation	
	Spiritual and religious values	
	Aesthetic values	

Notes: Enhancement is defined as either increased production of or change in the ecosystem good or service that leads to greater benefits for people.
Degradation is defined as current use exceeding sustainable levels, or a reduction in the benefits obtained from the good or service due to either some human-induced change or use exceeding its limits.
Mixed status implies that the condition of the good or service globally has experienced enhancement in some regions but degradation in others.
Source: Adapted from MEA (2005, Table 1).

purification and waste treatment, wild foods, genetic resources, bio-chemicals, wood fuel, pollination, spiritual, religious, and aesthetic values, and the regulation of regional and local climate, erosion, pests, and natural hazards.

    As we have seen throughout this book, one major difficulty is that the increasing costs associated with this rising ecological scarcity are not routinely reflected in markets. Almost all the degraded ecosystem goods and services listed in Table 8.1 are not marketed. Some goods, such as capture fisheries, fresh water, wild foods, and wood fuel, are commercially marketed, but due to the poor management of the biological resources and ecosystems that are the source of these goods, the market prices do not reflect unsustainable use and overexploitation. Nor have adequate policies and institutions been developed to handle the costs associated with worsening ecological scarcity globally. All too often, policy distortions and failures compound these problems by encouraging wasteful use of natural resources and environmental degradation.

Thus, the unique challenge posed by rising ecological scarcity today is to overcome a vast array of market, policy, and institutional failures that prevents recognition of the economic significance of this scarcity in the first place. As argued by Pearce and Barbier (2000, p. 157):

efficient and sustainable management of environmental resources, or natural capital, is essential to the long-term development of economies and human welfare. We refer to this as environmentally sustainable development. Unfortunately, we find little evidence that sustainability is actually being achieved. Important environmental values are generally not reflected in markets, and despite much rhetoric to the contrary, are routinely ignored in policy decisions. Institutional failures, such as the lack of property rights, inefficient and corrupt governance, political instability and the absence of public authority or institutions, also compound this problem. The result is economic development that produces excessive environmental degradation and increasing ecological scarcity. As we have demonstrated, the economic and social costs associated with these impacts can be significant. However, possibly the greatest threat posed by unsustainable development may be the long-term, potentially serious impacts on the welfare of future generations.

Figure 8.1 highlights the policy challenge that the world faces. At the core is the vicious cycle of unsustainable growth whereby the failure of environmental values to be reflected in markets and policy decisions leads to economic development with excessive environmental degradation. If environmental values are not reflected in market and policy actions, then any increasing ecological scarcity will also be ignored in decision making. The result is that the vicious cycle will be reinforced, and the current pattern of economic development will continue on its unsustainable path.

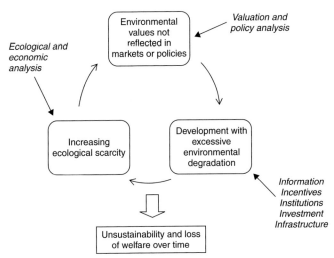

Figure 8.1 Reversing the vicious cycle of "unsustainable" development
Source: Adapted from Pearce and Barbier (2000, Figure 7.1).

Reversing this process of unsustainable development requires transforming the vicious cycle displayed in Figure 8.1 into a virtuous one. Three important steps are involved.

First, improvements in environmental valuation and policy analysis are required to ensure that markets and policies incorporate the full costs and benefits of environmental impacts. Environmental valuation and accounting for natural capital depreciation must be fully integrated into economic development policy and strategy. As discussed throughout this book, and especially in Chapter 2, the most undervalued components of natural capital are ecosystems and the myriad goods and services they provide. Valuing ecosystem goods and services is not easy, yet it is fundamental to ensuring the sustainability of global economic development efforts.

Second, the role of policy in controlling excessive environmental degradation requires implementation of effective and appropriate information, incentives, institutions, investments, and infrastructure (the five *i*'s indicated in Figure 8.1). Better information on the state of the environment, ecosystems, and biodiversity is essential for both private and public decision making that determines the allocation of natural capital for economic development. The use of market-based instruments, the creation of markets and, where appropriate,

regulatory measures have a role to play in internalizing this information in everyday allocation decisions in the economy. Such instruments are also important in correcting the market and policy failures
that distort the economic incentives for improved environmental and
ecosystems management. However, overcoming institutional distortions and encouraging more effective property rights, good governance, and support for local communities, is also critical. Reducing
government inefficiency, corruption, and poor accountability are also
important in reversing excessive environmental degradation in many
countries. But there is also a positive role for government in providing an appropriate and effective infrastructure through public investment, protecting critical ecosystems and biodiversity conservation,
new incentive mechanisms such as payment for ecosystem services,
and fostering the technologies and knowledge necessary for improving ecosystem restoration and ecological transitions.

   Third, continuing environmental degradation and ecological landscape conversion affects the functioning, diversity, and resilience of
ecological systems and the goods and services they supply. The ecological scarcity of these goods and services, and their potential long-
term impacts on the health and stability of ecosystems, are difficult
to quantify and value. As stressed in Chapter 7, increasing collaboration between environmental scientists, ecologists, and economists
will be required to assess and monitor these impacts. As indicated in
Figure 8.1, such interdisciplinary ecological and economic analysis is
necessary to identify and assess problems associated with increasing
ecological scarcity. Further progress in reversing unsustainable development calls for more widespread interdisciplinary collaboration
across the existing fields of economics, ecology, and other social and
natural sciences in order to analyze complex problems of environmental degradation, biodiversity loss, and ecosystem decline.

   Articulating the steps needed to overcome various market, policy,
and institutional failures that are contributing to ecological scarcity is
relatively straightforward. Yet implementing these steps is still prov-
ing to be very difficult.

   The problem may lie in the intransigence of social institutions – the
mechanisms and structures for ordering economic behavior and the
means of production within society.

   One reason why today's mounting ecological scarcity problems
seem so intractable is the numerous market, policy, and institutional

failures that prevent recognition of the economic significance of this scarcity. But why has it proven so difficult to overcome these failures? An explanation for this intransigence may be the result of what New Institutional Economists (NIE) view as the tendency of many important social institutions, broadly defined, to be highly invariant over long periods of time (see, for example, Dixit 1996, 2003; Hodgson 1998; McCann *et al.* 2005; North 1990, 1991; Williamson 2000).

The NIE define institutions as all the mechanisms and structures for ordering the behavior and ensuring the cooperation of individuals within society. They are the formal and informal "rules" that govern and organize social behavior and relationships, including reinforcing the existing social order, which is a stable system of institutions and structure that characterizes society for a considerable period of time. Consequently, as societies develop, they become more complex, and their institutions are more difficult to change. Institutions help structure the means of production, and how goods and services are produced influences the development of certain institutions. This is a cumulative causative, or mutually reinforcing, process. This process is self-reinforcing because institutions and the social order become geared toward reducing the *transaction costs* – the costs other than the money price that are incurred in existing production and market relationships. For example, typical transaction costs include search and information costs, bargaining and decision costs, and policing and enforcement costs.

Since the means of production include the endowment of natural capital, and the way in which an economy uses this endowment, it follows that the existing system of social institutions and structure – the "social order" – becomes fixed around a stable set of economic institutions. These institutions in turn determine how production is organized and all inputs are combined, including the environment, natural resources, technology, and human skills.

The result, however, is that, despite rising ecological scarcity, the economy continues to use and exploit ecosystem goods and services in the same manner as before.[1]

---

[1] This institutional intransigence may not be solely a problem of the current Age of Ecological Scarcity but may explain why so many economies historically have had difficulties in overcoming natural resource scarcity problems. See Barbier (2011).

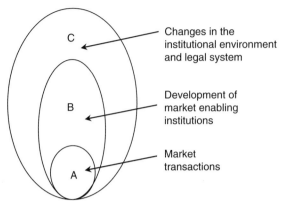

Figure 8.2 The transaction costs of environmental policy change
Source: Adapted from McCann *et al.* (2005).

As ecosystem goods and services become scarce, the transaction costs of finding, using and developing either 1) completely different ways of using the environment and natural resources or 2) novel ways of substituting other inputs for scarce ecosystem goods and services are extremely high, because our institutions and social order are oriented not towards reducing these new transaction costs but are instead built up around reducing the transaction costs of the existing production and exchange relationships. These relationships depend, in turn, on *perpetuating* the same way in which we use ecosystem goods and services in combination with other inputs.

Thus, from a social perspective, the transaction costs of continuing the same production patterns, including replicating the pattern of finding, exploiting, and using the same set of environmental and natural resources, are significantly lower. As a consequence, we may become more aware of the rising ecological scarcity associated with maintaining environmentally unsustainable economic development. But the high relative transaction costs involved in making the necessary corrections to the market, policy, and institutional failures, compared to keeping the same pattern of production and environmental use, seem prohibitive.

Figure 8.2 illustrates the difficulty of instigating policies to correct market, institutional, and policy failures contributing to environmental problems. When a new policy is implemented, such as a tax on pollution or implementing licenses for resource harvest or establishing a new protected area, additional market transaction costs in the form of search and information costs, bargaining and decision costs, and policing and enforcement costs are bound to occur (Area A). However, establishing some market-based instruments and trading mechanisms, such as taxes, tradable permit systems, and new environmental markets, such as payments for ecosystem services, will also require the establishment or reallocation of property rights to facilitate these instruments, and the setting up of new public agencies and administrative procedures to record, monitor, and enforce trades. Thus the full transaction costs of the policies will be areas A and B in the figure. Finally, if additional changes in the institutional environment and legal system are required, the transaction costs will be larger still, including areas A, B, and C. Of course, if the type of new mechanism required is at the global level, such as the implementation of an international payments scheme for ecosystem services, then the magnitude of these transaction costs will be even larger, especially area C.

These transaction costs associated with correcting market, institutional, and policy changes are significant but not insurmountable. What is clearly needed is more research illustrating the consequences of *not* making these changes. As illustrated in Figure 8.1, that means more ecological and economic analysis of the consequences of increasing ecological scarcity, more valuation and policy analysis of the effects of failing to incorporate the value of ecosystem goods and services in market and policy decisions, and more studies of how the "five *i*'s" can help alleviate the excessive environmental degradation and ecosystem loss associated with the current pattern of economic development.[2]

Funding challenge

The wide gap between the global benefits that humankind receives from ecosystems and what we are willing to pay to maintain and conserve them is a critical symptom of how oblivious we are to the risks arising from the excessive ecological deterioration arising from the

---

[2] A good example of an attempt to make progress in these areas of research is the international project The Economics of Ecosystems and Biodiversity (TEEB). See, for example, Sukhdev (2008) and TEEB (2010).

current pattern of economic development. Yet, as we saw in Chapter 5 in discussing the establishment of an international payment scheme for ecosystem services, there are many disincentives working against the creation of such schemes. Although progress has been made in establishing international payments for global ecosystem services, most notably a nascent financial mechanism to reduce emissions from deforestation and forest degradation (REDD), several important concerns have arisen. Monitoring and verifying changes in deforestation rates in developing countries and their impacts on carbon emissions could increase substantially the transaction costs of implementing a REDD scheme on a global scale. In addition, a carbon market for avoided deforestation may not necessarily be the best way of protecting forests that yield other global ecosystem services. There is also concern over the high opportunity costs faced by many developing countries from losses in foregone agricultural and timber benefits. These issues need to be resolved if there is to be a successful REDD financial mechanism implemented on a global scale.

With regard to a more comprehensive international scheme for payment of ecosystem services, as we concluded in Chapter 5, the most likely result from current negotiations is a scheme that is underwritten by only a handful of rich countries and that pays for only a modest increase in global ecosystem protection. Although they may be supported through multilateral and bilateral assistance, developing countries will continue to bear the direct and opportunity costs of ecosystem conservation for the foreseeable future. Clearly, this perpetuates the unsustainability problem, especially given rising global ecological scarcity. But to overcome the economic disincentives that are reinforcing such an outcome, the international community needs to think more creatively as to how to agree, design, implement, and verify international mechanisms for payment of ecosystem services. We also need to develop more innovative ways of financing such schemes, other than relying on conventional development assistance.

Table 8.2 outlines actual and potential funding mechanisms for global ecosystem conservation. One of the funding sources, the Global Environmental Facility (GEF) of the United Nations (UN), is a multidonor funding mechanism for environmental protection that has been in operation since 1991. To date the GEF has allocated $8.8 billion,

Table 8.2 *Financing mechanisms for funding global ecosystem conservation*

Mechanism	Description
Global Environmental Facility (GEF)	A multi-donor global mechanism to meet the additional costs of developing countries in achieving global environmental benefits from biological diversity, climate change, international waters, ozone layer depletion, reduced land degradation, and abatement of persistent organic pollution.
International payment for ecosystem services (IPES)	A global mechanism for raising and distributing funds from beneficiaries of ecosystem services to those who conserve them.
Reduced emissions from deforestation and forest degradation (REDD) scheme	A specific IPES aimed at reducing greenhouse gas emissions from deforestation and forest degradation (REDD) in developing countries.
Global carbon cap and auction systems	Allocating a proportion of funds raised from a cap and auction scheme for CO_2 emissions among wealthy nations.
Global carbon tax	Allocating a proportion of funds raised from taxes on CO_2 emissions among wealthy nations.
Financial transaction taxes (FTT)	Taxes collected on the sale of specific financial assets, such as stock, bonds, or futures.
Currency transaction taxes (CTT or Tobin tax)	Taxes applied to currency exchange transactions
International Finance Facility (IFF)	Mobilizing financing from international capital markets by issuing long-term bonds repaid by donor countries.
Taxes on airline travel or fuel	Taxes applied to international airline ticket sales or fuel use.
Taxes on global arms trade	Taxes applied to international export sales of armaments.

supplemented by more than $38.7 billion in co-financing, for over 2,400 projects in 165 developing economies.[3] The REDD mechanism, which has been operating as a pilot initiative with a budget of $75 million, represents one possible scheme for international payment of ecosystem services (IPES). The other financing mechanisms listed in Table 8.2 have yet to be implemented, but have been discussed and debated as potential ways of providing substantial additional funding for the GEF, REDD, new IPES schemes, or possibly a direct source of financing ecosystem conservation globally.

Such additional funding is clearly needed in the case of the GEF. Although the GEF has provided additional financing for a variety of environmental projects with global benefits in developing countries, since 1994 its total budget allocation has declined in real terms (Clemençon 2006). Thus, concerns have been raised about its future role, as well as the need to raise additional funds other than conventional development assistance (Clemençon 2006; Mee *et al.* 2008). Increasing significantly the resources of the GEF is essential if it is to be transformed into an innovative mechanism for delivering global ecosystem benefits, which can only be accomplished if the GEF has sufficient funds to compensate developing countries for land use change and other economic activities that are the cause of ecological degradation worldwide. Currently, the GEF is incapable of doing the latter. As summarized by Clemençon (2006, p. 69): "The GEF's capacity to fund new initiatives and sustain results during the long term is questionable without a gradual but predictable increase in the flow of resources."

As we saw in Chapter 5, IPES and REDD in particular may represent new sources of financing of global ecosystem conservation. For example, Farley *et al.* (2010) argue that some of the funds raised through a global cap and auction system for greenhouse (GHG) emissions among wealthy nations could be diverted to fund international payment for ecosystem services, with the financing apportioned to

---

[3] From the website www.theGeF.org as of November 2010. The GEF partnership includes ten international donor agencies: the UN Development Programme; the UN Environment Programme; the World Bank; the UN Food and Agriculture Organization; the UN Industrial Development Organization; the African Development Bank; the Asian Development Bank; the European Bank for Reconstruction and Development; the Inter-American Development Bank; and the International Fund for Agricultural Development.

targeted countries in accordance with how well they meet specific criteria for the provision of global ecosystem services. Similarly, in the case of REDD, the annual cost of reducing global deforestation by 10 percent may be around $0.4–1.7 billion but the additional financing through carbon markets could earn developing countries $2.2–13.5 billion annually (Ebeling and Yasué 2008; Kindermann *et al.* 2008). But the same disincentives that work against negotiating an international agreement for IPES mechanisms would also have to be overcome to set up an international cap and auction system for GHG emissions (Aldy and Stavins 2007; Olmstead and Stavins 2006).

An alternative to raising funds through an international cap and auction scheme would be to implement a global carbon tax on GHG emissions (Hyder 2008; Nordhaus 2007, 2010). As suggested by Nordhaus (2007), countries set market penalties on GHG emissions at levels that are equalized across different regions and industries. The tax would be set low initially, and rise steadily over time to reflect the rising damages from global warming. Estimated revenues from such a scheme could range from $318 to $980 billion by 2015 (in 2005 prices) and $527–1,763 billion by 2030 (Hyder 2008). Conceivably, some of these revenues could be used to finance IPES schemes, the GEF, and other global initiatives for ecosystem conservation. However, as Nordhaus (2010, pp. 5–6) maintains, international agreements on harmonized taxes on GHG emissions are proving to be more elusive than for IPES or carbon cap and trade: "Economists often point to harmonized carbon taxes as a more efficient and attractive regime, but these have been generally shunned in negotiations, particularly in the United States, because of the taboo on considering tax-based systems."

The idea of an International Finance Facility (IFF) is to mobilize resources from international capital markets by issuing long-term bonds that are repaid by donor countries over twenty to thirty years. This approach has already been applied to the IFF for Immunization (IFFIm), which was launched in 2006 by the UK and supported by France, Italy, Spain, Sweden, the Netherlands, Norway, and South Africa. These countries have pledged to contribute $5.9 billion over twenty-three years.[4] IFFIm raises finance by issuing bonds in the

---

[4] Information on the IFFIm can be obtained from its website www.iff-immunisation.org.

capital markets to convert these long-term government pledges into funds for immediate investment. The government pledges are then used to repay the IFFIm. So far IFFIm bonds have raised $2.6 billion in financial resources through its bonds, which receive a triple-A rating. The investments are disbursed through the Global Alliance on Vaccines and Immunization (GAVI), a public–private partnership of major stakeholders in immunization in the developing world. Since inception, IFFIm has approved immunization programs of $2 billion and disbursed $1.2 billion to support vaccine purchases and delivery to seventy developing countries. The World Bank acts as financial advisory and treasury manager to the IFFIm.

One of the perceived advantages of the IFF approach is that, unlike other potential new sources of global financing or mechanisms, it can be started by a handful of donor countries without the need of an international agreement involving many countries (Addison *et al.* 2005). On the other hand, if the IFFIm is any guide, the funds raised are more likely to be in the tens of billions rather than hundreds of billions. Doubts have therefore been raised over the ability of the IFF approach to overcome on its own major shortfalls in international assistance, such as for global ecosystem conservation (Moss 2005). Still, an IFF for global ecosystem protection would be an innovative and potentially viable financial mechanism and, as the IFFIm has shown, can easily work with existing development institutions, such as the World Bank. A similar funding relationship could easily be worked out between any IFF and the GEF, or possibly a new IPES scheme such as REDD.

A financial transaction tax (FTT) is gaining ground as one possible long-term funding source for global public goods, such as ecosystem conservation (Addison *et al.* 2005; Clemençon 2006; Griffith-Jones 2010; Koch-Weser 2002; Spahn 2010). An FTT is a tax collected on the sale of specific financial assets, such as stock, bonds, or futures. A variant is a currency transaction tax (CTT), or *Tobin tax*, named after the economist James Tobin who first proposed it in the 1970s. This is a tax applied to any foreign currency exchange transaction.

An FTT would be implemented nationally and, in fact, such taxes already exist, as in the case of the stamp duty tax in the United Kingdom. However, the 2008–2009 global recession has renewed interest in establishing FTTs more widely. For example, the UN-sponsored Leading Group on Innovative Financing for

Development has concluded that a CTT is the most desirable and feasible option for overcoming the chronic underfunding of global public goods, partly because it would be relatively easy and cheap to implement (Griffith-Jones 2010). There are concerns that a CTT or any other FTT could disrupt trading liquidity and fail to curb speculation, but as argued by Spahn (2010, p. 12): "A very small tax rate (0.005% or less) is unlikely to affect liquidity seriously. And there are ways of distinguishing between liquidity trading and speculation in practice." Yet such a small tax rate could raise substantial funds globally for ecosystem conservation. Foreign exchange transactions worldwide totaled $800 trillion in 2007, which means that even a negligible tax rate could raise substantial revenues for global public goods (Spahn 2010).

The major obstacle to an international FTT is implementation. Any global FTT or CTT would still involve some form of negotiated international agreement involving many countries (Addison *et al.* 2005; Spahn 2010). France and Belgium have adopted CTT legislation, but its implementation is contingent on other European Union (EU) countries adopting the tax, which is still an unlikely prospect (Spahn 2010). Initially, then, an FTT or CTT is likely to be collected nationally, with a proportion of revenues transferred to international agencies, such as the World Bank or GEF, for disbursement. But national collection increases the likelihood that revenues will be diverted to support public budgets and reduce fiscal deficits, which would limit the funding available for ecosystem conservation. As an alternative, proceeds from a CTT or FTT could be channeled to a global solidarity fund, which would then use the proceeds to fund international conservation and similar investments (Griffith-Jones 2010). Negotiating and establishing such an international funding mechanism would be yet another major policy challenge.

As in the case of an FTT or CTT, an arms trade or airline travel tax to raise revenues for global public goods has been proposed for some time (Addison *et al.* 2005; Brzoska 2004; Koch-Weser 2002). For example, a 10 percent tax on global arms exports could raise up to $5 billion (Brzoska 2004). However, compared to a CTT or FTT, this is not a negligible tax for revenue-raising purposes and, as a result, perhaps more difficult to implement politically and would create more incentives to evade or avoid, especially by arms importing developing countries. In the case of taxes on airline travel or fuel, national governments have already raised substantially such rates, and there are concerns of how further tax increases would affect a struggling international air travel industry. For an arms trade tax there is also the problem of low level of transparency, especially for the trade in small arms and light weapons (Brzoska 2004). Finally, any tax on the arms trade or on airline travel or fuel would require a negotiated international agreement, which as we have seen is very difficult to negotiate successfully.

To summarize, there are a number of possible innovative financial mechanisms available to fund the current shortfall in global biodiversity and ecosystem conservation funding (see Table 8.2). Perhaps the most promising way forward is some form of intervention in the global financial sector, either a financial transaction tax (FTT), a currency transaction tax (CTT), or an international financial facility (IFF). One advantage of the IFF approach to other potential sources of financing is that an IFF does not require an international agreement involving many countries (Addison *et al.* 2005). As the current IFF for Immunization (IFFIm) has shown, such a financing mechanism can be started by a handful of donor countries. Recall from Chapter 5 that the most likely outcome for implementing an IPES scheme for global ecosystem benefits may be a scheme that is underwritten by only a limited number of rich countries. If these potential donors are also willing to use an IFF to fund an IPES, then the long-term financing of such a mechanism is more likely to be secured.

Of course, the financing raised through an IFF is likely to be insufficient. Only $2.6 billion in additional investment funding has been leveraged by the sale of bonds by the IFFIm. Although not an insubstantial amount, it is still much less than the "hundreds of billions" required for ecosystem and biodiversity conservation globally (Pearce 2007). The only likely alternative that would raise more substantial funds quickly is a currency transaction tax (CTT). Although support for a global CTT scheme is growing in the international community, major implementation obstacles remain: the need for an international agreement on its operation and governance, as well as rules and procedures for the collection and disbursement of revenues. But there are still two reasons why a CTT might be attractive. First, there is the appeal of recycling funds collected from the growth of currency transactions to reinvest back in the conservation of natural capital for the greater global public good. Second, as argued by Griffith-Jones

(2010, p. 17): "Improving the net contribution of the financial sector to the real economy, and to the welfare of ordinary people, would significantly rehabilitate the financial sector's battered image, a desirable aim for the financial sector itself."

Equity challenge

Most developing countries, and certainly the majority of the populations living within them, depend directly on natural resources. The livelihoods of much of the world's rural poor are also intricately linked with exploiting fragile environments and ecosystems. Thus, finding ways to protect global ecosystems and simultaneously improve the livelihoods of the poor is an important policy challenge for the Age of Ecological Scarcity.

To address this policy challenge requires understanding the linkages between the livelihoods of the poor and their use of surrounding ecosystems. Many key global habitats appear to be important to poor households in developing countries.

For example, as we saw in Chapter 2, estimates from Thailand suggest that the net present value (in 1996 $) over 1996–2004 arising from the net income to local communities from collected forest, shellfish, and other products from coastal mangroves range from $484 to $584 per hectare (ha). The net present value of mangroves as breeding and nursery habitat in support of off-shore artisanal fisheries ranged from $708 to $987 per ha, and the storm protection service was $8,966–10,821 per ha (see Table 2.5). Such benefits are considerable when compared to the average incomes of coastal households; a survey conducted in July 2000 of four mangrove-dependent communities in two different coastal provinces of Thailand indicates that the average household income per village ranged from $2,606 to $6,623 per annum, and the overall incidence of poverty (corresponding to an annual income of $180 or lower) in all but three villages exceeded the average incidence rate of 8% found across all rural areas of Thailand (Sarntisart and Sathirathai 2004). The authors also found that excluding the income from collecting mangrove forest products would have raised the incidence of poverty to 55.3% and 48.1% in two of the villages, and to 20.7% and 13.64% in the other two communities.

The Thailand example is not unusual; poor households across the developing world typically display considerable direct and indirect use values for mangroves.[5] However, there is also evidence that coastal people hold important nonuse values associated with mangroves. A contingent valuation study of mangrove-dependent coastal communities in Micronesia demonstrated that the communities "place some value on the existence and ecosystem functions of mangroves over and above the value of mangroves' marketable products" (Naylor and Drew 1998, p. 488).

Coral reefs are another critical habitat throughout the developing world that both support near-shore fisheries harvested by poor coastal communities, generate revenues for local communities from ecotourism, and provide valuable shoreline protection.[6] For example, Cesar (2000) estimates the losses, in net present value per square kilometer (sq. km), in terms of support for near-shore artisanal fisheries and coastal protection from the destruction of coral reefs in Indonesia. The main threats to coral reefs are from poison fishing, blast fishing, coral mining, sedimentation from logging onshore, and overfishing. Together, these threats account for present value losses in coastal fisheries of around $0.41 million per sq. km of coral reef destroyed, and present value losses in coastal protection of $0.011–0.453 million per sq. km of coral reef destroyed. In contrast, reliable values for the sustainable production of coral reef fish for local consumption and the aquarium trade are rare. White *et al.* (2000) provide some estimates for the Philippines. The potential annual revenue for sustainable fish production could be $15–45,000 sq. km of healthy coral reef for local consumption and $5–10,000 sq. km for live fish export. Revenues from coral reef tourism in the Pulau Payar Marine Park, Malaysia, are estimated at $390,000 per year (Yeo *et al.* 2002), and coral reef diving earns gross revenue of $10,500–45,540 per year in the Bohol Marine Triangle in the Philippines (Samonte-Tan *et al.* 2007). Coral reefs also have important cultural and nonuse value to neighboring coastal communities; many cultural and religious traditions have evolved in tropical coastal zones that honor the dependence of local

---

[5] Badola and Hussain (2005); Bandaranayake (1998); Barbier and Strand (1998); Das and Vincent (2009); Naylor and Drew (1998); Othman *et al.* (2004); Rönnbäck *et al.* (2007); Ruitenbeek (1994); Walters *et al.* (2008); and Walton *et al.* (2006).

[6] Brander *et al.* (2007); Cesar (2000); Mathieu *et al.* (2003); Moberg and Folke (1999); Moberg and Rönnbäck (2003); Samonte-Tan *et al.* (2007); White *et al.* (2000); Wilkinson *et al.* (1999); and Yeo *et al.* (2002).

communities on adjacent reefs and reflect the "bequest value" of preserving this way of life into the future (Moberg and Folke 1999).

Forested watersheds in developing regions also provide a number of hydrological services that can impact the livelihoods of the poor, such as water filtration/purification; seasonal flow regulation; erosion and sediment control; and habitat preservation.[7] These services will become increasingly important as more and more river basins in developing areas experience rising water use relative to freshwater supplies (Rosegrant *et al.* 2002). In addition, forests, especially forests of upper watersheds, provide a number of direct uses to adjacent poor communities, including timber, collected nontimber products, and community forestry (Guo *et al.* 2001; Kremen *et al.* 2000; Pagiola *et al.* 2005).

Some of the most important benefits of maintaining and improving land uses in upper watersheds accrue to poor communities living downstream. In the central highlands of Bolivia, for example, Richards (1997) finds that a project to improve watershed protection and reduce soil erosion on farmers' fields in the uplands yields a net present value of nearly $34.9 million, with the majority of the benefits due to flood prevention and the increased water availability due to aquifer recharge in the lower watershed. Similarly, improvements to the upper watersheds in Karnataka, India through afforestation and construction of tanks, artificial ponds, check dams, and other reclamation structures leads to significant benefits to downstream farmers through improving groundwater recharge and availability, thus reducing the cost of irrigation and the need for developing new wells or extending existing wells (Diwakara and Chandrakanth 2007). Pattanayak and Kramer (2001) estimate that increased water flows associated with afforestation of watersheds in Eastern Indonesia yield economic values for downstream farmers equivalent to 1–10 percent ($3.5–35) of annual agricultural profits. However, land uses other than forests in some tropical watersheds may also yield beneficial hydrological flows; for example, Aylward and Echeverría (2001) show that conversion of forests to pasture for livestock in the upper watersheds of Río Chiquito, Costa Rica actually increases water flow

---

[7] Chomitz and Kumari (1998); Chopra and Adhikari (2004); Diwakara and Chandrakanth (2007); Guo *et al.* (2001); Kremen *et al.* (2000); Pattanayak and Kramer (2001); Postel and Thompson (2005); Richards (1997); Silvano *et al.* (2005).

downstream, generating net present values in the range of $250–1,000 per hectare of pasture.

In many poor countries, an economically important natural environment downstream is the seasonally inundated savanna or forested floodplains located in the lower river basins. During seasonal flood events, water often leaves the main river channel and inundates these floodplains. As the floods abate and recede, crops are planted in the naturally irrigated soils, fish are caught more easily in the retreating waters, and the increased alluvial deposits increase the biological productivity of forests, wildlife, and other harvested resources. Around half of Africa's total wetland area consists of floodplains, including huge large-scale ecosystems of several thousand square kilometers such as the Inner Niger Delta in Mali, the Okavango Delta in Botswana, the Sudd of the Upper Nile in Sudan, and the Kafue Flats in Zambia (Lemley *et al.* 2000). Millions of people across the continent are dependent directly on the floodplains for their economic livelihoods through production activities such as flood-recession agriculture, fishing, grazing, and wood and non-wood harvesting of riparian forest resources, and millions more in surrounding arid land depend on the groundwater recharge service of floodplains for drinking water and irrigation (Barbier 2003). Similar benefits are found in other extremely poor countries, such as Bangladesh, where 80 percent of the country consists of floodplains created by the confluence of the Ganges, Brahmaputra, Meghna, and other rivers (Islam and Braden 2006). Chopra and Adhikari (2004) show how upland economic activity, such as intensified agriculture, in Northern India can affect hydrological flows into the wetlands comprising Keoladeo National Park, thus affecting the income gained by downstream villagers from tourism and extracting biomass, fodder, and other products.

As we saw in Chapter 2, upstream dam developments are also threatening the economic livelihoods of millions of poor agricultural households dependent on the Hadejia–Jama'are floodplain in Northeast Nigeria. Full implementation of all the upstream dams and large-scale irrigation schemes is estimated to produce overall net losses in terms of agricultural, fuelwood, and fish production to these households of around $20.2–20.9 million in net present value terms (Barbier 2003). In addition, the reduction in mean peak flood extent is predicted to cause a one-meter fall in groundwater levels in the shallow aquifers that are recharged by the standing water in the floodplain wetlands, leading to additional annual losses of around $1.2 million in tube-well irrigated dry season agriculture and $4.76 million in domestic water consumption for rural households. Islam and Braden (2006) show that, in Bangladesh, fishing and flood-recession agriculture are important joint products to poor rural households utilizing natural floodplains, although it is largely the landless who benefit from floodplain fish production rather than agricultural landowners. As a consequence, a natural floodplain contains more land devoted to fishing than agriculture but actually yields higher overall net economic returns, especially compared to traditional management scenarios of upstream dam developments to limit flooding, increase agricultural area, and expand crop production downstream.

A commonly held view is that, because many of the poor people in developing regions are located in fragile environments, they must be responsible for the majority of the world's ecosystem degradation and loss – even though their livelihoods are directly affected by such environmental destruction. This perspective that poor people are mired in a two-way "poverty–environment trap" has gained credence ever since it was asserted by the World Commission on Environment and Development (1987, p. 27): "poor people are forced to overuse environmental resources to survive from day to day, and their impoverishment of their environment further impoverishes them, making their survival ever more uncertain and difficult."

However, studies of poor households and communities suggest that their behavior with respect to the environment is more complex. The range of choices and tradeoffs available to the poor is affected by their access to key markets (e.g., for land, labor, credit, as well as goods and services) as well as the quality and state of the surrounding environment on which their livelihoods depend.[8] As summarized by Dasgupta (1993, p. 475) "in rural communities of poor countries a great many markets of significance (e.g. credit, capital, and insurance) are missing, and a number of commodities of vital importance for household production (potable water, sources of fuel and fodder, and so forth) are available only at considerable time and labour cost." In the absence of local labor markets capable of absorbing all the poor

---

[8] For reviews, see Barbier (2008b, 2010); Barrett (2004); Carter and Barrett (2006); Caviglia-Harris (2004); Dasgupta (1993, 2003); Gray and Mosley (2005); Pattanayak *et al.* (2003); Reardon and Vosti (1995); and World Bank (2008).

and landless households looking for work, or well-functioning rural credit markets to lend needed capital, the landless and near landless in rural communities depend critically on the use of common-property and open access resources for their income and nutritional needs. Thus, it may be the "assetless" poor who end up most dependent on exploiting the surrounding environment and its ecological goods and services for survival.

A survey of the extremely poor and poor households across 13 countries sheds some light on how they survive (Banerjee and Duflo 2007).[9] Although the survey did not include how the poor used their surrounding natural environment, it does reinforce that the poorest rural households have very few productive assets. First, land is one of the few productive assets owned by the rural poor, and almost all households engage in some form of agriculture, but the size of land-holdings tends to be very small. The median landholding among the poor who own land is one hectare (ha) or less in India, Indonesia, Guatemala, and Timor Leste; between one and two hectares in Peru, Tanzania, and Pakistan; and between two and three hectares in Nicaragua, Côte d'Ivoire, and Panama. Second, poor rural households tend to rely on selling their only other asset, unskilled labor. Agriculture is generally not the mainstay of most of these households; instead, they generally obtain most of their income from off-farm work as agricultural laborers or in unskilled paid work or occupations outside of agriculture. However, when households do engage in outside employment, they tend to migrate only temporarily and for short distances. Permanent migration for work is rare for most poor rural households. Thus, given the lack of ownership of assets by the rural poor, and their tendency to stay where they are located, it is not surprising that the livelihoods of the "assetless" poor are often the most dependent on their surrounding natural environments.

The scale of this dependence may be very extensive in some developing regions. For example, in Southern Malawi it was found that

---

[9] The thirteen countries are Côte d'Ivoire, Guatemala, India, Indonesia, Mexico, Nicaragua, Pakistan, Panama, Papua New Guinea, Peru, South Africa, Tanzania, and Timor Leste. The survey identified the extremely poor as those living in households where the consumption per capita is less than $1.08 per person per day, using 1993 purchasing power parity (PPP), whereas the poor were defined as those living in households where the consumption per capita is less than $2.16 per day.

surveyed households derive 30 percent of their income on average from exploiting "common" forests (Fisher 2004). Households that are especially lacking in land, education, and goat holdings are more reliant on "low return" forest activities, such as sales of "forest-based" crafts (bamboo baskets and mats, grass brooms, and wood-fired pots), roof thatching and brick-burning, sales of prepared foods and drink, sales of firewood and bamboo, and traditional medicines. Similarly, in South Africa the poorest households used more nontimber forest products, such as fuelwood, wild fruits, edible herbs, and grass hand brushes, per capita than wealthier households (Shackleton and Shackleton 2006). Such findings appear to be consistent with studies of income diversification across Africa, which show that the "assetless" poor diversify into low-return activities based on exploiting common property environmental resources, but with little hope of escaping the "poverty trap" (Barrett *et al.* 2001; Dercon 1998).

This link between asset poverty, lack of income opportunities, and resource extraction as insurance may also be very significant in many tropical forest regions, where the livelihoods of the poor often depend on the extraction of biological resources in fragile environments.[10] For example, Vedeld *et al.* (2004) conduct a meta-analysis of fifty-four case studies globally of rural communities that live in or near tropical forests, and find that on average 22 percent of household income in these communities depends on forest resources. However, the proportion of forest income was significantly higher for poorer households (32 percent) compared to the nonpoor (17 percent). Similarly, López-Feldman and Wilen (2008) find that nontimber forest product use is mainly conducted by households in Chiapas, Mexico with low opportunity costs of time and fewer income generation opportunities. And, in Palawan (the Philippines), hunting pressure on fauna was shown to be inversely related to farm size and agricultural productivity, but positively correlated with labor availability (Shively 1997). The state of the local environment may also affect how the poor utilize its resources, and in turn, their livelihood strategies. In India, Narain *et al.* (2008a) find that, in villages surrounded by good quality forests, the poorest households depend on forest resources for as much as 41

---

[10] See, for example, Adhikari (2005); McSweeney (2005); Shone and Caviglia-Harris (2006); Pattanayak and Sills (2001); Takasaki *et al.* (2004); Vedeld *et al.* (2004); World Bank (2008); Wunder (2001).

Adhikari, B. 2005. "Poverty, property rights, and collective action: understanding the distributive aspects of common property resource management." *Environment and Development Economics* 10(1):7–31.

Aksornkoae, S. and R. Tokrisna 2004. "Overview of shrimp farming and mangrove loss in Thailand." In E.B. Barbier and S. Sathirathai, eds. *Shrimp Farming and Mangrove Loss in Thailand*. Edward Elgar, London, pp. 37–51.

Aldy, J.E. and R. Stavins, eds. 2007. *Architectures for Agreement: Addressing Global Climate Change in the Post-Kyoto World.* Cambridge University Press.

Alix-Garcia, J., A. De Janvry, and E. Sadoulet. 2008. "The role of deforestation risk and calibrated compensation in designing payments for environmental services." *Environment and Development Economics* 13:375–394.

Aylward, B. and J. Echeverría. 2001. "Synergies between livestock production and hydrological function in Arenal, Costa Rica." *Environment and Development Economics* 6:359–381.

Badola, R., and S.A. Hussain. 2005. "Valuing ecosystems functions: an empirical study on the storm protection function of Bhitarkanika mangrove ecosystem, India." *Environmental Conservation* 32(1):85–92.

Bandaranayake, W.M. 1998. "Traditional and medicinal uses of mangroves." *Mangroves and Salt Marsh* 2:133–148.

Banerjee, A.V. and E. Duflo. 2007. "The economic lives of the poor." *Journal of Economic Perspectives* 21(1):141–168.

Barbier, E.B. 2003. "Upstream dams and downstream water allocation – the case of the Hadejia-Jama'are floodplain, Northern Nigeria." *Water Resources Research* 39(11):1311–1319.

2006. "Natural barriers to natural disasters; replanting mangroves after the tsunami." *Frontiers in Ecology and the Environment* 4:124–131.

2007. "Natural capital and labor allocation: mangrove-dependent households in Thailand." *The Journal of Environment and Development* 16(December):398–431.

2008a. "In the wake of the tsunami: lessons learned from the household decision to replant mangroves in Thailand." *Resource and Energy Economics* 30:229–249.

2008b. "Poverty, development, and ecological services." *International Review of Environmental and Resource Economics* 2:1–27.

2010. "Poverty, development, and environment." *Environment and Development Economics* 15:635–660.

2011. *Scarcity and Frontiers: How Economies Have Developed Through Natural Resource Exploitation.* Cambridge University Press.

Barbier, E.B. and I. Strand. 1998. "Valuing mangrove-fishery linkages: a case study of Campeche, Mexico." *Environmental and Resource Economics* 12:151–166.

Barbier, E.B. and S. Sathirathai, eds. 2004. *Shrimp Farming and Mangrove Loss in Thailand*. Edward Elgar, London.

Barrett, C.B. 2004. "Rural-poverty dynamics: development policy implications." *Agricultural Economics* 32(1):43–58.

Barrett, C.B., T. Reardon, and P. Webb. 2001. "Nonfarm income diversification and household livelihood strategies in rural Africa: concepts, dynamics and policy implications." *Food Policy* 26: 315–331.

Bluffstone, R.A. 1995. "The effect of labor market performance on deforestation in developing countries under open access: an example from rural Nepal." *Journal of Environmental Economics and Management* 29:42–63.

Brander, L.M., P. Van Beukering, and H.S.J. Cesar. 2007. "The recreational value of coral reefs: a meta-analysis." *Ecological Economics* 63:209–218.

Brzoska, M. 2004. "Taxation of the global arms trade? An overview of the issues." *Kyklos* 57:149–172.

Bulte, E.H., R.B. Boone, R. Stringer, and P.K. Thornton. 2008. "Elephants or onions? Paying for nature in Amboseli, Kenya." *Environment and Development Economics* 13:395–414.

Carter, M.R. and C.B. Barrett. 2006. "The economics of poverty traps and persistent poverty: an asset-based approach." *Journal of Development Studies* 42(2):178–199.

Carter, M.R., P.D. Little, T. Mogues, and W. Negatu. 2007. "Poverty traps and natural disasters in Ethiopia and Honduras." *World Development* 35(5):835–856.

Caviglia-Harris, J.L. 2004. "Household production and forest clearing: the role of farming in the development of the Amazon." *Environment and Development Economics* 9:181–202.

Cesar, H.S.J. 2000. "Coral reefs: their functions, threats and economic value." In H.S.J. Cesar, ed. *Collected Essays on the Economics of Coral Reefs*. CORDIO, Kalmar, Sweden.

Chhatre, A. and A. Agrawal. 2008. "Forest commons and local enforcement." *Proceedings of the National Academy of Sciences* 105:13286–13291.

Chomitz, K.M. and K. Kumari. 1998. "The domestic benefits of tropical forests: a critical review." *The World Bank Research Observer* 13(1):13–35.

Chopra, K. and S.K. Adhikari. 2004. "Environment development linkages: modeling a wetland system for ecological and economic value." *Environment and Development Economics* 9:19–45.

Hodgson, G.M. 1998. "The approach of institutional economics." *Journal of Economic Literature* 36(1):166–192.

Holden, S., B. Shiferaw, and J. Pender. 2004. "Non-farm income, household welfare, and sustainable land management in a less-favoured area in the Ethiopian highlands." *Food Policy* 29:369–392.

Hyder, P. 2008. "Recycling revenue from an international carbon tax to fund an international investment programme in sustainable energy and poverty reduction." *Global Environmental Change* 18:521–538.

Islam, M. and J.B. Braden. 2006. "Bio-economic development of floodplains: farming versus fishing in Bangladesh." *Environment and Development Economics* 11:95–126.

Jansen, H.G.P., A. Rodriguez, A. Damon *et al.* 2006. "Determinants of income-earning strategies and adoption of conservation practices in hillside communities in rural Honduras." *Agricultural Systems* 88:92–110.

Jindal, R., B. Swallow, and J. Kerr. 2008. "Forestry-based carbon sequestration projects in Africa: potential benefits and challenges." *Natural Resources Forum* 32:116–130.

Johnson, C. and T. Forsyth. 2002. "In the eyes of the state: negotiating a 'rights-based approach' to forest conservation in Thailand." *World Development* 30:1591–1605.

Kindermann, G., **M.** Obersteiner, B. Sohngen *et al.* 2008. "Global cost estimates of reducing carbon emissions through avoided deforestation." *Proceedings of the National Academy of Sciences* 105(30):10302–10307.

Koch-Weser, M.R.v.B. 2002. "Sustaining global environmental governance: innovation in environment and development finance." In D. Esty and M. Ivanova, eds. *Global Environmental Governance*, Yale University Press, New Haven, CT, pp. 1–23.

Kremen, C., J.O. Niles, M.G. Dalton *et al.* 2000. "Economic incentives for rainforest conversion across scales." *Science* 288:1828–1832.

Lemley, A.D., R.T. Kingsford, and J.R. Thompson. 2000. "Irrigated agriculture and wildlife conservation: conflict on a global scale." *Environmental Management* 25(5):485–512.

López-Feldman, A. and J.E. Wilen. 2008. "Poverty and spatial dimensions of non-timber forest extraction." *Environment and Development Economics* 13:621–642.

Mathieu, L.F., I.H. Langford, and W. Kenyon. 2003. "Valuing marine parks in a developing country: a case study of the Seychelles." *Environment and Development Economics* 8:373–390.

McCann, L., B. Colby, K.W. Easter, A. Kasterine, and K.V. Kuperan. 2005. "Transaction cost measurement for evaluation environmental policies." *Ecological Economics* 52:527–542.

McSweeney, K. 2005. "Natural insurance, forest access, and compound misfortune: forest resources in smallholder coping strategies before and after Hurricane Mitch in northeastern Honduras." *World Development* 33(9):1453–1471.

Mee, L.D., H.T. Dublin, and A.A. Eberhard. 2008. "Evaluating the Global Environmental Facility: a goodwill gesture or a serious attempt to deliver global benefits?" *Global Environmental Change* 18:800–810.

Moberg, F. and C. Folke. 1999. "Ecological goods and services of coral reef ecosystems." *Ecological Economics* 29:215–233.

Moberg, F. and P. Rönnbäck. 2003. "Ecosystem services of the tropical sea-scape: interactions, substitutions, and restoration." *Ocean & Coastal Management* 46:27–46.

Moss, T. 2005. "Ten myths of the international finance facility." Working Paper Number 60, Center for Global Development, Washington, DC, May.

Millennium Ecosystem Assessment (MEA). 2005. *Ecosystems and Human Well-being: Synthesis.* Island Press, Washington, DC.

Narain, U., S. Gupta, and K. van 't Veld. 2008a. "Poverty and resource dependence in rural India." *Ecological Economics* 66(1):161–176.

2008b. "Poverty and the environment: exploring the relationship between household incomes, private assets, and natural assets." *Land Economics* 84(1):148–167.

Naylor, R. and M. Drew. 1998. "Valuing mangrove resources in Kosrae, Micronesia." *Environment and Development Economics* 3:471–490.

Nordhaus, W.D. 2007. "To tax or not to tax: alternative approaches to slowing global warming." *Review of Environmental Economics and Policy* 1:26–44.

2010. "Economic aspects of global warming in a post-Copenhagen environment." *Proceedings of the National Academy of Sciences* 107(26):11721–11726.

North, D.C. 1990. "A transaction cost theory of politics." *Journal of Theoretical Politics* 2(4):355–367.

1991. "Institutions." *Journal of Economic Perspectives* 5(1):97–112.

Olmstead, S.M. and R.N. Stavins. 2006. "An international policy architecture for the post-Kyoto era." *American Economic Review: Papers & Proceedings* 96:35–38.

Othman, J., J. Bennett, and R. Blamey. 2004. "Environmental management and resource management options: a choice modelling experience in Malaysia." *Environment and Development Economics* 9:803–824.

Pagiola, S., A. Arcenas, and G. Platais. 2005. "Can payments for environmental services help reduce poverty? An exploration of the issues and the evidence to date from Latin America." *World Development* 33(2):237–253.

Pascual, U. and E.B. Barbier. 2006. "Deprived land-use intensification in shifting cultivation: the population pressure hypothesis revisited." *Agricultural Economics* 34:155–165.

——— 2007. "On price liberalization, poverty, and shifting cultivation: an example from Mexico." *Land Economics* 83(2):192–216.

Pattanayak, S.K. and R.A. Kramer. 2001. "Worth of watersheds: a producer surplus approach for valuing drought mitigation in Eastern Indonesia." *Environment and Development Economics* 6:123–146.

Pattanayak, S.K. and E. Sills. 2001. "Do tropical forests provide natural insurance? The microeconomics of non-timber forest products collection in the Brazilian Amazon." *Land Economics* 77(4):595–612.

Pattanayak, S.K., D.E. Mercer, E. Sills, and J.-C. Yang. 2003. "Taking stock of agroforestry adoption studies." *Agroforestry Systems* 57:173–186.

Pearce, D.W. 2007. "Do we really care about biodiversity?" *Environmental and Resource Economics* 37:313–333.

Pearce, D.W. and Barbier, E.B. 2000. *Blueprint for a Sustainable Economy*. Earthscan, London.

Pearce, D.W., A. Markandya and E.B. Barbier. 1989. *Blueprint for a Green Economy*. Earthscan Publications, London.

Pender, J. 2004. "Development pathways for hillsides and highlands: some lessons from Central America and East Africa." *Food Policy* 29:339–367.

Postel, S.L. and B.H. Thompson, Jr. 2005. "Watershed protection: capturing the benefits of nature's water supply services." *Natural Resources Forum* 29:98–108.

Ravallion, M. 2008. *Bailing out the World's Poorest*. Policy Research Working Paper 4763. World Bank, Washington, DC.

Reardon, T. and S.A. Vosti. 1995. "Links between rural poverty and the environment in developing countries – asset categories and investment poverty." *World Development* 23:1495–1506.

Richards, M. 1997. "The potential for economic valuation of watershed protection in mountainous areas: a case study from Bolivia." *Mountain Research and Development* 17(1):19–30.

Rönnbäck, P., B. Crona, and L. Ingwall. 2007. "The return of ecosystem goods and services in replanted mangrove forests: perspectives from local communities in Kenya." *Environmental Conservation* 34(4):313–324.

Rosegrant, M.W., X. Cai, and S.A. Cline. 2002. *World Water and Food to 2025: Dealing with Scarcity*. International Food Policy Research Institute, Washington, DC.

Ruitenbeek, H.J. 1994. "Modeling economy-ecology linkages in mangroves: economic evidence for promoting conservation in Bintuni Bay, Indonesia." *Ecological Economics* 10(3):233–247.

Saengsupavanich, C., S. Chonwattana, and T. Naimsampao. 2009. "Coastal erosion through integrated management: a case of Southern Thailand." *Ocean & Coastal Management* 52:307–318.

Samonte-Tan, G.P.B., A.T. White, M.T.J. Diviva, E. Tabara, and C. Caballes. 2007. "Economic valuation of coastal and marine resources: Bohol Marine Triangle, Philippines." *Coastal Management* 35:319–338.

Sarntisart, I. and S. Sathirathai. 2004. "Mangrove dependency, income distribution and conservation." Chapter 6 in E.B. Barbier and S. Sathirathai, eds. *Shrimp Farming and Mangrove Loss in Thailand.* Edward Elgar, London.

Shackleton, C.M. and S.E. Shackleton. 2006. "Household wealth status and natural resource use in the Kat River valley, South Africa." *Ecological Economics* 57:306–317.

Shively, G.E. 1997. "Poverty, technology, and wildlife hunting in Palawan." *Environmental Conservation* 24(1):57–63.

Shively, G.E. and M. Fisher. 2004. "Smallholder labor and deforestation: a systems approach." *American Journal of Agricultural Economics* 86(5):1361–1366.

Shone, B.M. and J. Caviglia-Harris. 2006. "Quantifying and comparing the value of non-timber forest products in the Amazon." *Ecological Economics* 58:249–267.

Silvano, R., A.M.S. Udvardy, M. Ceroni, and J. Farley. 2005. "An ecological integrity assessment of a Brazilian Atlantic Forest watershed based on surveys of stream health and local farmers' perceptions: implications for management." *Ecological Economics* 53:369–385.

Spahn, P.B. 2010. "A double dividend." *The Broker* 22(Oct/Nov):8–14.

Stone, R. 2006. "A rescue effort for tsunami-ravaged mangrove forests." *Science* 314: 404.

Sukhdev, P. 2008. *The Economics of Ecosystems & Biodiversity: An Interim Report.* European Communities, Brussels.

Sudtongkong, C. and E.L. Webb. 2008. "Outcomes of state- vs. community-based mangrove management in southern Thailand." *Ecology and Society* 13:27. www.ecologyandsociety.org/vol.13/iss2/art27/, accessed April 4, 2011.

Sugunnasil, W. and S. Sathirathai. 2004. "Coastal communities, mangrove loss and shrimp farming: social and institutional perspectives." Chapter 10 in E.B. Barbier and S. Sathirathai, eds. *Shrimp Farming and Mangrove Loss in Thailand.* Edward Elgar, London, pp. 191–209.

Takasaki, Y., B.L. Barham, and O.T. Coomes. 2004. "Risk coping strategies in tropical forests: floods, illness, and resource extraction." *Environment and Development Economics* 9:203–224.

Braden, J.B., 35, 289
Brazil, 105n.9, 176, 249
Brock, W.A., 258–259
Bulte, E.H., 105–106

Cadenasso, M.L., 38
Cambodia, 155–158, 162, 296
cap and auction system for GHG
    emissions, 280–281
capital *see* natural capital
capital approach to sustainability of
    development, 235–240
carbon emissions, 179–183, 184, 190–
    191, 251–252, 278, 280–281
carbon sequestration, 66–70, 177
carbon tax, 280, 281
Caribbean, 156, 244, 245
Carpenter, S.R., 258–259
Carter, M.R., 296
Catskills watershed, 55–56
Cesar, H.S.J., 286
Challawa Gorge Dam, 57–62
China, 17–18, 99–100, 103, 158, 162,
    164
choice modelling, 52 *see also* stated
    preference valuation method
Chopra, K., 288
Clark, C.W., 129, 241
Clean Development Mechanism
    (CDM), 177, 179n.11,
    180–181n.13
Clemençon, R., 280
climate regulation, 270–271
coastal ecosystems, 18–20, 216,
    243–246, 256–257
coastal landscapes, 131–134, 145
coastal protection, 66
coastal wetlands, 62–66, 108
    see also wetlands
Common, M., 217–218
compensation, 237–239
    see also payment for ecosystem
    services
competing land use model, 89–92
Congo, Democratic Republic of,
    180n.12
contingent valuation method, 50–52,
    70n.11 *see also* stated preference
    valuation method
continuous conversion of landscape
    model, 86, 89–92, 119

Coombes, O., 180–181n.13
coral reefs
    dependence of the poor on,
    286–287
    interconnected systems, 244–246
    loss of, 154
    nearshore coral reefs, 131–132
    regime shift in, 214
    storm protection, 131–132
    synergies across seascapes, 143–144
corruption, 176–177
Costa Rica, 99–100, 178, 287–288
Côte d'Ivoire, 162, 290
Cox, M., 250–251
cropland, 13–16 *see also* agricultural
    land
Cuba, 99–100
currency transaction taxes (CTTs),
    280, 282–283, 284–285

Daily, G.C., 8
Dasgupta, Partha, 47, 232, 239, 254,
    259, 289, 293
David, P.A., 300
deforestation, 103–107, 179–
    183, 224–227, 249–250
    see also REDD (reduce emissions
    from deforestation and forest
    degradation)
degeneracy in ecosystems, 256–257
Denmark, 72–73, 180, 190
depletion of ecosystem services, 42
detoxification, 50, 55 *see also* water
    quality
developing countries
    equitable treatment, policies for,
        270, 285–300
    incentives for preservation of
        ecosystems, 184–189, 295–300
    linkages between ecosystems and
        the poor, 285–295
    loss of ecosystems in, 153–154
    payment for ecosystem services,
        152–153, 189–191, 250–253
    REDD, 179–183, 190–191,
        251–252, 278
    resource dependency, 154, 160–167
    rural poverty, 154–160, 285–295
    trade, effects of, 152–153, 174–177,
        189, 249–250
direct use values, 48–49, 50

disturbances *see* ecosystem resilience
diversity, 256–257
  see also biodiversity
Dobson, A., 199–200, 206, 211,
  254–255
Dominican Republic, 99–100, 162
drainage, 50
Duffy, J.E., 256–258

Ebeling, J., 181
Echeverría, J., 287–288
ecological collapse
  and ecosystem resilience, 200,
    213–217
  factors affecting, 199–201
  future research, 254–259
  natural asset model, 201–206
  resistance to, 227–228
  spatial landscape model, 206–213
  valuation of future flows of
    ecosystem services, 47
ecological landscapes
  allocation between competing
    users, 41–48
  and ecosystems, 13–16, 27, 40–41,
    73–74
  loss of, 153–154, 249–250
  meaning of, 41n.6
  natural asset model, basis of, 85–86
  payment for ecosystem services,
    152–153, 189–191
  and resource dependency, 154,
    160–167
  and rural poverty, 154–160
  spatial variation in, 129–131,
    145–146
  and trade, 152–153, 189
  trade-off between competing uses,
    66–70
  and wetland valuations, 35–38
  see also landscapes; restoration of
    ecological landscapes
ecological scarcity
  acceleration of, 11–20
  Age of Ecological Scarcity, 1–4,
    269–270
  and economic development, 6–11,
    269, 270–285, 297–301
  as economic problem, 6–11, 20–22
  equitable treatment of the poor,
    270, 285–300

funding policies, 269–270, 277–285
meaning of, 7
policy challenges, 4, 269–270,
  297–301
sustainable development policies,
  269, 270–285, 297–300
ecological transition
  forest transitions, 13–16, 96–103,
    120, 247–249
  future research, 246–249
  mangroves, replanting, 112–118,
    120–121
  natural asset model, 86, 92–96,
    119
  tropical deforestation, 103–107,
    120, 179–183
  wetland restoration, 107–111,
    120–121, 246–247
economic development
  and ecological scarcity, 6–11, 269,
    270–285, 297–301
  and ecosystem services, 20–22, 44,
    45, 240–246
  and ecosystems, 11–20, 152–153
  forest transitions, 96–103, 120,
    247–250
  loss of ecosystems, 153–154,
    249–250
  mangroves, effects on, 112–118,
    120–121, 250–251
  and resource dependency, 154,
    160–167
  spatial variation effect on marginal
    gains, 137–142, 145–146
  sustainability of, 233–240
  sustainable development, meaning
    of, 235–237
  tropical deforestation, 103–107,
    120
  wetland restoration, 107–111,
    120–121, 246–247
ecosystem rehabilitation
  ecological transition model,
    92–96
  forests, 96–103, 120, 247–249
  future research, 246–249
  mangroves, 62–66, 108, 112–118,
    120–121, 246
  valuation methodologies, 45
  wetlands, 107–111, 120–121,
    246–247

International Finance Facility (IFF),
    280, 281–282, 284
International Finance Facility for
    Immunization (IFFIm), 281–282,
    284
international payment for ecosystem
    services (IPES), 280–281
international trade *see* trade
International Union for Conservation
    of Nature and Natural Resources
    (IUCN), 112
invading species, 224–227
investments, role of, 4, 273–274, 296
Ireland, 103
irrigation, 50, 55–62
Islam, M., 35, 289

Jack, B.K., 253
Jama'are River, 55–62
Japan, 99
Jenkins, W.A., 35, 110
Johnston, R.J., 35, 143, 242, 246
Jordan, 162, 164

Kafin Zaki Dam, 57–62
Kano River Irrigation Project (KRIP),
    57–62
Karsenty, A., 179n.11, 182, 183
Kenya, 144, 158, 162
Kihslinger, R.L., 109
Kindermann, G., 181, 183
Knowler, D J., 221–222
Koch, E.W., 133
Kramer, R.A., 287
Krutilla, J.V., 45, 85
Kyoto Protocol, 177, 179n.11, 179–
    183, 180–181n.13, 190–191

lakes, 214
land area, 27, 153, 199–201
    see also spatial landscape model;
    spatial variation in ecological
    landscapes
land use model *see* natural asset
    model
landscapes
    biodiversity, 216–217
    deforestation, resilience valuation,
        224–227
    and ecosystems, 13–16, 41n.6

Goulburn–Broken Catchment
    (GBC), resilience valuation,
    222–224, 258
measurement of ecosystems, 27,
    40–41
payment for ecosystem services,
    177
spatial models of, 241–242
    see also ecological landscapes;
    restoration of ecological
    landscapes
Laos, 155–158, 162
Latin America
    deforestation, 105–106
    forest transitions, 100
    funding of protected areas, 184
    land use, 13–16
    payment for ecosystem services,
        177, 178
    resource dependency, 160, 162
    rural poverty, 156, 159–160
Levin, S.A., 129, 213, 215–216n.7,
    216, 256–257
livestock grazing, 100
local communities, 116–118
López, R., 176
López-Feldman, A., 291
Lozon, J.D., 225
Lubchenco, J., 213, 215–216n.7, 216,
    256–257

MacIsaac, H.J., 225
Madagascar, 162, 296
Malawi, 290–291, 295
Malaysia, 99–100, 162, 164, 176,
    245, 286
Mäler, K-G., 47, 223, 227–228n.9
mangroves
    dependence of the poor on,
        285–286
    economic development, effects of,
        112–118, 120–121, 250–251
    employment, 293
    institutional framework, 297–300
    interconnected systems, 244–246
    land use, Thailand, 62–66,
        116–118
    loss of, 154
    replanting as ecological transition,
        112–118, 120–121

restoration of, 62–66, 108,
112–118, 120–121, 246
spatial landscape model, 139–142,
210–213
storm protection, 112–116,
131–133, 134–137, 292–293
synergies across seascapes, 143–144
valuation methodologies, 50–52,
54–55
marginal cost of developing ecological
land *see* continuous conversion of
landscape
marine ecosystems, 18–20, 214, 216,
241, 242–243, 256–257
market value of ecosystem services, 43
markets, 271–285, 296–297, 300
Mather, A.S., 248
Matthews, J.W., 109
Mazda, Y., 133, 136–137
Mendelsohn, R., 30
Mexico
employment, 293, 294–295
payment for ecosystem services, 178
resource dependency, 162
rural poverty, 158
tropical forests, 291
water withdrawal, 18
Micronesia, 50–52, 286
Middle East, 156, 160, 162, 184
Millennium Ecosystem Assessment
(MEA), 2–3, 30, 270–271
Milon, J.W., 111
Mitsch, W.J., 35
Moberg, F., 244
modularity in ecosystems, 256–257
Morocco, 99–100, 162
mudflats, 143, 242
Mumby, P.J., 35, 143–144, 245–246

Naidoo, R., 176
Narain, U., 291–292
national land use transition, 96–103
National Research Council (NRC),
34, 48
natural asset model
continuous conversion of landscape,
86, 89–92, 119
ecological collapse, risk of,
201–206
ecological transition, 86, 92–96,
119

forest transitions, 96–103, 120
incentives to participate, 184–189
mangroves, replanting, 112–118,
120–121
one-time development of landscape,
86, 87–89, 118–119
payment for ecosystem services,
172–174, 177–179, 189–191,
250–253
resilience of the ecosystem, 217–221
role of, 85–86
tropical deforestation, 103–107,
120
wetland restoration, 107–111,
120–121
see also open economy natural asset
model
natural capital
capital approach to sustainability of
development, 235–240
compensation for loss of, 237–239
concept of, 6–7
ecosystems as, 3, 6–11, 20–22,
232–233, 259–260, 297–301
future research, 232–233
sustainable development,
233–240
valuation of, 26–27
Natural Capital Project, 66–67
natural resource dependency, 154,
160–167
nearshore coral reefs, 131–132
see also coral reefs
Needle, C.L., 248
Nelson, E., 67–70
Nepal, 162, 294
New York City water supply, 55–56
New Zealand, 99
Nicaragua, 290
Nigeria, 55–62, 162, 288–289
nonuse values from ecosystem
services, 48–49
Nordhaus, W.D., 281
North America, 99
Norway, 180, 190

Odum, E.P., 28, 40
Olmstead, S., 30
O'Neill, R.V., 27–28
one-time development of landscape
model, 86, 87–89, 118–119

open economies
and ecological landscapes, 152–153
ecosystems, loss of, 153–154
incentives for preservation of
ecosystems, 184–189
payment for ecosystem services,
177–179, 189–191, 250–253
REDD, 179–183, 190–191,
251–252, 278
resource dependency in developing
countries, 160–167
and rural poverty, 154–160
trade, effects of, 169–171, 174–177,
189, 249–250
open economy natural asset model
development of, 167–169
payment for ecosystem services,
172–174, 177–179
trade, effects of, 169–171, 174–177,
189
see also natural asset model
opportunity cost, 41–48, 66–70, 183
see also natural asset model
option value, 49n.10

Pakistan, 18, 162, 290
Panama, 162, 180n.12, 180–181, 290
Papua New Guinea, 162, 180n.12
Paraguay, 180n.12
Pascual, U., 294–295
Pattanayak, S.K., 287, 292
payment for ecosystem services
and ecological landscapes, 152–
153, 189–191
future research, 250–253
incentives to participate, 184–189,
295–300
open economies, 172–174, 177–179,
189–191, 250–253
and the poor, 177–179, 190,
252–253, 295
REDD, 179–183, 184, 190–191,
251–252, 278
supply curve, 253
Pearce, D.W., 152, 184, 259–260,
269–270, 272
Peconic Estuary, Long Island, 242,
246
Pensacola Beach, Florida, 240–241
Perrings, C., 214n.5, 217–218
Peru, 162, 290

pest regulation, 270–271
Peterson, G.D., 214–215
Peterson, G.W., 132
Philippines, 18, 176, 286, 291, 294
Pickett, S.T.A., 38
Pimm, S.L., 214n.5
Pitsuwan, Surin, 112
plantations *see* timber
Polasky, S., 30–31, 34, 257
policy challenges
of ecological scarcity, 4, 269–270,
297–301
equitable treatment of the poor,
270, 285–300
funding ecosystem conservation,
269–270, 277–285
sustainable development, 269,
270–285, 297–300
pollination, 270–271
pollution control, 50, 55, 221–222,
270–271
Portugal, 103
Posthumus, H., 110
poverty
and ecological scarcity policies,
270, 285–300
in fragile environments, 154–160
incentives for preservation of
ecosystems, 295–300
linkages between ecosystems and
the poor, 285–295
payment for ecosystem services,
177–179, 190, 252–253, 295
and resource dependency, 162–167
see also rural poverty
predator–prey relationships, 144
primary products, 154, 160–167
production function valuation
method, 50, 52–54
productive ecosystems, 50
Puerto Rico, 99–100, 133–134, 245

Ramsar Convention on Wetlands of
International Importance, 34
Rauscher, M., 167
recreational benefits, 70–73, 270–271
REDD (reduce emissions from
deforestation and forest
degradation), 179–183, 184, 190–
191, 251–252, 278, 280–281
redundancy in ecosystems, 256–257

Reed, W.J., 201, 202, 204, 227–228n.9
reforestation, 99, 102–103, 247–249
regime shift
  and ecological collapse, 200, 213–217
  natural asset model, 217–221
  resilience, meaning of, 213–214
  valuation methodologies, 221–227
replacement cost valuation method, 50, 54–55
research *see* future research
resilience
  and ecological collapse, 200, 213–217
  future research, 254–259
  importance of, 227–228
  meaning of, 213–214
  natural asset model, 217–221
  valuation methodologies, 221–227
resource dependency in developing countries, 154, 160–167
restoration of ecological landscapes
  ecological transition model, 92–96
  forests, 96–103, 120, 247–249
  future research, 246–249
  mangroves, 62–66, 108, 112–118, 120–121, 246
  valuation methodologies, 45
  wetlands, 107–111, 120–121, 246–247
Richards, M., 287
robustness
  and ecological collapse, 200, 213–217
  future research, 254–259
  importance of, 227–228
  meaning of, 213–214
  natural asset model, 217–221
  valuation methodologies, 221–227
Rönnbäck, P., 244
Rosenzweig, M., 103
Rudel, T.K., 103–104, 247–248
rural poverty
  and ecological scarcity policies, 270, 285–300
  in fragile environments, 154–160
  incentives for preservation of ecosystems, 295–300
  linkages between ecosystems and the poor, 285–295

payment for ecosystem services, 177–179, 190, 252–253, 295
  and resource dependency, 162–167
Rwanda, 99–100, 162

salt marshes, 131–132, 143, 242
Sanchirico, J.N., 35, 143–144, 245–246
sand dunes, 131–132
Sandler, T., 185, 186
Sathirathai, S., 35, 65
scale, and ecosystem services, 130
scarcity *see* ecological scarcity
Schneider, D.C., 130
Schulz, C.E., 167
Scrogin, D., 111
seagrass beds, 33, 131–132, 143–144, 242, 244–246
sealions, 144
seascapes, 27, 142–144, 146, 244–246
Segerson, K., 30–31, 34, 257
Settle, C., 243
Seychelles, 244
Shabman, L.A., 54–55
Shively, G.E., 296–297
shocks *see* ecosystem resilience
Shogren, J.F., 243
shrimp farms, 62–66, 116–118, 134–137, 139–142, 246, 250–251
  see also fisheries
siltation, prevention of, 50
social institutions, 274–285
Sohngen, B., 175, 250
soil conservation, 66–70
Solow, R.M., 239n.5
South Africa, 162, 291
South Korea, 18, 99–100
Spahn, P.B., 283
Spain, 180, 190
spatial landscape model, 137–142, 206–213
spatial variation in ecological landscapes
  coastal landscapes, 131–134
  influence of, 129–131, 145–146
  mangrove services, 139–142, 210–213
  seascape synergies, 142–144, 146
  storm protection, 134–137, 139–142
  valuation of ecosystem services, 240–242

Sri Lanka, 162, 164
stated preference valuation method,
    50–52, 70n.11, 71, 72–73
states, role of, 104–106
storm protection
    coastal landscapes, 131–132
    mangroves, 112–116, 131–133,
        134–137, 292–293
    spatial landscape model, 134–137,
        139–142
    valuation methodologies, 50, 54–55
    Willamette Basin, Oregon, US,
        66–70
strong sustainability, 237–239
Sumatra, 253
supply curve for ecosystem services,
    253
sustainable development
    capital approach to, 235–240
    future research, 274
    meaning of, 235–237
    policy challenge, 269, 270–285,
        297–300
    systems approach to, 233–235
    value of ecosystem services,
        240–246, 273
Swaziland, 162, 164
Sweden, 52, 55
systems approach to sustainability of
    development, 233–235

Tansley, T.G., 28
Tanzania, 162, 180n.12, 290
taxes
    carbon tax, 280, 281
    currency transaction taxes (CTTs),
        280, 282–283, 284–285
    financial transaction taxes (FTTs),
        280, 282–283
    on global arms trade, 280, 283–284
    on travel, 280, 283–284
temporal variation in ecological
    landscapes, 240–241
terrestrial ecosystems, 216–217
Thailand
    institutional framework, 297–300
    local communities and mangroves,
        116–118, 285, 293
    mangrove land use, 62–66,
        116–118

mangrove restoration, 246
spatial landscape model, 139–142
storm protection provided by
    mangroves, 114–116, 134–137,
    292–293
The Economics of Ecosystems and
    Biodiversity (TEEB), 3, 277n.2
Thompson, J.R., 58–61
Tiga Dam, 57–62
timber, 99, 102–103, 139–142, 175,
    250, 270–271
Timor Leste, 290
Tobin tax, 280, 282–283
total energy flow, 38–40
trade
    and ecological landscapes, 152–
        153, 189
    effects of, 174–177, 249–250
    open economies, 152–153, 169–
        171, 174–177, 189, 249–250
transaction costs, 275–285
transition *see* ecological transition
travel, taxes on, 280, 283–284
travel cost valuation method, 50,
    71–72
tropical forests
    deforestation, 103–107, 120,
        179–183
    dependence of the poor on,
        291–292
    incentives for preservation of, 185
    loss of, 154
    REDD, 179–183
    regime shift in, 224–227
    spatial models of, 241–242
Tschirhart, J., 243
Tunisia, 162, 164
Turkey, 221–222
Turner, M.G., 41, 41n.6, 130
Turner, R.E., 132

Uganda, 162, 294
United Kingdom (UK), 71–72, 110,
    241
United Nations (UN), 112, 179–183,
    190–191, 278–280
United States (US)
    ecological collapse, 258–259
    funding ecosystem conservation,
        281

habitat-fishery linkages, 132
synergies across seascapes, 143, 144
valuation of ecosystem services,
  66–70, 240–241, 242, 243,
  246–247
water supplies, 55–56, 146
wetland restoration, 107, 108–111
use values from ecosystem services,
  48–49

valuation of ecosystem services
  assessment, 29–34
  forests, recreational benefits of,
    70–73
  further case studies, 74
  future research, 240–246
  Hadejia–Jama'are floodplain case
    study, 55–62, 288–289
  mangroves, 50–52, 54–55, 62–66
  methodologies, 48–55, 66–67, 74,
    240–246
  opportunity cost, 41–48, 66–70,
    183
  sustainable development role,
    240–246, 273
  wetlands, valuation of, 34–38, 52,
    55
  Willamette Basin, Oregon, US,
    66–70
  see also ecosystem services
Vedeld, P., 291
Venn diagram of sustainable
  development, 234–235
Ventner, O., 183
Vietnam, 155–158, 162, 180n.12

Walker, B., 213–214, 222–224
Wassenaar, T., 100n.6, 105n.9
water quality, 55–56, 66–70,
  270–271

water withdrawal, 16–20, 154
watersheds, 177, 287–288
weak sustainability, 237–239
wetlands
  decline of, 20
  definition, 34–35
  Hadejia–Jama'are floodplain,
    55–62, 288–289
  loss of, 153, 154
  restoration of, 107–111, 120–121,
    246–247
  valuation of, 34–38, 52, 55
  see also mangroves
whales, 144
White, A.T., 286
Wilen, J.E., 291
Willamette Basin, US, 66–70
willingness to pay (WTP), 70, 111,
  187n.15
Willis, K.G., 70n.11
wood, sources of, 139–142
  see also timber
woodland, 13–16, 70–73
  see also forests
World Commission on Environment
  and Development (WCED), 3,
  235, 289
World Conservation Union
  see International Union for
  Conservation of Nature and
  Natural Resources (IUCN)
Worm, B., 256–258
Wright, G., 300
Wunder, S., 176, 253

Yasué, M., 181
Yellowstone Lake, 243

Zambia, 162, 180n.12
Zandersen, M., 72–73